# SILENT POETRY

*Essays in numerological analysis*

# Silent Poetry

*Essays in numerological analysis*

EDITED BY ALASTAIR FOWLER

NEW YORK
BARNES & NOBLE, INC.

First published in Great Britain 1970

Published in the United States of America 1970
by Barnes & Noble Inc., New York, N.Y., 10003

© Routledge and Kegan Paul Ltd 1970

ISBN 0 389 03596 3

Printed in Great Britain

O learne to read what silent love hath writ,
To heare with eies belongs to loves fine wit.

Shakespeare, *Sonnets* xxiii

Though no man hear't, though no man it reherse,
Yet will there still be *Musik* in my *Verse*.

Cowley, *Davideis* I

# CONTRIBUTORS

Christopher Butler
*Lecturer in English, Christ Church, Oxford*

Maren-Sofie Røstvig
*Professor of English Literature, University of Oslo*

Russell A. Peck
*Associate Professor of English, University of Rochester*

A. Kent Hieatt
*Professor of English, University of Western Ontario*

Alexander Dunlop
*University of North Carolina, Chapel Hill*

Alastair Fowler
*Fellow of Brasenose College, Oxford*

H. Neville Davies
*Lecturer in English, University of Birmingham*

Douglas Brooks
*Lecturer in English, University of Leeds*

# CONTENTS

# PREFACE

Numerological criticism analyses literary structures of various kinds, ordered by numerical symmetries or expressing number symbolisms. In poetry, numerological structure often forms a level of organization intermediate in scale and externality between metrical patterns on the one hand and structure as ordinarily understood on the other. As such, it constitutes a huge subject – perhaps, even, larger than most medieval and Renaissance scholars working today have begun to realize. It is probably no exaggeration to say that most good literary works – indeed, most craftsmanlike works – were organized at this stratum from antiquity until the eighteenth century at least. Moreover, numerological criticism is potentially a more fruitful subject than large-scale prosody, since it has more bearing on meaning, thematic content, structure and other adjacent strata.

This book collects essays on a wide variety of numerological topics. It begins with general essays tracing two distinct but related traditions of arithmological thought, the first philosophical (Pythagorean and Platonic), the second theological (Augustinian and exegetical). Subsequently the arrangement is chronological, but intended also to represent a variety of approaches. Professor Peck's study of Chaucer's *Book of the Duchess* is concerned with large-scale structural organization and with sequences of thought themselves tinged with number symbolism. Professor Hieatt's paper on *Sir Gawain*, though it too will affect interpretation of the poem as a whole, deals with more elaborately gothic patterns of stanzas and lines. The paper on *The Faerie Queene*, on the other hand, concentrates on simpler architectural symmetries and significant spatial mid-points, while that on *Amoretti* describes a predominantly calendrical structure. The next three articles, on *Lycidas* and on late-seventeenth-century Cecilian Odes, explore some possibilities of numerological organization in lyric poetry. And finally Douglas Brooks shows that numerology in prose fiction was still relatively intricate as late as Fielding's *Joseph Andrews*.

Six of the essays are new, four have already appeared in print. Acknowledgments are due to *Papers in Language & Literature* for permission to reprint 'Sir Gawain: pentangle, *luf-lace*, numerical structure', in a slightly altered form, and 'Placement "in the middest" in *The Faerie Queene*' in a considerably altered form. 'The structure of Dryden's *Song for St Cecilia's Day, 1687*' first appeared in *Essays in Criticism*, 'Structure as prophecy' in *Renaissance and Modern Studies*.

In a composite volume such as the present, no complete uniformity of style or styling is possible or desirable. American and British spellings co-exist, and some variation has been allowed in forms of reference. For the convenience of the reader, however, quotations have been made throughout according to the same plan. Original spelling and punctuation have been retained, except for normalizing of *s* and *f*, *v* and *u*, *i* and *j* in printed texts. The usual journal abbreviations have been employed, as well as such familiar abbreviations as *PL* (Migne, *Patrologia latina*) and *EETS* (*Early English Text Society*). In the notes, omission of a place of publication from a reference implies a London imprint.

ALASTAIR FOWLER
*Brasenose College, Oxford*

# Numerological thought

CHRISTOPHER BUTLER

I

In this essay I wish to explain to the reader those few technical concepts and procedures which are central to the tradition of numerological thought, and then to offer a very brief historical account of the use of these ideas by some early medieval and Renaissance writers. It must be emphasized that the presentation of the material given here is extremely selective.[1]

Pythagoras and Plato believed that mathematics would furnish the key to philosophic contemplation of the cosmos, as devoutly as Russell and others later believed that mathematics provided the key to the foundations of logic. In the *Republic* we are told that the study of arithmetic must be enforced by law, 'not cultivating it with a view to buying and selling, as merchants and shopkeepers, but for purposes of war, and to facilitate the conversion of the soul itself from the changeable to the true and the real'.[2] For mathematics 'draws the soul upwards' from the changeable things of this world to the contemplation of the pure Forms, which are its plan. Plato is thus impressed, not so much by the very extensive practical achievements of the mathematics of his time, despite the admitted usefulness of mathematics in time of war, but more by the status of number as somehow both underlying and transcending reality. In this he is indebted to his predecessor Pythagoras.

Very little is known about Pythagoras as an historical personage; in giving an account of his thought we have to rely principally upon the account of 'the Pythagoreans' or 'the Italians', as he calls them, given by his hostile critic Aristotle. It is not even certain that Pythagoras made the major discoveries attributed to him. Nevertheless, it is possible to give some account of what the Pythagoreans, as a religious sect, believed about mathematics.

They believed, for example, that limit (*peras*) was good, since it represented the imposition of order upon the cosmos, and that unlimit (*apeiron*) was evil. These two concepts, along with those of the monad (unit) as the principle from which the number series was generated, and of odd and even, are basic in the long tradition stemming from Pythagoras. In this tradition the monad comes to represent a creative god, and the distinction between limit and unlimit, odd and even, to symbolize a Manichaean opposition of good and bad principles – straight and crooked, light and dark, even male and female.[3]

In default of the system of notation for numbers that we have inherited from the Arabs, the Greeks thought of particular numbers in geometrical fashion, for example as pebbles laid out in patterns on the ground. This method revealed to them a number of facts about numerical series that their designation of numbers by the letters of the alphabet tended to conceal. Thus they could construct progressions of numbers that appeared to be 'triangular' in nature:

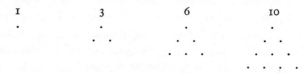

And square numbers, of which we still speak, can be represented by dots laid out in squares. This association of numbers with geometrical forms that could be held to describe objects, may have been a factor in leading the Pythagoreans to assert that things *were* number: in Aristotelian terms, both the material and formal cause of things. This view was reinforced when they saw that the first four numbers could be used to represent a point, a line, a triangle (or surface), and a solid (the tetrahedron):

They also had a reverence for certain numbers that had particular factorizing possibilities, for example 'perfect' numbers, which are the sum of their divisors exclusive of themselves, such as 6 (= 1 + 2 + 3) and 28. By the same token, there were 'deficient' numbers, such as 14, whose aliquot parts add up to less than 14, and 'abundant' numbers, such as 12, whose aliquot parts add up to 16. There were also 'circular' numbers whose property was that they perpetually reproduced themselves when raised to their powers, such as 5 and 6.

The Pythagoreans' greatest respect was kept for the 'divine *tetraktus*', the number 10 considered as the sum of 1, 2, 3, 4. In its triangular form it became a sacred symbol by which they swore in their initiation ceremonies. Its importance was due to Pythagoras' greatest and most influential discovery. For he first stated the mathematical ratios involved in musical harmonic relationships, and these all turned out to be contained within the number 10, and to be expressible as ratios between the first four numbers. In Greek music, which was essentially melodic, notes were not sounded simultaneously to give harmonic chordal effects in our modern sense. Thus instruments were tuned to particular intervals according to the mode, or scale, needed for a particular piece of music. These intervals were, for the 7-stringed lyre, the octave, the fifth, and the fourth, the tuning of the remaining strings varying according to the scale required. Pythagoras saw that this basic framework depended upon fixed and simple numerical ratios – 2:1 for the octave or diapason, 3:2 for the fifth or diapente, 4:3 for the fourth or diatessaron, and 9:8 for the tone. These intervals are sometimes expressed by Nicomachus and other later commentators as 12:9:8:6; Pietro Bongo, for example, in his *De numerorum mysteria* (1585) tells us that the Pythagoreans called 35, the sum of these, 'harmony', since all the harmonic intervals were contained within it.[4]

The *tetraktus* was even involved in the Pythagoreans' astronomical thinking. They had maintained that the astronomical model for the universe should be based on a system of 9 concentric spherical shells (earth, moon, sun, Venus, Mercury, Mars,

Jupiter, Saturn – this is the order such as we have it in Plato, with the addition of the sphere of the fixed stars). But the Pythagoreans added a mythical 'counter earth' or central fire, which was always opposite to the unpopulated parts of the earth, hence unobservable, to make up the tetraktic number 10. This conception certainly had some value as an actual working model for astronomy. As an attempt to visualize the planetary system as a whole it was an advance upon the simple recording of the disparate positions of the stars in the sky, which the Greeks had inherited from the Babylonians. It is also remarkable in its displacement of the earth from the centre of the universe. It was further asserted that the stars as they moved gave forth musical sounds. In Aristotle's words, 'they supposed the elements of number to be the elements of all things, and the whole heaven to be a musical scale [*harmonia*] and number'.⁵ (Aristotle mocks the Pythagoreans both for this and for bringing in the counter earth – simply, as he thinks, to make up the number 10.⁶)

Plato in his *Timaeus* also describes a working model of a musicalized universe; but in doing so he goes further than Pythagoras, for the 'harmonic series' he holds to underly it is far more complicated. This was the '*lambda* series', so called because early commentators on Plato laid it out in the form of the Greek letter:

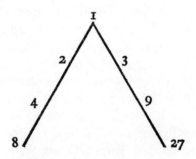

These numbers, according to Plato, constitute the 'world soul', which is the cause of the reasonable, circular motions of the heavenly bodies. He in fact thinks of the world soul as a kind of long strip which can be slit and then bent out into 2 circles, corresponding to the sidereal equator and the zodiac. One of these rings is then cut into 7 concentric rings for the individual planets.[7] These rings then revolve in appropriate directions and at appropriate speeds to simulate the movements of the planets and of the fixed stars. The whole thing in the end looks very much like an armillary sphere.

The *lambda* series stops at the cube, since this can symbolize body in 3 dimensions; there have to be 2 series since Pythagorean theory demanded that the odd numbers should be represented as well as the even ones.[8] Plato treats the series from 1 to 27 as if it defines a musical scale – and Cornford has shown that harmonic and arithmetic means can be inserted between the numbers to give a scale with intervals of a tone or a semitone, over a compass of 4 octaves and a major sixth.[9] Thus the soul of the world is itself musical. The numbers are also used to define the sizes of the planetary orbits (*Timaeus* 36D): exactly how, Plato does not specify, but it is reasonable to assume that the figures measured the radii of the successive orbits of the planets round a common centre. (Perhaps the Spindle of Necessity of the myth of Er; but if the account in the *Timaeus* is carried through, this would have to be rather grievously bent, as the axis of the earth is at an angle to that of the fixed stars.) Plato does not in fact tell us in the *Timaeus* that the stars give forth musical notes. For this we have to go to the myth of Er at the end of the *Republic*.[10] This did not prevent Renaissance commentators, who were following Macrobius' commentary on *The Dream of Scipio* rather than the original Platonic conception in the *Timaeus*, from speculating at length about the connection between these planetary distances, and the musical harmony in the world soul.

Plato also described in the *Timaeus* the constitution of matter and of the 4 elements, which make up the body of the world. The 2 primary elements of matter, earth to give solidity and fire to confer visibility, he thought would be best held together in a geometrical *analogia* or proportion, and he looked for sequences of numbers which would do this in the 'tightest' and most satisfactory way. Now the primary bodies, or elements, must be represented by cubes to symbolize their solidity – and between 2 cubes there can be inserted 2 mean proportional numbers to make a lock. As Cornford remarks, a simpler sequence, such as 2, 4, 6, 8, is more easily understood for the purposes of illustration.[11] These form several satisfying interrelations, as $2:4::4:8$, $8:4::4:2$, and $4:2::8:4$, and can be used to express the interrelationship of elements in the universe. 'So God placed water and air between fire and earth, and made them as far as possible proportional to one another; so that air is to water as water is to earth; and in this way he bound the earth into a visible and tangible whole.'[12] Empedocles had earlier made the elements equal in amount; but since his time it had been realized that the universe was much larger than previously supposed. Since the heavenly bodies are composed of fire, Plato logically gives them the largest place in his scheme. He is not, however, trying to say what the actual proportions were in terms of quantity. He is only convinced that they must be in some proportion which will reflect a rational design, in which, moreover, the elements are in concord, or amity.

Plato further distributes 4 of the Euclidean regular solids among the elements – giving the cube to earth (as most immobile), the pyramid to fire (as most sharp and penetrating), the icosahedron to water and the octahedron to air. The fifth solid, the dodecahedron, as approximating most closely to the sphere, is used for the constellations.[13] Thus we are given an extended description of a mathematically planned universe, of the eternal model, whose mere changing likeness (*eikon*) we actually experience. Plato hovers uneasily between scientific description and the symbolic force of myth. The actual status of the Demiurge as divine creator is disputed by commentators. Aristotle in the *De caelo* (279 b 33) suggests that the description of the actual process of construction is only for the purposes of understanding. (Rather similar suggestions are made by Renaissance commentators concerning the 6 days of creation in Genesis, which, they say, was really instantaneous.) In fact Plato did not attempt, for example in suggesting the sizes of the planetary orbits, to conform to the best observations of his time, though the Academy itself was probably encouraging such attempts, e.g. by Eudoxus. However, this did not prevent the

*Timaeus* from being one of the prime sources for any attempt at scientific cosmology all through the Middle Ages, along of course with the 'purer' observational data of Ptolemy, Manilius and others. For Plato had provided the basic scientific assumption of order, along with some of its details. We shall see just how strong this suggestion could be, when we come to discuss Kepler.

It was of course chiefly as a challenging account of divine creation that the *Timaeus* intrigued men of all religions in the centuries immediately after Christ. The great problem for many of these was to reconcile Christian belief with Greek wisdom, and from then on numerological thinking was always syncretic in cast. From Philo (*c.* 30 B.C.–A.D. 50) to Henry More's *Coniectura cabbalistica* (1653), it is asserted that Pythagoras and Moses were influenced by one another. This meant in effect that the Bible had to be made to yield up the desired, more civilized Greek meaning; it had in particular to be shown that the Mosaic Pentateuch took account of all that was best in Greek theology, science and ethics. The Bible was supposed to give some direct clues, for example in the book of Solomon – 'thou hast ordered all things in number and measure and weight' (Wisdom xi. 21). The '*harmonia mundi*' was also supposed to be alluded to in the Lord's challenge to Job – 'Where were you when I laid the foundation of the earth? . . . On what were its bases sunk, or who had its cornerstone, when the morning stars sang together, and all the sons of god shouted for joy?' (Job xxxviii. 4–7). But numerological elements were best discovered in the Bible by allegorical exegesis. Thus Philo (and many writers after him) explains that Creation as described in Genesis took 6 days, since 6 is a perfect number, suitable to a perfect creation. It is also, as a multiple of 2 the first female number, and 3 the first masculine one, peculiarly suitable for the creation of a world containing 'beings that sprang from a coupling together'.[14] One could use a similar type of analysis, based on the *tetraktus*, to show for example that the 4 gospels of the New Testament 'contained' the Decalogue of the Old. It cannot be over-emphasized that this continued assimilation of Greek and Biblical thought was both widespread, and until the critical examination of the Old and

7

New Testaments by Erasmus and others, which finally destroyed any possible historical correspondence, completely orthodox. The numerological approach to the Bible was an integral part of Christian education, and encouraged by the fathers of the Church, especially St Augustine. Throughout the Middle Ages too, the machinery of the *Timaeus* was taken over and elaborated upon. Klibansky reports that 'there was hardly a medieval library of any standing which had not a copy of the fragment translated by Cicero'.[15] Indeed the chief sources for Platonism of any kind in this period were Chalcidius, and the commentary on *The Dream of Scipio* by Macrobius. The latter projects the mediaeval 'world picture' on the model of Plato, who is 'the sanctuary of truth itself', and lays special emphasis (certainly in so far as it influenced writers like Chaucer) upon the music of the spheres:

> Thus the world soul, which stirred the body of the universe to the motion we now witness, must have been interwoven with those numbers which produce musical harmony in order to make harmonious the sounds which it instilled by its own quickening impulse. It discovered the source of these sounds in the fabric of its own composition.[16]

Perhaps the influence of Gnosticism, with its extremely abstract progressions and emanations, reinforced the identification of God with the monad, which as One, or unity, was for the Greeks not itself a number, but its principle and source. (This can be understood if we see that in the absence of a notation for zero, 1 lay at the convergence of the positive and negative series of integers.) Thus Macrobius identifies the monad with God, or *Mens*: 'although the monad is itself not numbered, it nevertheless produces from itself, and contains within itself, innumerable patterns of created things'.[17] This conception of God creating according to a mathematical plan became part of the tradition. In Boethius also we find that *omnia quaecumque a primaeva rerum natura constructa sunt, numerorum vedentur ratione formata*.[18] In the Renaissance Pietro Bongo tells us *nam mundus uterque numeris est dispositus*; Cornelius Agrippa believes that 'proportion of numbers' was 'the principall pattern in the mind of the Creator'; and the astronomer Kepler believed that God was *geometriae fons ipsissimus, et ut Plato scripsit, aeternam exercens Geometriam.*[19] The concept of the *harmonia mundi* was hugely elaborated in this period, notably by Francesco Giorgio in his *De harmonia mundi* (Venice, 1525), by Kepler in his *Harmonices mundi* (Linz, 1619), by Mersenne in his *Traite l'harmonie universelle* (Paris, 1627) and by Kircher in his *Musurgia universalis* (Rome, 1650).

This use of mathematics to project a theological cosmogony had even carried over into the handing down of 'ordinary' arithmetic as one of the intellectual disciplines, in the *artes* or *teknai* which preserved classical learning for the Middle Ages, for instance by Nicomachus in his *Introduction to Arithmetic* and by Capella in his *De nuptiis Philologii et Mercurii*, which was influential in determining the 7 liberal arts and their scope.[20] The 'divine arithmetic' of these writers generally treats fairly systematically of the nature of the integers within the decad, assigns them to their corresponding pagan deities (usually planetary ones) and outlines their function in cosmological thinking, the latter nearly always strictly derived from the *Timaeus*. It is interesting to note that the Jesuit Athanasius Kircher in his *Arithmologia* (Rome, 1665) hands down what are nevertheless very similar doctrines, as *vera et licita numerorum mystica significationis*, having supposedly shorn them of their 'magic' and 'impious' Cabbalistic and Gnostic connotations. This does not prevent him from following Boethius and the spurious Hermes Trismegistus in asserting that all comes from the monad, or from citing many examples of 'magic squares' (in which the numbers added together in the horizontal and vertical dimensions, and along the diagonals of the square always come to the same total). These squares were assigned to planetary deities; for example that depicted in Dürer's *Melancolia I*, to Saturn.[21] In these treatises the numbers are given symbolic properties of the type originally bestowed upon them by Pythagoreans, who for instance called the number 4 Justice, since as a square number it signified reciprocity. Such systems of symbolic associations, as Guthrie remarks, led the Pythagoreans 'into all sorts of difficulties which cannot be said to have been counterbalanced by any advantages for the development of human thought'.[22] This is true only from a scientific point of view. Aristotle of course had a pertinent criticism – 'if everything must partake in number, many things will turn out to be the same'. [23] But this syncretic aspect of number symbolism seemed to those who used it to be one of its main advantages.

Thus Capella tells us that 2 makes a line, is called Juno, and signifies separation and discord, for it breaks away from the monad. (This doctrine was easily assimilated by Christians, for God failed to say that he saw that it was good on the second day of Creation.) The number 7 is virgin and Minerva; 'virgin' because it neither generates nor is generated within the decad; that is, is neither the product of numbers below 10, nor will multiply with a number below 10 to produce a number below 10, except of course 1, which was not considered a number in the ordinary sense. There are also 7 forms of the moon, and the number signifies the moon's course, for the numbers from 1 to 7 added together make 28. Capella gives similar accounts of the other numbers within the decad, and only then goes to explain elementary arithmetic, defining prime numbers, perfect numbers, types of ratio, and so on. Thus even simple textbooks of arithmetic explained the symbolic accretions of number, and we find this throughout the period under discussion. Even so practical a book as Euclid's *Elements* is introduced by John Dee in 1570 as able to 'winde and draw' the reader 'into the inward and deep search and vew, of all creatures distinct vertues, properties, and *Formes*'.[24]

For 'divine arithmetic' of this type was popularly supposed to provide a key to the comprehension of the whole world, its contents included. It was both an arch-synthesizer of all useful knowledge, and also the especially privileged language of the Creator. Giorgio tells us that *'celuy qui veut etre heureux, et qui desire de sonder et rechercher les choses celestes et divines, ne doit point ignorer le nombre'*.[25] And William Ingpen, on the title-page to his *Secrets of Numbers* published in 1624, which treats for the most part of numbers within the decad, advertises his book as 'pleasing to read, profitable to understand, opening themselves to the capacities of both Learned and Unlearned. Being no other than a key to lead a man to any doctrinall knowledge whatsoever.'

This knowledge, however, was not always won at the cost of any particular philosophical insight. For a great use of numerology was for categorization. This is why even supposedly systematic treatises like Giorgio's sometimes read like dictionaries. Lists of things were made that fell under a certain number, and thenceforth that number could connote the things in the list. The earliest commentators used numbers in this way. Thus Theon, writing in the first century A.D., has a chapter 'On the *tetraktus* and the decad' enumerating, appropriately enough, 10 sets of things that the *tetraktus* was held to symbolize:

Numbers: 1, 2, 3, 4.
Magnitudes: point, line, surface, solid.
Simple Bodies: fire, air, water, earth.
Figures of Simple Bodies: pyramid, octahedron, icosahedron, cube.
Living things: seed, growth in length, in breadth, in thickness.
Societies: man, village, city, nation.
Faculties: reason, knowledge, opinion, sensation.
Seasons of the Year: spring, summer, autumn, winter.
Ages: infancy, youth, manhood, old age.
Parts of the human being: body and the 3 parts of the soul.

Later authorities, such as Bongo and Agrippa, carried this tendency to an extreme. The latter, for example, pursues triads right through the triple world scheme of his time. The highest or original meaning of 3 is the 3 lettered name of God (given in Hebrew, God's own language), and signifies the Christian Trinity of Father, Son, and Holy Ghost. In the intellectual (ultramundane) world 3 signifies the 3 hierarchies of angels grouped into 3 to represent the Trinity. In the celestial world 3 represents the 3 quaternions of the zodiacal signs of the Houses used in casting a horoscope. Agrippa then divides the sublunary world

into two, the elemental (physical) world, in which 3 represents
the 3 degrees of the elements, and the minor or microcosmic
world of man, in which 3 represents the main parts of man's body:
the head, containing the intellect corresponding to the intellectual
world, the breast containing the heart, the 'seat of life', corresponding to the celestial world, and the belly with its genitals
corresponding to the elemental world. He also as a 'negromantike'
finds triplicities in the infernal world, in the 3 infernal furies, the
3 judges, and the 3 degrees of the damned.[26]

It should not be assumed, however, that all this is just irre-
sponsible list-making. It is a genuine philosophical aim to seek
generality in understanding one's world, and in doing so these
writers in fact observed a strict numerological decorum. For the
numbers involved had to correspond in some intelligible symbolic
way to the entities they grouped; and furthermore, since numbers
were part of God's plan, they could show, correctly interpreted,
*why* things were as they were. Thus Bongo makes the very
strong claim that numerology will show why there are 4 elements, since 4 is a number fit for generation (for it is generated
and generates within the decad), and why there are 7 planets –
7, being a number that does not thus generate, as we have seen, is
obviously suitable for the immutable celestial bodies.[27]

The numerological style of thinking was not only used for this
sort of categorization: we also find it being used to explain far
more complicated and closely observed phenomena in the
scientific investigation of the period. Copernicus, and Kepler,
at least, were influenced by the Neoplatonic humanist belief that
the universe was ordered in a mathematically satisfying way.
Being religious men, they believed that the universe carried upon
it the 'signature' of its creator. Thus Kepler follows Nicholas of
Cusa in taking the sphere as a symbol of the Trinity, its centre
being the Father, its surface the Son ('the visible body'), and the
intermediate ether-filled sphere the Holy Ghost. These 3 also
correspond in the Copernican system to the central sun, the fixed
stars and the planetary system in between.[28] In treating the sphere
as the most appropriate model, Kepler was of course following the
*Timaeus*: and in trying to explain the sizes of the orbits of the

planets within the new Copernican sun-centred system, he hit upon an amazing reapplication of the Platonic doctrine concerning the regular solids. He thought that by treating the planetary orbits as if they took place upon solid spheres, the distance between the spheres, and hence the distance between the planets and the sun, was determinable by the insertion of one of these Platonic solids between the successive spheres, each solid having a circumscribed and an inscribed planetary sphere contiguous to it. Thus the planet on an inner sphere would be at its greatest distance from the sun upon the inscribed sphere of the solid, but the next planet further out would lie on the circumscribed sphere of that solid when at its least distance from the sun. Kepler describes this theoretical solution of the observations of Copernicus at length in his *Mysterium cosmographicum* (Tübingen, 1596). In doing this he appeals quite explicitly to the conception of a God proceeding *more geometrico*, and further thought, that since there could be only 5 regular solids thus disposed, he had shown why there were 6 circum-solar planets, echoing Bongo's view that numerological arguments can explain to us the 'why' of things.[29]

In the latest phase of his career Kepler vastly extended his search for numerical correspondences in the universe in his *Harmonices mundi* (1619), in which he published his third law of planetary motion. The fact that Kepler managed to evolve these laws from numerological premises, shows that this type of thinking was very far from being confined to mystagogues and cranks, but a genuine part of the world picture of a religious age, in which all thinking, from scientific to aesthetic, tended to be theologically motivated. In this book also Kepler revives the Pythagorean and Macrobian doctrines of the music of the spheres in an entirely new guise, using a vastly extended conception of the possible harmonic ratios.[30] He attempts to show how all the very complicated observational data concerning the positions and velocities of the stars which he had inherited largely from his erstwhile colleague Tycho Brahe, fall within a single system of musical harmony. He differs from Plato and Pythagoras in that he insists that it is the *speeds* of the planets and not their distances from a common centre of revolution (the sun) that determine the celestial harmony. For the numbers that he correlated with musical intervals are derived from the sizes of the angles a planet sweeps out in a given period, when observed from the sun. (Even though his system seems to be a purely mathematical one, he cannot at times resist an analogical speculation. 'The Earth sings Mi Fa Mi so that you may infer even from the syllables that in this our domicile MIsery and FAmine obtain.') Kepler thus articulates in scientific form that conception of the *harmonia mundi* that we find throughout the philosophy and literature of the age.

It is also significant, in view of the developments in the arts to be described further on, that Kepler sees the universe as a kind of work of art, which we can attempt to imitate upon our own human, microcosmic level. For he concludes:

> Accordingly the movements of the heavens are nothing but a kind of everlasting polyphony (intelligible not audible) with dissonant tunings, like certain syncopations or cadences (where-with man imitates these natural dissonances), which tends towards fixed and prescribed clauses – the single clauses having 6 terms (like voices) – and which marks out and distinguishes the immensity of time with these notes.

Kepler here shows that he is quite aware that the harmonic system he has employed is an advance upon that of the ancients, when he describes the universe as giving forth polyphonic strands of melody, such as we find in the church music of his time. (In this way he avoids an awkward problem that faced Plato, who could not guarantee that if all the notes of the *lambda* scale were sounded together, they would in fact be concordant.) He goes on to say that:

> it is no longer a surprise that man, the ape of his Creator, should finally have discovered the art of singing polyphonically (*per concentum*), which was unknown to the ancients, namely in order that he might play the everlastingness of all created time in some short part of an hour by means of an artistic concord of many voices and that he might to some extent taste the satis-

faction of God the Workman with his own works, in that very sweet sense of delight elicited from this music which imitates God.[31]

So far I have tried to explain, though very briefly, the development of numerological thinking as it proceeded on cosmological assumptions which would have been intelligible to Pythagoras and to Plato. But as we saw in the case of Philo, there was a second great source of number symbolism, also with divine authority, and that was the Bible. All the early exegetes would have agreed with John Donne's dictum that:

Nothing . . . seems so much to endanger the Scriptures, and to submit and render them obnoxious to censure and calumniation, as the apparence of Error in Chronology, or other limbs and numbers of Arithmetick; for, since Error is an approbation of false for true, or incertain for certain, the Author hath erred, (and then the Author is not God) if any number be falsely delivered, . . . [32]

In many cases, a number used in the Bible took on a symbolic connotation from the context in which it was used: thus 23 was the number of judgment since in Exodus (Vulgate xxxii.28) and I Corinthians (x.8) 23,000 men were punished for fornication and idolatry. The number also had overtones of the 'eleventh hour' of the world, before the eighth day of eternity, in which God would come to judge man. A more extended and ingenious use was made of numerology in reconciling the Old and New Testaments. St Augustine was the most influential of the Church Fathers in making this kind of exegesis respectable. Thus, to give a famous instance, in *De Civitate Dei* XV xxvi and xxvii, he explains how 'Noah's Ark signifies Christ and his Church in all things'. This was because the dimensions of the ark signified the ideal proportions of a man's body, 'in which the Saviour was prophesied to come', Christ being also the Ark of Salvation.

Lay a man prone and measure him, and you shall find his length from head to foot to contain his breadth from side to side 6 times, and his height from the earth on which he lies, 10 times; therefore the ark was made 300 cubits long, 50 broad, and 30 deep. And the door in the side was the wound that the soldier's spear made in our Saviour. . . . And the ark was made of all square wood, signifying the unmoved constancy of the Saints; for cast a cube or square body which way you will, it will ever stand firm.

This type of numerological analysis was very widely practised, and would have made some knowledge of numerology the possession of every educated Christian. Thus Bongo relentlessly tracks down and collates and explains what must be nearly all the numbers mentioned in the Bible. For example, he says that since 2 is the number of discord, evil and division, the division of the sheep from the goats at the last judgment is prefigured by the 2 sons of Adam the father of mankind, one *iustus* (Abel), the other *reprobus* (Cain).[33] It is important to remember that in doing this sort of thing, Bongo is following a large number of authorities, whom he cites. (It is indeed a pronounced characteristic of many Renaissance treatises, that the original contribution of their authors is often remarkably small, and that they are really summarizing and ordering the common property of learned men.)

Numerology was less orthodox, however, in the hands of those who had a liking for the occult. From Pythagoras onwards knowledge of the properties of number had been regarded as a secret mystery. Pythagoras was popularly supposed to have made his initiates vow silence for 3 years, and thus in the Renaissance 1095 (i.e. $3 \times 365$), was the 'number of silence'. Even Copernicus doubted whether he ought to reveal his discoveries, on explicitly Pythagorean grounds. In his prefatory letter to Pope Paul he says:

I hesitated long whether, on the one hand, I should give to the light these my Commentaries written to prove the Earth's motion, or whether, on the other hand, it were better to follow the example of the Pythagoreans, and others who were wont to impart their philosophic mysteries only to initiates and friends, and then not in writing but by word of mouth, as the letter of Lysis to Hipparchus witnesses.[34]

And Bongo emphasizes that the tradition handed down from Plato, through Aglaophemus, Philolaus and Iamblichus, is secret knowledge, *occultam arithmeticam*, not for the vulgar (*ne mitte margaritas ante porcos*).

Renaissance magi such as Cornelius Agrippa believed that this knowledge was potentially very powerful in celestial magic, since all things were 'formed by number' in the first place:

> For it is a generall opinion of the Pythagoreans, that as Mathematicall things are more formall than Naturall, so also they are more efficacious, as they have less dependence in their being, also in their operation.[35]

The magus believed that by the correct arrangement of 'lower' things he could draw down the power of 'higher' ones. Granted his triple world scheme, such as we saw it expressed by Agrippa earlier, he sought to activate influences between those worlds which for him were of a genuinely sacred character. Thus Agrippa tells us that 'There is no member in man [*sc.* in the proportioning of his body] which hath not correspondence with some sign, star, intelligence, divine name, sometimes in God himself the Archetype.'[36] As D. P. Walker remarks, 'Magic was always upon the point of turning into art, science, practical psychology, or above all religion.'[37] The supposedly magical effects of number become of aesthetic relevance when we notice that Comus' 'words set off by some adjuring power', by which he attempts to ensnare the Lady are in fact numerologically structured.[38]

In the Renaissance numerological tradition the prime emphasis was not simply on the elucidation of the facts – the structure of the cosmos, the explanation of a text – but also on the effects of this knowledge upon man. Plato's doctrine of Ideas or Forms had ensured that the Timaean system remained for a long time an object of religious contemplation, rather than a schema for practical investigation. Pythagoras and Plato taught further that just as the universe was harmonic in constitution, so is the soul of man who contemplates it; who, as he gains knowledge, orders and cultivates the divine elements in himself. They believed in fact that 'like was known by like' (Plato writes in a fragment 'with earth we see earth, with water water'). The idea of man as microcosm is thus of very considerable antiquity. The philosopher who contemplates the *kosmos* becomes *kosmios* in his own soul.

Ever since Plato it was believed that this harmony could be achieved through the arts. Crucial here is the passage on music and the soul in the *Timaeus*:

> The sight of day and night, the months and returning years, the equinoxes and solstices, has caused the invention of number, given us the notion of time, and made us enquire into the nature of the universe; thence we have derived philosophy. . . . We should see the revolutions of intelligence in the heavens and use their untroubled courses to guide the troubled revolutions in our own understanding, which are akin to them. . . . And all audible musical sound is given us for the sake of harmony, which has motions akin to the orbits within our soul and which, as anyone who makes intelligent use of the arts knows, is not to be used, as is commonly thought, to give irrational pleasure, but as a heaven-sent ally in reducing to order and harmony the revolutions within us.[39]

In the *Phaedo*, Plato extends this conception of harmony in the soul to include the balance of the 'elements', subsequently interpreted as the 'humours':

> [Simmias speaks] We mostly hold a view of this sort about the soul: we regard the body as held together in a state of tension by the hot, the cold, the dry, the moist, and so forth, and the soul as that blending or attunement of these in the right and due proportions.[40]

In Pythagorean thought, of course, the soul *was* number, and this more fundamental category would underlie the humours.

Renaissance philosophers were led by considerations such as these to elaborate doctrines concerning the 'harmony of the passions' in man: thus the Third Canto of Giorgio's *De harmonia mundi* is concerned with the harmony between and within the soul and the body; showing how a harmony between Intelligence and the heavens gives power over all things. But the Holy Ghost alone can harmonize the tetrachord of the humours and the passions, reconciling the order in man with the grand and divine *tetraktus*. And Agrippa's Twenty-eighth Chapter is 'Of the composition of harmony in the human soul' in a very practical sense – for example: 'Reason to concupiscence hath the proportion diapason, but to anger diatesseron.' Kircher in his *Musurgia universalis* develops these themes at length.[41]

2

Up to this point I have concentrated upon the purely philosophical aspects of the numerological tradition; but all these had an aesthetic significance. They provided not only a world picture to be imitated in the arts, but also influenced the way in which works of art were created and experienced.

There seem to be two main influences here: the great wealth of symbolic meaning released by numerological allegorical exegesis, and the interaction of the various disciplines within which numerology had an influence. In the Renaissance these were eventually integrated with artistic activity. Ever since Pythagoras, as we saw, numbers had been given symbolic connotations – I cited above the number 4 as signifying Justice or Reciprocity. By the time Du Bartas came to write on mathematics in his *Second sepmaine* (1584), he could allude quite freely to these accretions of meaning developed by the early arithmologists, such as Nicomachus and Capella. Thus he says that 1 is 'the right / Root of all Number; and of Infinite', 2 the 'first number, and the Parent / Of female pains', 4 the 'Number of Gods great Name, Seasons, Complexions / Winds Elements, and Cardinall Perfections', and so on.[42] Simon Goulart in his commentary on Du Bartas tells us, with some truth, that:

In forty verses or there abouts, the Poet comprehendeth the principall grounds of the infinite secrets of Arithmetike, who list to examine that which the Ancients and Moderns have written, should find matter enough for a large book.[43]

The integers within the decad had computational as well as 'static', symbolic, properties. Hugh of St-Victor, in a work expressly designed to show how the disciplines of the quadrivium could be brought to bear upon the exegesis of the Bible, outlines these. It is worth giving his account in some detail here, since it describes fairly exhaustively the possible techniques a literary critic can bring to bear on a text in order to extract from it its numerological allegory. For Hugh, numbers can come into relation in 9 different ways. (i) *Secundum ordinem positionis*; as when 2 after 1 signifies sin, a breaking away from the *primo bono*. (ii) *Secundum qualitatem compositionis*; 2 can be divided, signifying corruption and transitory things. (iii) *Secundum modum porrectionis*; 8 after 7 signifies eternity after mutability. (This in accord with the doctrine of the eighth age after judgment, when we shall be with God in eternity after our stay on earth, which is subject to the 7-day week.) Similarly, according to Hugh, 9 within 10 signifies defect within perfection (a falling short) and 11 after 10 a transgression of the measure (of the 10 commandments). (iv) *Secundum formam dispositionis*; 100 in breadth can signify the breadth of charity ('largesse', presumably). (v) *Secundum computationem*; 10 is perfect since it contains within itself all computations. (vi) *Secundum multiplicationem*; 12 signifies the universe, being a multiple of the corporeal 4 of the elements, and the spiritual 3. (vii) *Secundum partium aggregationem*; thus 6 is perfect. (viii) *Secundum multidudinem partium*; thus 3 signifies the Trinity, 4 the seasons. (ix) *Secundum exaggerationem*; Hugh is here thinking of the occasions, '70 times 7' and so on, when a number is used to mean 'a great number of times'.[44]

It is therefore in the light of a quite traditional type of exegesis, that Renaissance writers looked for numerological allegory in the Bible. Guy Le Fèvre, introducing Giorgio's *De harmonia mundi* in French translation, tells us that the accounts of the building of the ark, of the tabernacle, of the temple of Solomon, Ezekiel's vision, and the Apocalypse:

> ne chantent qu'une mesme chanson, bien que diversement, comme fort bien entendent qui savent Pythagorifer et Philosopher par la Mathematique, qui comme elle soit trenchée d'un quarrefourc, nous monstre pour expliquer les choses naturelles et divines quatre voyes et grands chemins tous issans de l'unité et de ses nombres . . .

Just after the passage quoted, Le Fèvre goes on, like Nicomachus, to attach a specific type of mathematics to different intellectual disciplines, which also provide 4 approaches to understanding; number (arithmetic proper), measuring (geometry), music (harmony) and celestial arithmetic (astronomy). The reasoning here is complex. Le Fèvre believes that all number comes from the Pythagorean *tetraktus*, the number 4 which 'contains' the decad, hence all numbers. He also accepts that the 4 modes of understanding a text are all contained in the senses of allegory, which are 4 (literal, allegorical, tropological, anagogical), and that these come into conjunction with the 4 disciplines of the quadrivium. But he gives numerology precedence, saying that an understanding of divine and natural things all really comes from number. He says this because he believes that only a numerological key can unlock the secrets of divine writings, such as those concerning the tabernacle and so on.

This tendency to unify the disciplines had a profound effect on all the arts in the Renaissance period. Not only was music allied to mathematics and astronomy in the tradition stemming from Pythagoras and Plato, but it was also held to include poetry and the dance.[45] Raphael's 'School of Athens' thus shows poetry on the side of mathematics, in the group of 5 plus 2 people standing beside Aristotle, symbolizing the number of tones sounded in the octave. (The grouping beside Plato is 7 plus 2, to symbolize the planets and fixed spheres towards which he points.) Poetry was not simply associated with logic and rhetoric, as the sequence of Aristotle's *Organon*, *Rhetoric* and *Poetics* had suggested. St Augustine's *De musica* was probably the first major post-classical

CHRISTOPHER BUTLER

text to emphasize this close association of poetry and mathematics. In Book vi, St Augustine analyses all the metrical feet of Latin poetry in detail, showing how, when divided into *arsis* and *thesis*, they all reduce to ratios within the *tetraktus* – 1 : 1, 2 : 1, 3 : 7, 4 : 3 – and express musical consonances. All, that is, except the amphibrach, 3 : 1, which both skips a number in the interval of the ratio and fails to make a consonance within the octave. The interpretations of the legends of Orpheus, Linus, Musaeus and particularly of the lyre of David,[46] showed the extraordinary power of poetry allied to harmony. Poetry indeed became for the Italian Humanist the most important and comprehensive of the arts. Ficino tells us that:

> poetry is superior to music, since through the words it speaks not only to the ear but also directly to the mind. Therefore its origin is not in the harmony of the spheres, but rather in the music of the divine mind itself, and through its effect it can lead the listener directly to God himself.[47]

The visual arts also, under the influence of this type of thinking, rose above their earlier lowly status as mechanical arts. Leonardo treats painting as a science, and emphasizes its close relationship with mathematics.[48] Dürer's *Melancholia I* portrays a seated melancholiac under Saturn, along with a magic square of numbers, a truncated Platonic solid, a compass, and, in Panofsky's words, 'these symbols and emblems bear witness to the fact that the terrestrial craftsman, like the Architect of the Universe, applies in his work the rules of mathematics'.[49] Theories of proportion based on the Pythagorean consonances abounded, for example in Pacioli's *Divina Proportione* (Venice, 1509) and Lomazzo's *Trattato della Pittura* (Milan, 1584, Richard Haydocke's English translation, Oxford, 1598).[50] Musical proportions were also embodied in architecture: Alberti and others, explicitly following Pythagoras, believed that the consonances of proportion in stone would affect our minds in exactly the same way as musical sounds affect our ears.[51] In this they follow Boethius, who says that 'The ear is affected by sounds in quite the same way

22

as the eye is by optical impressions' – showing once more the surprising continuity of numerological thinking.[52]

Thus it was believed that works of art could be constructed that gave pleasure by virtue of their Pythagorean proportions, and further, that these proportions reflected laws of nature, which Plato had restated in his *Timaeus*. As various disciplines were unified through the common language of mathematics found in them (I am thinking particularly of music, astronomy and Biblical exegesis) so also there arose the conception, or perception, of a common bond of symbolic import, between such apparently disparate subjects as music and astronomy (as we saw in Kepler – the association was of course a traditional one, but Kepler used a *modern* harmonic series), between music and architecture, poetry and the Bible, and poetry and music.

The background of ideas of traditional philosophical aesthetics was extremely hospitable to this sort of alliance. In the *Philebus*, Socrates, discussing sublime types of pleasures, tells us that the 'surfaces and solids which a lathe, or a carpenter's rule and square' produce are absolutely not relatively beautiful because of their mathematical form. He goes on to say:

> Any compound, whatever it be, that does not by some means or other exhibit measure and proportion, is the ruin both of its ingredients, and, first and foremost, of itself; what you are bound to get in such cases is no real mixture, but literally a miserable mess of unmixed messiness.
> *Protagoras* True.
> *Socrates* So now we find that the Good has taken refuge in the character of the Beautiful: for the qualities of measure and proportion invariably, I imagine, constitute beauty and excellence.[53]

From Plato onwards, measure, proportion and harmony were the main constituents of beauty, both in the moral and artistic senses – which in fact were not closely distinguished, *pulchrum* and *to kalon* standing for either. Indeed Pythagoras may be said to have provided one of the earliest aesthetic theories of formal

23

beauty in so far as he believed that a numerical structure underlay the qualitatively pleasing intervals of music. The conflict in our own day between 'traditional' harmony and the Schoenbergian 12-tone system and its derivatives turns in its essentials upon the validity of the original Pythagorean discovery as demonstrating the most 'natural' foundation for music, to which we, as listeners, are best adapted.

For St Augustine, physical objects participate in the forms that exist in the mind of God by virtue of their numerical properties: in the rhythm of the metres of poetry (*numerosus* is his word for this) or even in dancing:

> Ask what delights you in dancing and number will reply, 'Lo, here am I.' Examine the beauty of bodily form, and you will find that everything is in its place by number. Examine the beauty of bodily motion, and you will find everything is in its due time by number.[54]

It is important to emphasize the theological motivation of this type of analysis. Through works of art we can create according to God's own pattern. Plotinus, following the *Timaeus*, tells us that 'the measures of our sensible music are not arbitrary but are determined by the Principle whose labour is to dominate matter and to bring pattern into being'.[55] According to this theory works of art have two very desirable qualities. They are formally organized: for Augustine, composite things only become wholes once they are harmonized or given symmetry, which consists in the likeness of one part to another.[56] Secondly, in contemplating works of art, the soul is drawn upwards, for as Plotinus tells us, the soul by its very nature has a kinship to 'the noblest existents in the hierarchy of being'.[57]

In practice, this meant that works of art with the pleasurable aesthetic qualities of harmony and proportion and symmetry (what Alberti calls *concinnitas*) could also have a 'hidden sense'. For the actual proportions chosen could refer us to the macrocosm of creation in various ways: for example, to those numbers discovered by Pythagoras and Plato as underlying creation (the

*tetraktus* and the *lambda* series especially), or to the actually observ-
able measures traced out by the heavenly bodies. Thus a church
designed by Giorgio and a poem written by Spenser have actually
been demonstrated to do this.[58]

The connection between structural numerical properties and
literary texts was most strongly made in Biblical exegesis – for
here again the analysis was held to be a means for entering into the
mind of God. His interest in architectural matters was held to be
sufficiently shown by his extended directions for the construction
of the tabernacle, its altar and courtyard, in Exodus xxv–xxvii.
Bongo frequently refers to this passage, showing for example how
the 3 worlds are figured in the construction of the tabernacle – a
doctrine in which he follows Pico in his *Heptaplus*.[59] The Psalms
in particular were supposed to be numbered symbolically according to their contents, and even more importantly, *structured*
with the same decorum. Miss Røstvig demonstrates this, with
particular reference to Cassiodorus, in the present volume.[60]

It is thus reasonable to look for numerological allegory, not
only in the architecture and music of the Renaissance, but also in
its literary works. Guy Le Fèvre, in his second introductory essay
to Giorgio, talks about an *allegorie symbolique par les nombres*,
giving as examples the ark, Ezekiel, and so on. So far, he seems
concerned only with a number symbolic content in the Bible.
But later he praises Ezekiel and St John for following the laws of
music in their *compositions*:

> car qui ne void que tous les Prophètes ont este instruits et bien
> appris en la vraye poesie? Qui est ce qui ne recognoist en
> Moyse, Ezechiel, et Sainct Jean les plus exquises et subtiles
> mesures de la geometrie. Et de rechef en Moyse, Daniel et St
> Jean les proportions des nombres . . . Ce sont donc ceux qu'il
> nous convient suivre pour nos guides: ce sont les docteurs que
> nous devons imiter et ceux à la mesure desquels nous devons
> former tout ce que nous entreprenons.

Thus Ezekiel's vision of the chariot has a structure of 27 verses –
the number of deity cubed – and Giorgio's own last tone of the

third canto is an ode according to a musical pattern, thus ful-filling the precept of his translator.[61] These ideas are also found in English sources, for George Puttenham, in his *Arte of English Poesie* (1589), argues that by varying the lengths of the lines of a poem and their distribution the poet 'by measure and concordes of sundry Proportions doth counter fait the harmonicall tunes of the vocal and instrumentall Musickes'.[62] And Cowley, annotating a passage in his own *Davideis* (1656), which describes creation according to a musical plan, says, 'the *Scripture* witnesses, that the World was made in *Number, Weight* and *Measure*; which are all qualities of a good *Poem*. This order and proportion of things is the true Musick of the world. . . .'[63]

# NOTES

1 I have attempted a rather more extended account in my *Number Symbolism* (1970).

2 *Republic* VII. 525 D.

3 For an extended list of opposed principles, see Aristotle, *Metaphysica* 986 a 22. The doctrine of limit had a peculiar effect on the history of the concept of Infinity. Even as late as the Renaissance, only brave thinkers such as Bruno and Digges thought that the universe might be infinite in extent. Plotinus summarized the feelings of most people: 'Doubtless the universe is both great and beautiful, but it is beautiful only in so far as its unity holds it from dissipating into infinity' (*Enneads* VI. VI. 1).

4 Pietro Bongo, *De numerorum mysteria* (Basel, 1618) p. 492 (a later, supplemented edition). On the peculiar history of the interval of the third (6:5), missing from the mediaeval scale as defined by Boethius yet fundamental to modern systems of harmony, see L. Spitzer, *Classical and Christian Ideas of World Harmony* (Baltimore, Md., 1963), p. 37.

5 *Harmonia* for the Greeks meant originally a joining or fitting together, e.g. of a mortise and tenon joint. The passage quoted is from *Metaphysica* 985 b.

6 Cf. *Metaphysica* 986 a 3, and *De Caelo* 293 a 25. The counter earth emitting light was in fact of some use to the Pythagoreans in explaining eclipses; though what occupied the centre was a problem for Plato when he came to describe the movements made by the earth (*Timaeus* 40 B–C). See also Cornford's commentary on this, *Plato's Cosmology* (1937), pp. 120–34, esp. 123–4.

7 E.g. *Timaeus* 36 B–D.

8 Both series emanate from unity via the first odd, and the first even, number; Plato perhaps chooses the 7 numbers as he will need them later for fixing the sizes of the planetary orbits. As Cornford points out, *op. cit.*, pp. 68ff., they are certainly not chosen with the primary purpose of defining a musical scale.

9 Cornford, *op. cit.*, p. 71.

10 *Republic* x. 617, the first extant description of the music of the spheres in Greek literature. Pythagoras' most famous doctrine is in

fact only found briefly alluded to in Plato and Aristotle: the main descriptions of the music of the spheres date from the Greco-Roman period, most notably in Macrobius' commentary on *The Dream of Scipio*.

11 Cornford discusses this fully, *op. cit.*, p. 45f.

12 *Timaeus* 32 C; I have used the translation by H. D. P. Lee (1965).

13 *Timaeus* 55 D.

14 *De opificio mundi*, in *Philo*, ed. with an English translation by F. H. Colson and G. H. Whitaker, Loeb edn, i (Cambridge, Mass. and London, 1929) 13f.

15 R. Klibansky, *The Continuity of the Platonic Tradition* (1939), p. 28.

16 Macrobius, *Commentary on the Dream of Scipio*, tr. and ed. W. H. Stahl (New York, 1952), II. i. 19; p. 193. On the bonds between the bodies, see I. vi. 23; on the *lambda* and the world soul, see I. vi. 45–7.

17 *In somn. Scip.* I. v. 7–8, ed. Stahl, pp. 100–1. The mixture of religious influences in the period in fact makes it difficult to say whether Macrobius was Christian or pagan. On the monad as God or a god, see also Nichomachus, *Introduction to Arithmetic*, tr. M. L. d'Ooge, Univ. of Michigan Studies in the Human Sciences, xvi (1926), vi. 8; and Plotinus, *Enneads* VI ix. 6; V. i. 7.

18 Boethius, *Institutio arithmetica* i. 2.

19 Pietro Bongo, *De numerorum mysteria*, p. 2. Cornelius Agrippa, *De occulta philosophia* (written in 1510 but published Antwerp and Paris, 1531), quoted from J. F.'s 1651 translation, *Three Books of Occult Philosophy,,* II. ii. 170. Kepler, *Harmonices mundi* (Linz, 1619), in *Ges. Werke*, ed. M. Caspar, 12 vols (Munich, 1938–55), vi. 299.

20 Nicomachus, *ed. cit.;* Capella, ed. A. Dick (Leipzig, 1925). The 7 liberal arts as defined by Capella were: grammar, dialectic, rhetoric, geometry, arithmetic, astronomy, harmony.

21 Athanasius Kircher, *Arithmologia* (Rome, 1665), p. 241. Some works were written exclusively for the purpose of explaining Plato: e.g. Theon of Smyrna, *Expositio rerum mathematicarum ad legendum Platonem utilium*. There is an edn with French translation by J. Dupuis (Paris, 1892).

22 W. K. C. Guthrie, *A History of Greek Philosophy*, i. (1962) pp. 301–2.

23 *Metaphysica*, 1093 a 1.

24 John Dee, Pref. to *The Elements of Geometrie of the Most Ancient Philosopher Euclid of Megara, faithfully (now first) translated into the*

28

*English toung by H. Billingsley, with a very fruitfull preface made by M. J. Dee* (1570). Billingsley was then an alderman, later Lord Mayor of London.

25 Giorgio, *L'Harmonie du Monde* (1579), Pref. to Canto I, p. 3.
26 Agrippa, II. vi. 186–7. Agrippa gives general descriptions, then scales (*sc.* diagrams) of the associations of numbers from 1 to 12.
27 Bongo, p. 283. Each chapter of the *De numerorum mysteria* is given up to a particular number, and the reader will get a far better impression of the multiplicity of meaning for a given number, and also of the rationale behind it, if any, by reading these chapters as a whole.
28 Cf., e.g., *Epitome*, Bk. IV. i. I. Tr. C. G. Wallis, pp. 853–4, in *Great Books of the Western World*, xvi (Chicago, London and Toronto, 1952).
29 Cf. *Epitome*, IV. i. 2.
30 Elliot Carter Jr. gives an extremely good description of Kepler's harmonic system, and compares it with the modern one, on pp. 1026–8 of the Wallis translation.
31 *Harmonices mundi*, v. 7, tr. Wallis, p. 1048.
32 *Essays in Divinity*, ed. E. M. Simpson (Oxford, 1952), p. 55. Donne goes on to write a chapter on the occurrence of the number 70 in the Bible.
33 Bongo, pp. 62–3.
34 As quoted in T. S. Kuhn, *The Copernican Revolution* (New York, 1959), p. 137.
35 Bongo, Pref., p. 2. Cf. Agrippa, II. ii. 170.
36 Agrippa, II. ii. 264; in this he follows Ficino's *De triplice vita*.
37 D. P. Walker, *Spiritual and Demonic Magic from Ficino to Campanella* (1958), pp. 75–6.
38 Miss Røstvig analyses some speeches from *Comus* in 'The Hidden Sense', in *The Hidden Sense and Other Essays* (Oslo, 1963).
39 *Timaeus* 47 A; tr. Lee, pp. 64–5. Cf. Aristotle, *Politics*, 1340 b 18: 'There seems to be in us a sort of affinity to musical modes and rhymes, which makes many philosophers say that the soul is a harmonia, others that it possesses harmonia.'
40 *Phaedo* 86 B. See R. Hackforth, *Plato's Phaedo translated with introduction and commentary* (Cambridge, 1955).
41 Agrippa, p. 277. Kircher, *Musurgia universalis* (Rome, 1650), I. vii, Pt I. v–viii; and *ibid.*, Pt 3 *passim*; also II. ix, Pts 1 and 3. Douglas Brooks and Alastair Fowler have shown the relevance of such

doctrines to the structure of Dryden's ode for St Cecilia's Day (see pp. 185–200 below).

42 Cf. *The Columns*, 11. 136ff.

43 S. Goulart, tr. Thomas Lodge, *A learned summary upon the famous poeme of W. of Saluste* (1621), p. 248.

44 Hugh of St-Victor, *Exegetica*, (*PL*, clxxv, cols 22–3).

45 Cf. *Republic* vii; 531A and 376A.

46 See Miss Røstvig, 'Structure as Prophecy', p. 46. Poetry and music were especially closely allied in Baïf's Academy; see Frances A. Yates, *French Acadamies of the Sixteenth Century* (1947), esp. Ch. iii.

47 Ficino, *Opera* i (Basel, 1576), p. 614.

48 E.g., *Literary Works of Leonardo da Vinci*, ed. J. P. Richter, i (London, 1939), pp. 31f.

49 Erwin Panofsky gives a full analysis of the picture in *The Life and Art of Albrecht Dürer* (Princeton, N. J., 1955), pp. 156–71.

50 For an interesting short history of the theory of human proportions see Panofsky, *Meaning in the Visual Arts* (Garden City, N.Y., 1955), Ch. 2.

51 Cf. *De re aedificatoria*, IX. v. tr. Leoni as *The Architecture of . . . Alberti in Ten Books* (1726, facs. ed. J. Rykwert, 1955), pp. 196–7. For an extended treatment of the use of harmonic proportions in Renaissance architecture, see R. Wittkower, *Architectural Principles in the Age of Humanism* (rev. edn, 1962).

52 Boethius, *De musica* i. 32 (*PL*, lviii, cols 1194).

53 *Philebus* 51 C and 64 D; tr. Hackforth, *Plato's Examination of Pleasure* (Cambridge, 1958), pp. 100–1, 136. Cf. Ficino's interesting commentary, *In Philebum*, in *Opera*, ii (1576), 1234ff., 1248ff.

54 *De libero arbitrio* II. xvi. 42, tr. J. H. S. Burleigh, The Library of Christian Classics, vi (Philadelphia, Pa., 1953).

55 *Enneads* I. v. 3.

56 *De vera religio*, xxx. 55.

57 *Enneads* I. vi. 2.

58 Wittkower discusses Giorgio's church at pp. 102f. and prints Giorgio's memorandum at pp. 155f.; Hieatt describes the astronomical symbolism in the structure of Spenser's *Epithalamion* in *Short Time's Endless Monument* (New York, 1960).

59 Bongo, p. 137. Cf. pp. 136, 370, 377, 414, 434, 473, 532, 578, 580. Bongo's discussion of separate numbers, rather than of particular Biblical instances of their use, makes his analysis of Exodus xxv–xxvii very scattered.

60 See pp. 41–3.
61 Analysed by Miss Røstvig in 'The Hidden Sense', *op. cit.*, pp. 33ff.
   Cf. also the 3 nuptial songs on pp. 119–21 of the 1525 Latin edn
   of Giorgio.
62 G. Gregory Smith (ed.), *Elizabethan Critical Essays*, 2 vols (Oxford,
   1937), ii, 88.
63 *Davideis* i in *Works* (1668), p. 36.

# Structure as prophecy:
# the influence of biblical exegesis
# upon theories of literary structure

MAREN-SOFIE RØSTVIG

If the poet's task is to imitate nature, we must necessarily ask ourselves how this well-known classical formula would be likely to be interpreted by a particular poet or period. Whenever nature is defined as the existing order of things, and when this order is believed to have been created by God according to a specific pattern, nature may be 'imitated' by reproducing this pattern in the structure of the literary composition. This interpretation would be bound to recommend itself most strongly in periods influenced by Neoplatonic thought and by a general tendency, among artists, to consider form as meaningful.

Pico della Mirandola's *Heptaplus* (1489) provides an explicit and emphatic Renaissance statement of the view that poetry should reproduce the order of the universe. In his second proem Pico connects the classical doctrine of poetry as imitation with his philosophical interpretation of that nature which is to be imitated, and he characterizes Moses as the perfect poet because his narrative presents an exact image of the world. It was possible for Moses to do this, because God had revealed this image to him on the mountain, and then commanded him to make everything according to this image, as we may read in Exodus xxv. 40 and in Hebrews viii. 5. St Paul repeats the story because he wants to underline the difference between mere shadows of heavenly things (i.e. the tabernacle and the old covenant) and 'the pattern of things in the heavens' (ix. 23) or the new covenant. Pico's thought, therefore, has Apostolic sanction; his Platonizing interpretation of Exodus xxv. 40 is supported by St Paul's use of phrases that seem distinctly Platonic. Pico's own phrasing, in *Heptaplus*, is admirably clear; to imitate is to copy or reproduce an arrangement:

32

Since a writer copies nature, if he is learned about nature – as we believe this writer of ours was if anyone ever has been – it is believable that his teaching about the worlds is arranged just as God, the almighty artificer, arranged them in themselves, so that the scripture of Moses truly is the exact image of the world; just as we also read that on the mountain where he learned these things, he was commanded to make everything according to the pattern that he had seen on the mountain.[1]

As so often, Pico is repeating an argument advanced by the great theologians of our Church, St Augustine being the most famous exponent in antiquity of this view, which links poetic theory with a Platonic or Neoplatonic interpretation of the Mosaic account of creation. St Augustine's description of the world as God's poem is no mere metaphor; to him the book of God's words and the book of his works were parallel texts in the most literal sense. He assumed that God is the author of the Bible as well as of the universe, that the two are constructed in much the same manner, and that the divinely inspired poet would imitate the creative procedure of the Deity. The technique employed had been defined by Solomon in a phrase that came to echo down the centuries with ever-increasing authority: *omnia in mensura, et numero, et pondere disposuisti* (Wisdom xi. 21). Since God, then, has created everything in number, weight, and measure, so must the poet – an argument advanced by Andrew Marvell as his final compliment to John Milton in the poem written to celebrate the publication of *Paradise Lost*: 'Thy verse created like thy *Theme* sublime, / In Number, Weight, and Measure, needs not *Rhime*.'

The familiarity of this concept of an alignment between the artistic and the divine act of creation is shown by the fact that George Puttenham (*The Arte of English Poesie*, 1589) prefaced his discussion of the beauty inherent in structure or 'Proportion poetical' with a praise of the order imposed upon the universe by means of number, weight, and measure. Puttenham attributes this definition of order to the mathematicians and theologians instead of to Solomon, which shows that it had become one of

33

those all-pervasive concepts whose original source is less important than its subsequent history. However, although Puttenham in this manner connects the harmony of poetry with that of the Creation, he affirms the orthodox view that God created *ex nihilo* and not by 'any paterne or moulde as the Platonicks with their Idees do phantastically suppose'.

That Puttenham should have argued so forcibly against a Platonic theory of creation is an indication of its prevalence during the last few decades of the sixteenth century. While in the 1550s Thomas Wilson was content to praise the concept of order in general in his *Arte of Rhetorique* (1553), the 1570s and 1580s tended to associate order with the harmony of creation as propounded by the Neoplatonists. It is possible that Puttenham's firm statement about creation *ex nihilo* and without a pattern may have been a counterblast to the one-volume edition of Pico's *Heptaplus* and Francesco Giorgio's *De harmonia mundi* printed at Paris in 1579 in French translation by the brothers Guy and Nicholas le Fèvre de la Boderie. A more popular version of the same philosophy is found in the encyclopedic treatise on man, society, and the universe written by Pierre de la Primaudaye and translated into English under the title of *The French Academie*. The popularity of this treatise is revealed by the many editions that appeared on both sides of the English channel towards the end of the sixteenth century and the beginning of the seventeenth.[2]

The system of aesthetics advocated in these and similar works is based on the Platonic argument that all acts of creation require a preconceived mental pattern – a theory supported by referring to Exodus xxv. 40 – and that this pattern can be rendered in terms of certain numerical formulas. The insistence is not only on a plan, but on a special kind of plan, and on the meaningfulness of this plan. In expounding the plan and its meaningfulness, arguments from the Bible combine with concepts of classical origin in a thoroughly syncretistic manner, the supposition being that all of them contain the same divine revelation. And it is certainly easy enough to reconcile the Platonic and Mosaic accounts of creation; all that is required, is to follow Philo Judæus and St Augustine in interpreting the week of creation as a poetic metaphor used by Moses to indicate that the process of creation required 6 steps – which is what Plato, too, posits in his famous *lambda* formula.[3] Those who subscribe to this interpretation invariably invoke Solomon's statement about creation in number, weight, and measure as proof of the justness of this identification of the Mosaic week with the famous classical formula for the harmony of the universe.

Puttenham's protest against this sort of argument is only a partial one. He fully accepts the view that the beauty of the universe is a matter of number, weight, and measure; what he rejects is the theory that this pattern should be a reflection of a higher reality existing in the mind of God before creation. Puttenham, in other words, accepts the *substance* of St Augustine's aesthetic theory, but without committing himself to a Platonic interpretation of the act of creation. He accepts the validity of the pattern while rejecting the belief that this pattern existed before the world came into being.

Puttenham's extensive discussion of stanza pattern is evidence of his interest in structure, and this structural approach is even more marked in St Augustine's aesthetic theory as presented in his treatises *De ordine* and *De musica*. Evidence that St Augustine's *ars poetica* was well known to the Renaissance is provided by a book which appeared in the same year as Puttenham's – Fabius Paulinus' *Hebdomades* (Venice, 1589). This is a Renaissance handbook of Augustinian aesthetics, the main thesis being that beauty is a question of order, and that order in its turn is a question of numerical ratios or proportions. And the beauty of order imposed by God upon the created universe should be imitated by the artist. To put it quite briefly: the harmony in the mind of God, the harmony of the created universe, the harmony of music, and the harmony of poetry – all should be related to the famous numerical formulas for harmony given by Pythagoras and Plato as by Moses and the prophets. This is why St Augustine could maintain that if numbers were removed from the Creation, everything would perish – a statement frequently repeated by the Venerable Bede. Like St Augustine, Paulinus distinguishes sharply between vulgar and divine numbers. The divine numbers, as he puts it, are those ideas or principles which exist in the mind of God; they existed before the universe came into being, and they were the means whereby this was done. To the learned, therefore, the *scientia numerorum* has reference to form and matter (i.e. the science of numbers as expounded by Plato explains how form and matter combine in the *res creatae*). Poets have taken a particular delight in this science and have exploited it in their fables, which to the uninitiated have seemed to convey very little.[4] Paulinus makes an important point when he writes that mathematical terms alone are suited to express the nature of the deity, since they are plain and clear at the same time that they serve to veil the truth from the vulgar. Numbers are concepts, so that it is possible to philosophize by means of numbers, to borrow a phrase from Pierre de la Primaudaye who in his turn may have fetched it from Pico's famous *Oration on the Dignity of Man*. As Paulinus explains, this is why the Pythagoreans taught by means of numbers; their numbers were, in fact, allegories.

Paulinus combines Biblical with classical number symbolism in a manner typical of the syncretistically minded Renaissance Neoplatonists to whom Orpheus was *Theologus etiam Christianus*, and in this particular instance the proof adduced is a reference to the typological import of structural numbers: there are as many hymns by Orpheus *quantus est numerus cum quo Deus triplex creavit seculum sub Quaternarii Pythagorici forma numeratus*.[5] The juxtaposition of the Trinity (*Deus triplex*) with the Pythagorean *Quaternarius* is a typical example of Paulinus' fusion of Biblical (or theological) numbers with classical arithmology, and equally significant is his bland assumption that wherever the same number prevails, the same meaning is intended.

The Augustinian influence on Paulinus is strong. Book III, Chapter v, is virtually a summary of the most important points in St Augustine's *De musica*, and in Chapters ii–iv Paulinus applies the numerical ratios productive of harmony to poetry, in the manner of Augustine, when he traces the numbers contained in Plato's *lambda* formula in a single line from Virgil. These numbers are discovered, in correct sequence, by counting words, syllables, and letters. There is no doubt, in Paulinus' mind, that Virgil intended this line to imitate, or reflect, the numerical ratios responsible for the harmony of the universe. Similarly St Augustine, in *De musica* (vi. 17), had stated that the line *Deus creator omnium* spells health and truth to the soul because it incorporates the numerical ratios productive of the highest order, or harmony. Paulinus discovers significant structural numbers in many other literary works, the main point always being that the meaning invested in these numbers is correlated with the subject-matter. The author is credited with a conscious selection of these numbers *ut numerus cum re conveniret.*[6] This is a splendid phrase which defines the concept of numerical decorum with admirable clarity. In order that the subject-matter of his own book be expressed through its form Paulinus divided it into 7 books of 7 chapters each – a meaningful pattern already exploited by Pico della Mirandola in his *Heptaplus*. Pico explains, towards the end of the second proem, that he decided in favour of this organization, not to refresh the minds of his readers by frequent pauses, but in order to imitate St Basil and St Augustine. This casual reference indicates that Pico assumed that his readers were familiar with St Basil's and St Augustine's views concerning the meaningfulness of numbers.[7] A division into 7 times 7 was selected to permit the whole to correspond to the 7 days of creation, a most appropriate choice, since *Heptaplus* presents a sevenfold interpretation of the Mosaic week of creation. But Pico was not content with the imposition of an overall numerical structure capable of expressing the theme; numerical decorum required that the seventh chapter of each book must be concerned with Christ, because Christ 'is our Sabbath, our rest, and our felicity'. This literary principle follows from a consideration of the spiritual meaning attributed to the Mosaic account of creation. It is because Moses established the seventh day as a day of rest that 'we have taken care that every exposition of ours shall always in the seventh chapter be turned to Christ'.

Pico's works are a splendid source for a study of that syncretistic vision of the one truth which depends, to such a large extent, on a belief in the meaningfulness of numbers. Next to Pico must be placed Francesco Giorgio, a man whose fame outshone that of his professed master. Both the theory and the practice of meaningful literary structure can be studied in Giorgio's *De harmonia mundi* (Venice, 1525 and 1536) and *Problemata* (Venice, 1536 and Paris, 1574), so that Fabius Paulinus' *Hebdomades* (Venice, 1589) is a fairly late example of this general tradition.

These and similar works must not be dismissed as the product of an esoteric trend repugnant to reputable theologians. Much of what we find in Pico, Giorgio, Pontus de Tyard, Paulinus, or Pierre de la Primaudaye can be referred back to patristic sources, to medieval authorities such as St Thomas Aquinas, or again to Renaissance theologians, the reason being that orthodox theology was invaded by syncretistic thought to a much greater extent than we have been prepared to believe in the present century. Since the eighteenth century the absurdity of this type of reasoning has been only too apparent, largely because the syncretistic approach by then had become thoroughly discredited. The very word itself today has pejorative connotations implying a selection of bits and pieces from widely disparate sources. The vision prompting the selection has been forgotten, at the same time that the closely allied concept of meaningful form has been so effectively suppressed as to be virtually unknown. Our complete alienation from the syncretistic tradition is revealed by the irresistible tendency, even among reputable scholars, to associate number symbolism with a mystical rather than a rational approach to reality. Although the arithmologists (including St Augustine and Nicholas of Cusa) again and again define number as *ratio explicata*,[8] the application of number symbolism to the text of the Bible resulted in interpretations that many will find it difficult to refer to as rational. What can *seem* more nonsensical than to attribute a profound spiritual meaning to the dimensions of the Ark? or to the fact that there are 10 laws and 4 gospels? or that David appointed 4 chief musicians and played on a 10-stringed instrument? let alone trace a connection between these occurrences of 10 and 4 on the basis of the Pythagorean *tetraktus* formula? And who would agree that the *literary* structure of Psalm cxix (Authorized Version) – i.e. its division into 22 groups

38

of 8 verses – was designed by the Holy Ghost to permit an important prophecy to be conveyed through the symbolism invested in the form? Yet arguments like these can be traced through the pages of St Augustine and Gregory the Great to those of Cornelius à Lapide (1567–1637). This means that theologians whom we are compelled to consider rational nevertheless habitually attributed meaningfulness to structures described in the Bible, such as Noah's Ark, or to literary structures formed by the text itself. Temporal schemes, too, were important, and all these various structures were related to the structure of the universe.

The motivation for attributing meaningfulness to structures must have been very powerful. It must have been something of a psychological compulsion to believe that God had created a world where absolutely everything was meaningful. One overriding necessity seems to have been to relate the Old Testament to the New in such a manner that God is seen to present a gradual unveiling, through the course of human history, of the scheme of redemption. This scheme is revealed first through types and then in full clarity in the life of Christ, so that the spiritual significance of the chief Old Testament events is realized only when related to the gospels. Since classical number-lore could be used to support the typological interpretation of the Old Testament, the quest for types must have induced a syncretistic attitude. (The converse is also possible; the proposition that in proceeding from the Old Testament to the New we pass from shadowy types to truth was bound to appeal most strongly to minds influenced by Platonic thought.) If Pythagoras could help to prove that the 10 of the law is contained in the 4 of the gospels, then Pythagoras must somehow be admitted into the Christian fold. One way out was to believe that Moses had taught the Greek philosophers, another was to argue in favour of oral transmission in one way or another, in whatever sequence and through many links. It is enough to read the first few chapters of Sir Walter Ralegh's *A History of the World* (1614) to realize the importance attached to this syncretistic view, and it must be underlined that Ralegh fetched this material from reputable theologians such as Benedictus Pererius (*c.* 1535–1610) and Hieronymus Zanchius (1516–90). *A Woorke concerning the trewnesse of the Christian Religion* by Philip of Mornay and translated by Sir Philip Sidney and Arthur Golding (1587, 1592, 1604 and 1617) affirms that Pythagoras learnt his skill from the Hebrews. Moreover, Pythagoras and Plato were indebted to Hermes Trismegistus, and Hermes in his turn was taught by Moses. This means that those who father the sciences of arithmetic and geometry upon Trismegistus 'could not have led us more directly unto Moyses'.[9] These widely disseminated theories made it perfectly legitimate to use classical number-lore to gloss a biblical text.

The Psalms of David are a good starting-point for a study of the prophetic import often attributed by theologians to purely literary structures in the Bible. St Augustine believed that David had a 'mystical purpose in his arrangement of the Psalms', and that it was the Lord 'who inspired him in arranging this diversity, which is certainly not meaningless, however enigmatic it may seem'.[10] Whether the arrangement was attributed to David or to learned editors made no difference; whatever happened to the text was the work of the Holy Ghost.

In view of the great influence upon Protestant poets and theologians of St Augustine, it will be important to establish the kind of meaningfulness which he attributed to the arrangement of the Psalms. Did he consider the sum total, for example, as meaningful? or again the traditional divisions into 3 groups of 50, or into 70 plus 80? And what about the well-known groups formed by the Penitential Psalms (7) and the Psalms of Ascent (15), and the structure of Psalm cxviii (Vulgate)?[11] Finally, there is the point so strongly underlined by Fabius Paulinus that the number should correspond to the subject-matter. Is this, too, part of the theological concept of meaningful arrangement? Did St Augustine and those who followed him, believe that the Holy Ghost placed the Psalms in such a sequence that the symbolism invested in its ordinal number expresses its theme? If the answer should be yes, and if structures of this kind were proclaimed as meaningful by theologians usually considered as responsible or orthodox, then commentaries on the Psalms ought to be veritable handbooks in the art of numerical composition. And this is exactly what they are. Numerical analysis is the rule rather than the exception, which means that the possible presence of meaningful numerical structures in medieval or Renaissance religious verse must be viewed as evidence of the influence, upon literary theory and practice, of Biblical exegesis.

A systematic study must begin with St Augustine's powerful and moving sermons on the Psalms[12] and with the scholarly commentary written by Cassiodorus.[13] Cassiodorus was heavily indebted to St Augustine, and he pursues the latter's thesis concerning the 'mystical' purpose of the Holy Ghost in ordering the Psalms with extreme logical consistency. Whoever has read Cassiodorus, even in part, will have had it hammered home, again and again, that there is complete agreement between the theme of a Psalm and the symbolism of its ordinal number. The explanation is a reference to God's well-known method of creating the world: since God arranged everything in number, weight, and measure, we must also believe that He placed the Psalms in such an order that their 'virtue' is declared by their number (*in numeris positis atque definitis uirtutes omnium convenire psalmorum*). This general statement is found in Cassiodorus' comment on Psalm xxvi, and similar statements, relevant to a particular psalm, are often encountered. Thus the number of Psalm xviii declares its 'virtue' (*Numerus . . . virtutem psalmi declarare sentitur*), just as the number of Psalm xvii contains the 'mystery' (i.e. spiritual significance) of the Holy Law which is its subject (*Sic praecipua mysteria sanctae legis psalmi istius numero continentur*). The fact that editions of Cassiodorus' works appeared at Antwerp in 1566 and at Paris in 1579 and 1589 may explain why the late sixteenth-century theologian, Petrus Bongus (or Pietro Bongo), quotes so often from Cassiodorus in his systematic survey of the symbolic meaning of numbers – *De numerorum mysteria* – 5 editions of which appeared between 1584 and 1617. Bongo's chapter on the number 2 (*De Binario*) contains a long passage on the numerical decorum observed in the arrangement of the Psalms, and he assigns a prominent place to Cassiodorus' definition of numerical decorum as given in his comment on Psalm xxvi. After reading St Augustine and Cassiodorus, we realize that Bongo is merely repeating their argument when he writes that since the works of the Creator are distributed in number, weight, and measure, those who organized the Psalms into a proper sequence saw to it that the actions narrated in each always agreed with the 'mystery' of the number (*mysteriis numerorum gesta convenire curarunt*).[14]

A few examples must suffice to show how Augustine and Cassiodorus exploited number symbolism in their exposition of the Psalms.

After identifying the *beatus vir* and the tree described in Psalm i with Christ, Cassiodorus describes Christ as the creative monad. Decorum requires that Christ who is the beginning of numbers (i.e. of all created things) should be described in Psalm i:

> Nec vacat quod Dominus Christus est positus in principio numerorum. Unitas quippe specialis, simplex atque perfecta est, nullius indigna, in seipsa perenniter manens: a quo fonte multitudo numerorum sic egreditur, ut ad eam semper, quamvis multiplicata, revocetur. . . .

Christ, then, is the unity out of which issue all numbers, and unity is simple (i.e. not composed) and perfect and always remaining in itself. The multitude of numbers that issue out of unity as from a fountain do so in such a manner that they are capable of achieving a return; this numerical definition of Christ is supported by quoting Romans xi. 36 (*Ex ipso enim et per ipsum et in ipso sunt omnia*), and it is added that the Greeks referred to this unity as the monad.

Cassiodorus goes on to explain how the number of Psalm ii similarly relates to its theme, since this psalm describes the obstinacy of the Jews who refused to recognize Christ in his dual function as man and God. The third place in the sequence was given to the psalm which contains the mystery of the Trinity and the resurrection, since the liberation of David as described in this psalm signifies the resurrection of our Lord. Psalm iv is spoken by the Church, and its number admonishes us to take the gospel to the 4 parts of the world. Cassiodorus adds that the Pythagoreans considered this number as sacred because of its

importance in the structure of the created universe. Psalm vi –
the first Penitential Psalm – has a number well suited to represent
the truly penitent person, since 6 represents constant and un-
wavering perfection.[15] The number 6 also applies to man and to
redemption, since man was created the sixth day and Christ was
crucified on the sixth day of the week, so that the number most
aptly (*aptissime*) contains the beginning of man and the absolution
of sinners. On Psalm vii his comment is that the *septenarius*
admonishes us to think of our eternal rest (symbolized by the
seventh day), the promise of which is given in this psalm.

St Augustine often relates the theme of a psalm to the numerical
symbolism attributed to its heading. Thus Psalm xi is headed
'Unto the end, for the octave, a psalm for David', and St Augustine always interprets the *octave*, whenever it occurs, as the symbol
of our life in eternity. This symbolism follows when the octave is
seen as referring to the eighth age of bliss or again to that eighth
day on which Christ rose from the dead, thus securing eternal life
for man. Because the heading of Psalm xi suggests to St Augustine
that the psalm must be concerned with our life in eternity, he
introduces a numerical argument in his interpretation of verse 9
('The wicked walk round about'). The wicked are insatiable for
the goods of this world, 'and this thirst of theirs is like a wheel
which repeats its circle every 7 days and consequently never
arrives at that eighth day or the day of eternity, which forms the
title of the psalm'. And the world is defined numerically as
multiplicity, God as unity, when St Augustine adds: 'For in
things of time there is that multiplicity which separates us from
God's unity.'

St Augustine begins his sermon on Psalm cl by affirming his
belief that the arrangement contains 'the secret of a mighty
mystery'. Although he admits that it is scarcely possible to fathom
this mystery completely, the symbolism invested in numbers
apparently provides reliable clues. Thus the sum total of psalms
'signifieth the agreement of both Testaments' because 150 contains 15 tens, and 15 is the sum of 7 and 8, and these numbers
are the symbols of this life and of eternity. And since the Old
Testament is concerned with this life, the New Testament with

eternity, this numerical argument 'proves' that the Psalms are a summary of both Testaments. The same numerical symbolism is attributed to the 15 Psalms of Ascent, and the argument is reinforced by stating that there were 15 steps to the Temple for the same reason. The 15 steps symbolize all that is done in both Testaments to secure salvation for man. Although 7 usually represents the world of time, it may also signify the 7 Gifts of the Holy Ghost; the context must decide. Thus St Augustine goes on to say that the 150 psalms may be interpreted in terms of the meanings attributed to 3 and 50, since 150 is 3 times 50. The number 50 'containeth a great mystery' as it consists of a week of weeks (i.e. of $7 \times 7$) to which one adds unity 'to complete the number of fifty'. When we relate 50 to Pentecost and the sending of the Holy Ghost, 7 must be interpreted as a symbol of the Holy Ghost which 'is in Scripture especially spoken of by the number 7, whether in Isaiah or in the Apocalypse'. It is interesting to observe that St Augustine believes that the Holy Ghost came 'on the fiftieth day exactly' because of the appropriateness of the number. This is an exact parallel to the frequently repeated theological argument that God created the world in 6 days because 6 is a number of perfection and therefore capable of signifying the perfection of God's Creation. We find this argument in St Augustine as well as in Philo Judæus. It is amusing that St Augustine should have included it in his treatise *De Trinitate* for the reason that 6 represents the Trinity by virtue of the fact that it is the sum of the first 3 numbers.[16]

But this does not exhaust St Augustine's analysis of the meaningfulness of 50. When seen as the sum of 40 and 10, 50 becomes even more appropriate as a structural number conditioning the sum total of psalms. In this case the symbolism is derived from the fact that Christ ascended after 40 days, and that he sent the Holy Ghost after an interval of 10 days. St Augustine interprets these 40 days as a symbol of our earthly existence (a significance usually attributed to the 40 years in the desert after the exodus and before the entry into the Promised Land), and in doing so he refers to the fact that 'the number four prevaileth in forty; and the world and the year have each four parts'. And when we add 10 – the symbol of the fulfilment of the law in good works – 'eternity itself is figured'.

Because 150 contains 3 fifties, it is 'not unsuitable', since it suggests a multiplication 'by the Trinity'. Nor is it 'without significance, that the fiftieth [Psalm] is of penitence, the hundredth of mercy and judgment, the hundred and fiftieth of the praise of God in his saints. For thus do we advance to an everlasting life of happiness, first by condemning our own sins, then by living aright, that . . . we may attain to everlasting life.'

In view of St Augustine's unique position in the Church, it is perhaps scarcely surprising that St Thomas Aquinas repeats so many of St Augustine's numerical arguments concerning the structure of the Psalms.[17] Thus he agrees that the division into 70 plus 80 proves that the Psalms contain the mystery of the Old and the New Testament (*in hoc libro complentur mysteria veteris et novi testamenti*), but he avoids relating the triple structure to the Trinity, preferring, instead, to relate it to the triple state of the faithful (*triplicem statum populi fidelis*) – the state of penitence, the state of justice and mercy, and the state devoted to praise of the eternal glory of God. This division into 3 groups of 50 follows on analysing the subject-matter, and St Thomas puts the case for numerical decorum with admirable clarity and brevity when he writes that Psalm 1 describes the remission of debts because 50 is the number of the Year of Jubilee, *unde congruit hic numerus huic psalmo, in quo agit de plena remissione peccatorum.*[18]

Cassiodorus associates the sum total of psalms with the deluge, which lasted for 150 days, the reason being that the psalms take us through a spiritual abyss of sins, purifying us so that we may achieve salvation. And since 150 is 3 × 50, this means that remission of sins (symbolized by 50 or the Year of Jubilee) is achieved through the Trinity. Cassiodorus reminds his readers that the same numbers occur in the dimensions of the Ark (300, 50, and 30); which makes him conclude that the same prophetic message is intended. No wonder, therefore, that Cassiodorus ends his commentary on the Psalms by stating that it is quite apparent that the Creator, when he disposed all celestial and earthly things, did so in number, weight, and measure.

The faithfulness with which these structural arguments were repeated in the Renaissance is seen from the reprint of a medieval treatise such as the *Pia, brevis ac dilucida in omnes Psalmos explanatio sanctissimi viri D. Haymoniis* (Freiburg, 1533). The author explains that the 15 Gradual Psalms signify the virtues by which we ascend to the Heavenly Jerusalem, and it was for this reason that Solomon built 15 steps leading to the Holiest of Holies. These steps prefigure our ascent *ad supernam civitatem*, as the prophet shows in these 15 psalms. By this number David and Solomon prophesy the fulfilment of the Old Testament in the New, and they do so through the structure, as 15 is the sum of 7 and 8, and these numbers represent the Old and the New Testaments. The structure conveys another message as well, in that it tells us that the Law, or the Old Testament, cannot give us the eighth day, *id est, aeternum requiem*. Christ alone can give *requiem veram* after we have finished with the 7 days around which the entire world revolves, and so we see that the 15 degrees contain both Testaments.[19]

Before considering the meaningfulness attributed to the complex structure of Psalm cxviii, a few remarks must be inserted on the symbolism attributed to David's 10-stringed instrument. When Bede explains that the 10 strings are the Decalogue in which is comprehended both Testaments,[20] this is an argument which can be understood only by applying the Pythagorean *tetraktus* formula. This formula explains how the first 4 numbers create those mathematical ratios that produce musical harmony; when these numbers are added, they produce 10, which denotes a return to the number 1, or unity. The process can be reversed, so that 10 becomes 4 by being reduced to the sequence 1, 2, 3, and 4, and it is this simple arithmetical argument which explains why Bede can maintain that the 10 strings, or the Decalogue, should be taken to symbolize both Testaments – the Old Testament being represented by the 10 of the law, the New Testament by the 4 of the gospels.

Such is the prevalence of this argument that it is reasonable to assume that it prompted the emblematic frontispiece which adorns the title-page of several of Spenser's publications.[21]

46

Moses with the tables of the law confronts David with his harp, which means that Moses looks to David, the type of Christ, whose 'new song' is a prophecy of the gospels. Since 10 and 4 are inter-changeable in this manner, so that 10 is said to represent both Testaments, the original division of *Paradise Lost* (1667) into 10 Books may have been prompted by this theological version of classical number-lore. Certainly the symbolism is an attractive one. Marcus Vigerius exploited it when he wrote his *Rhetorica Divina* (Nuremberg, 1517), the 10 parts of which were designed as a *decachord* in imitation of David's 10-stringed instrument, as the author explains in his preface. The division into 10, moreover, is a reference to the 10 days of the scheme of redemption, beginning with the Annunciation and the Nativity and concluding with the Ascension and Pentecost; on this decachord of 10 days Christ played the 'new song', creating out of the disparate voices of the parts *unum concentum*. The English theologian Thomas Becon whose works, published in 1564, reveal a thoroughly Puritan bias, found this structural symbolism sufficiently appealing to divide one of his treatises into 10 'chords'; but in view of the Protestant fondness for the Psalms of David this is scarcely surprising.

These concepts of the interchangeability of 10 and 4, of the 'harmony' of the gospels, and of Christ himself as a musical instrument, should be connected with the idea of the creation of harmony from discord (*concentus ex dissonis*). The Fall is not merely *annulled* by the scheme of redemption, but out of the two is created a harmony superior to the one that was lost. This way of thinking about human history tends to impose balanced structures everywhere; the Fall must have occurred at high noon, since this was the hour of the crucifixion, and the two events must be exactly co-ordinated in order to create *concentus ex dissonis*.[22] For this reason the temporal scheme inferred from the Bible was deliberately manipulated to permit an exact correspondence between events associated with the Fall and those connected with the act of redemption; in addition, these antithetically poised temporal patterns were themselves invested with a symbolism derived from the numbers constituting the pattern. The most common observation is that man was both created and redeemed

47

on the sixth day, for reasons connected with the symbolism attributed to this number. Since the resurrection occurred on the eighth day, many assumed that this must also be the day of the Fall. And since the story of Exodus is the story, told through types, of man's fall and redemption (Egypt being the type of sin, the 40 years a type of all of human existence, and the entry into the Promised Land a type of our redeemed state in the Heavenly Jerusalem), then the temporal scheme of the exodus must be aligned with the events of Easter Week.

There are a great many such schemes based on numerical alignments of various kinds; it is virtually impossible to read a Renaissance book on theology or the Bible without coming across one or more. Thus the Israelites left Egypt before dawn, just as Christ rose from the dead before dawn – the first event being a prophecy, or type, of the second. The deluge lasted 40 days, just as Moses fasted for 40 days, the tribes wandered through the wilderness for 40 years, and Christ fasted for 40 days and was dead for 40 hours.[23] In his second discourse on Psalm xxix, St Augustine explains that man was sentenced by God in the evening, just as Christ was buried in the evening. Christ rose the third day in the morning, and so did man, since human history consists of 3 'days'. The first 2 ages in a state of Nature constitute the first 'day', the 2 ages under the Law the second, and the 2 ages under Grace the third and last 'day'. Augustine concludes that each of us must re-enact this sequence during the 3 'days' of our life (youth, maturity, and old age), an idea which Spenser exploited to advantage when he wrote *The Shepheardes Calender* (1579).[24] That Vigerius, in his *Rhetorica Divina* (1517), should compare the number 8 associated with the circumcision and the resurrection, with the Pythagorean interpretation of 8 as a number of Justice and a number representing solidity and permanence, is only one of many examples showing how theologians fused Biblical and classical number symbolism, finding support for the former in the latter.

Since such great importance was attached to chronological structures in the Bible, it is scarcely surprising that Milton should have manipulated the chronological scheme of *Paradise Lost*

48

so as to extract from it a maximum of meaningfulness.[25] The many obvious parallels or contrasts between the acts of Satan and those of Christ indicate how completely Milton thought in terms of a *concentus ex dissonis*. If Christ spends 7 days creating the universe, Satan must similarly use 7 days to undo what has been created, which he does by encircling the earth for 7 24-hour periods. This constitutes Satan's 'Week of Uncreation', and immediately afterwards follows the day of the Fall, a day specifically referred to in the text as the eighth. Hence Milton may be said to place the eighth day of the Fall against the eighth day of the resurrection.

If the presence of a concept in Aquinas is proof of its orthodoxy, then his interpretation of David's 10-stringed instrument in terms of Pythagorean number symbolism must be accepted as orthodox. Such is St Thomas's familiarity with numerical terminology that he uses the *quaternarius*, for example, as a term for our physical existence, referring, in so doing, to Plato and Boethius who related the number 4 to the first solid body (1 being a point, 2 a line, 3 a surface, and 4 a pyramid on a triangular base). Similarly St Thomas refers our spiritual existence to the *ternarius*, and he repeats one of St Augustine's favourite arguments when he considers 7 as a symbol of this life because it joins 4 to 3, body to soul or mind.[26]

The first chapter of the gospel according to St Matthew draws up a chronological scheme from Abraham to Christ consisting of 3 times 14 generations. In his *Triumphus veritatis* (Antwerp, 1609) the Jesuit de la Haye summarizes the chief interpretations advanced concerning the prophecy hidden in these numbers. The 14 judges from Abraham to David, the 14 kings from David to the Captivity, and the 14 priests from the Captivity to Christ indicate Christ's triple role as judge, king, and priest. St Jerome had argued that in the sacrament of this number 14 the parts of the world (symbolized by 4) achieve redemption (symbolized by 10). There are 42 generations in all, a number diligently investigated by the evangelist because of its spiritual significance (*Evangelista numerum hunc studiose notavit, et laboriose quaesivit propter mysterium*), and this significance is grasped on considering that 42 may be

49

resolved into 40 plus 2, or again 4 times 10 plus 2. These 3 numbers explain the symbolism: the *denarius* refers to the Decalogue, the *quaternarius* to this life (because of the 4 elements, the 4 humours, the 4 passions, etc.) in which Christ (associated with the 4 of the gospels) reigns by virtue of these 10 precepts. Taken as a whole the number 40 signifies our laborious existence (*vitae huius labores, tempus, ac decursum significat*) in which the 2 precepts of charity (the *binarius* or number 2) are to be observed so that Christ may reign in us.

The best example showing how a purely literary structure was invested with a symbolic meaning in keeping with the contents, is afforded by patristic and Renaissance commentaries on Psalm cxviii (A.V. cxix).

The structure of Psalm cxviii is alphabetical in that each group of 8 verses begins with the same letter of the alphabet, and there are as many groups of 8 as there are letters of the alphabet (22). Medieval and Renaissance commentators usually summarize patristic interpretations of the symbolic import attributed to the numbers that condition the structure, and this import is invariably related to the theme, which is the attainment of eternal bliss through obedience to the law. That the whole alphabet is used is supposed to indicate that the contents have universal validity. One of those who present this interpretation is the well-known Lutheran reformer, Dr Johann Bugenhagen (1485–1558). The relevant passage in Bugenhagen's commentary (*In librum Psalmorum interpretatio*, 1524) explains the symbolism attributed to the two numbers and then draws the conclusion that the structure conveys the message that only those who walk with God, keeping his law, will be resurrected with Christ to this new and eternal life. The medieval German bishop Haymo (*Pia, brevis ac dilucida in omnes Psalmos explanatio* (Freiburg, 1533), submits the same analysis, but also considers 22 as the sum of 12 (the Apostles) and 10 (the law), so that by this means the psalm can be taken to contain both the law of Moses and that of Christ as conveyed by the Apostles. The number 8 pertains to *aeternam requiem, quae post septem istos dies, per quos mundus iste volvitur, succedit,* and for this reason the structure tells us that the law and Apostolic doctrines lead to beatitude (8, or the *octonarius*). Baptista Spagnuolus Mantuanus (1448–1516) refers to the alphabetical arrangement as a *lusum poeticum*, but not a vain one, *sed admirabili obtectum mysterio, ut fere omnia sunt prophetica.*[27] In other words, the purpose of the arrangement is to make *everything* prophetic, including the form, and the fact that the author was such a well-known poet makes this statement particularly significant. It proves, beyond the shadow of a doubt, that to a major Renaissance poet the meaningfulness of structural numbers was a familiar concept invested with Biblical authority.

Many commentators remind their readers that St Augustine had compared the form of Psalm cviii to that of a tree with 22 large branches each of which had 8 smaller ones, and that he considered this form as a prophecy of the Tree of the Cross and of Christ the Saviour.[28] It is by means of this tree which is Christ that the Bible as a whole is given a circular structure reflecting the great circle of Eternity, the shadow of which is the circle of Time. This well-known argument is set out by Varlenius Sylvius in his *Commentarium libri tres omnes Psalmos Davidicos* (Louvain, 1557). The tree described in Psalm i is Christ, so that the first of David's psalms tells the same story as Genesis of the Garden of Eden in the midst of which is the Tree of Life which is Christ. And at the very end of the Bible, in Chapter xxii of Revelation, we are again confronted by a symbolic representation of Christ as a tree placed in the middle, this time of the Heavenly Jerusalem. The Psalms similarly proceed from the Garden of Eden to the Heavenly Jerusalem in that the 'new song' with which we are exhorted to praise the Lord in the last few psalms is identified with the new song sung by the 144,000 virgins in Revelation xiv. 1–3. The circularity of the overall structure of the Bible would have been even more apparent if one presumed, as many did at one time, that its contents fall into 22 groups or divisions. That such a structure should reflect the circular nature of the deity is apparent on remembering that God says of himself, in the first as in the last chapter of Revelation, that he is Alpha and Omega, the beginning and the end. On the basis of this statement commentators usually concluded that this was an indication that the nature of the deity

51

should be compared to a circle.[29] Cornelius à Lapide, no doubt thinking of the significance usually attributed to the 22 letters of the Hebrew alphabet, observed that St John had to use Greek letters since he was writing in Greek, but as the language of God was Hebrew, the text ought to have read: 'I am Aleph and Thau.'

In his *Problemata* (1536 and 1574) Francesco Giorgio queries the reason for the alphabetical method of composition sometimes encountered in the Old Testament.[30] Aristotle was familiar with the phenomenon, and the technique was a common one in Latin Nativity hymns, but can it be said to be meaningful? His answer is as one would expect; the alphabetical composition suggests that God is a fountain or river whence issue all creatures and everything that is good (*unde creaturae et omnis boni influxus*) in an ordered sequence, and the letters serve as a key to the divine influx which penetrates all who listen to the hymn. Although this statement should be associated with Cabalistic thought, according to which the act of creation was achieved through the letters of the alphabet, the concept was so well known as to be virtually a commonplace.

The preface to Giorgio's *Problemata* is in part an essay on the art of numerical composition, the argument being that the Holy Ghost, in whom are all numbers, composed the holy books in such an exact manner that those whose minds adhere to lower things cannot comprehend it. The original harmony of the world was lost through the Fall, but out of the Fall and the scheme of redemption God created a new consonance, which David well knew and rendered in his music by the power of God. Here, then, is yet another example of the close association between the concepts of meaningful literary form and of musical harmony, both being seen as a reflection of the 'consonance' created through the act of redemption. And, needless to say, this new harmony is a restoration of the harmony that was lost through the Fall of our first parents. The word of God itself assures us, in Job xxxviii, that the act of creation is associated with music, and it does so through the haunting cosmic image of the morning stars singing together and the sons of God shouting for joy. No wonder, therefore, that St Thomas Aquinas, in his gloss on this passage, refers the reader to the Pythagorean theory of the music of the spheres. It is interesting that he should connect this music with the ninefold angelic hierarchies as expounded by pseudo-Dionysius, since it indicates that he found it appropriate that the angelic hierarchies should be organized in terms of the most important of the numbers constituting Plato's formula for the harmony of the universe. And if we consult St Thomas's gloss on Job xl, we see that he, too, like Philo Judæus and St Augustine, associates the week of creation with an ordered numerical sequence; the days denote a sequence and not *temporis successionem*.[31]

The circumstance that Francesco Giorgio, like St Thomas, associates the act of creation both with the Pythagorean theory of the music of the spheres and with the angelic hierarchies[32] suggests that the association may have been traditional. Such an assumption would explain why Milton does exactly the same in Stanzas xii and xiii of his poem 'On the morning of Christ's Nativity. Compos'd 1629.' I have argued elsewhere that the structural numbers of Milton's 'Nativity Ode' (27 and 8) should be interpreted as an enactment of the harmony restored to man through Christ, since these are the crucial numbers in Plato's *lambda* formula.[33] It is now possible to see that the technique would have suggested itself to Milton as an appropriate one in view of the fact that Latin Nativity hymns traditionally employed the alphabetical technique of composition that we find in Psalm cxviii. Milton must clearly have thought in terms of some such preconceived pattern that would make the structure of his hymn to the Christ-child meaningful in the manner attributed to this psalm. And the reason why he used 27 8-line stanzas rather than 22 is found in the stanzas where he follows St Thomas and Giorgio in connecting the harmony of creation with the music of the spheres and the ninefold angelic hierarchies. As a result of this substitution of 27 for 22, the structural numbers enact the creation of consonance *ex dissonis* through the birth and passion of Christ, which is, of course, what the poem is about. To quote Mantuan's comment on Psalm cxviii: the numbers ensure that *omnia sunt prophetica.*

Numbers would scarcely have played such an important role in the exposition of the Psalms unless they had been considered of importance to the Bible as a whole. Thus Bede quotes Isidore's view (shared by Augustine) that the *ratio numerorum* illuminates the mystery contained in many parts of Scripture, whereupon, by way of proof, he quotes Wisdom xi. 21. And one applies the science of numbers to illuminate the text when one realizes that the work of creation is said to require 6 days (or steps) *because* 6 is a number of perfection and hence declares the perfection of the created world.[34] This is the archetypal Biblical instance of the technique of numerical composition, and it seems reasonable to assume that the belief that numerical decorum was observed in the act of creation prompted the similar belief that the Holy Ghost preserved a strict numerical decorum in the arrangement of the Psalms. That first great syncretist, Philo Judæus, who reconciled the Mosaic and Platonic accounts of creation, was the first to give clear expression to the thesis that there is perfect agreement between the work performed on a particular 'day' and its ordinal number. Since the acts of God necessarily are immediate and (to quote Milton) 'more swift / Than time or motion', they must be narrated 'as earthly notion can receive' (*Paradise Lost*, vii. 176 f. and 179); hence the metaphor of the 'week'. The 'days' are steps in a process, and the symbolism invested in the number given to each expresses the nature of its achievement. Animals, for example, were created on the fifth day because animals represent sense perception, and 5 is necessarily the number of the world of sense. The history of this numerical interpretation of the week of creation cannot be given here; suffice it to state that Philo Judæus exerted a profound influence on many theologians beginning with the early fathers, and that Pico's *Heptaplus* (1489) is an important Renaissance expression of this belief in the numerical decorum observed by God as he created the world.

The belief in the meaningfulness of the arrangement of the Psalms would also have been supported by the view that the narrative contained in them is a summary of both Testaments so that it contains all of time from the first day to the last in the great 'week' of human history. No belief was more firmly rooted than this, that the week of creation was a type, or prophecy, of the whole course of history. Thus the creation of the sun on the fourth day was a prophecy of the birth of Christ *in medio annorum*, as Pico explains in considerable detail. The same numerical pattern, therefore, applies to time as to space (or the created universe). The same numbers by means of which harmony was imposed upon the Creation also serve to shape the temporal pattern extending from Creation and the Fall to the final conflagration. The vision of cosmic order therefore fuses with the vision of the order imposed upon the stream of time by the hand of Providence. Moses, who was given a vision of this order, embedded it in his narrative, and so did David or the men who, under the inspiration of the Holy Ghost, placed the Psalms in such a sequence that the structure became as meaningful as that of the universe or the course of human history.

A good seventeenth-century summary of received opinion is provided by Cornelius à Lapide's *In Pentateuchum Mosis* (Antwerp, 1616), where Philo Judæus, St Augustine and Bede are invoked in support of the view that there are 6 days of creation for symbolical and arithmetical reasons. And if we turn to Bede, who is as good a source for this kind of thing as anybody, we learn that numbers derive from God, and from the beginning of the world and of time. The week of creation gives us an ordered progression from 1 to 7, and Bede compares this Mosaic sequence to the Platonic account of Creation as rendered by Boethius. If we exclude the monad, Plato's *lambda* sequence posits 6 steps. Out of the creative monad issue matter (symbolized by the divisible number 2) and form (symbolized by the indivisible number 3); these numbers are combined and then squared and cubed to form a 3-dimensional world. And so Bede concludes that the art of numbers is the art of philosophy, and philosophy is the knowledge of things divine and human.[35]

The circumstance that there are 10 laws and 4 gospels clearly caused many theologians to seek an explanation in Pythagorean number-lore. Cornelius à Lapide (*Commentarii in IV. Evangelia*, 1638) quotes Gregory the Great to the effect that there had to be 4 gospels in order to create a firm structure, since the *quaternarius* is *numerus solidus et quadratus* and thus aptly signifies the solidity and perfection of the gospel (*Evangeliorum soliditatem et perfectionem*). But what is even more important is the circumstance that the *quaternarius* is the *causa, basis, et fons* of the number 10 which represents everything that is perfect, so that the 4 of the gospels becomes the root of the 10 of the law.

It is fairly well known that the 4 rivers of Paradise were considered as a type or prophecy of the gospels, but it is nevertheless surprising that the same prophecy could be attributed to a purely literary structure simply because of the presence in this structure of the number 4. Lamentations consists of 5 chapters, all but the last of which display an alphabetical technique of composition. Because the contents were universally interpreted as a prophecy of the passion of Christ, the structural numbers (22 and 4) were interpreted accordingly. The form was taken to indicate that Jeremiah's lamentation was for the sins of the whole world, as the world is governed by the number 4 (the 4 seasons, the 4 humours, etc.). Both Cornelius à Lapide and Gasparius Sanctius[36] explain the symbolism attributed to the form, and both observe that the alphabetical technique is not found in the fifth and last chapter, although the number of verses is the same (22). They fail to remark that the structure is symmetrical, the pattern being one of 22, 22, 66, 22, and 22 verses, but the fact is sufficiently obvious.

That this is true also of Canticles (The Song of Solomon) is apparent only on studying the commentators. As Milton stated in *The Reason of Church-Government*, Origen 'rightly judges' that the Scriptures contain a divine pastoral drama in The Song of Solomon. And Cornelius à Lapide (*Commentarii in Canticum Canticorum*, 1637) refers to Origen and St Gregory and others who characterized Canticles as a *drama sponsale, sive nuptiale carmen*, written as an allegory *stylo comico et bucolico, quem post Salomonem secutus est Theocritus in Idylliis et Virgilius in Bucolicis*. After summarizing various ways of dividing the poem, the author decides in favour of a division into 5 acts, each of which describes the Church as it proceeds from a state of infancy and adolescence until it reaches maturity in the third act (*quasi virilem aetatem*). The fourth presents its sad decline (*senectutem*) after Constantine through luxury, ambition, schism, and heresy, caused by the pride and avarice of prelates. The fifth and last act, however, shows the renovation and reformation of the Church *ad felicit-atem et gloriam aeternam.*

There are here several points of resemblance with the scheme of Spenser's *The Shepheardes Calender* (1579). Spenser, too, connects the 4 ages of man with the theme of the progress and decay of the Church, and just as the Church in its full splendour is at the centre of Canticles, so Spenser designed a cycle of 12 eclogues where the sixth and seventh eclogues present Christ and the Church through types. Paradise is a type of the Church (our spiritual Paradise), and Eclogue vi (June) describes the landscape as the Paradise that Adam lost, while vii (July) summarizes the Old Testament, the focus being on the types of Christ. This Christocentric structure is beautifully aligned with the course of the sun, which reaches its highest point of elevation in June; the comparison between Christ and the sun is, of course, one of the great theological commonplaces. Thus Cornelius à Lapide's prefatory remarks on the gospels (*Commentarii in IV. Evangelia*, 1638) compares Christ and the Apostles to the sun in the midst of the planets in a manner which recalls Pico's comments, in *Heptaplus*, on the significance of the fourth day of creation. The number 4 applies with equal justice to the gospels, the sun, and Christ; the sun is fourth in the sequence of the planets and it was created on the fourth day, so that it holds the middle both temporally and spatially. Similarly Christ arrived in the fourth millennium *in medio annorum*, as Pico explains. It may seem odd that Cornelius à Lapide should compare the Apostles to the planets, but 7 and 12 were considered interchangeable, since both consist of 3 and 4 (7 being the sum and 12 the product).

Ezekiel's strange and powerful vision of the chariot of God (Ezekiel i and x) provides the most intriguing example of structure as prophecy, and the number 4 is again a key element in this structure. Before I summarize some representative comments on this vision, it will be useful to remember that Milton, in the passage in *The Reason of Church-Government* just referred to, proceeds from praise of the 'very critical art of composition' shown in the 'frequent songs' in the Old Testament,[37] to the

57

expression of his desire to celebrate 'the throne and equipage of God's almightiness, and what he works'. This praise recalls Francesco Giorgio's similar statement in the preface to his *Problemata*, many of which are concerned with questions concerning the possible meaning of Ezekiel's vision. The same association of ideas is found in the first proem to Pico's *Heptaplus*, where Pico first states his wish to 'illuminate' the Psalms of David 'with the torches of interpretation', next connects David's inspiration with that of Moses and both with Plato and Pythagoras, and finally considers 'the mystic pageant of Ezekiel' as an example of the way in which all these (and Christ, too) conveyed their doctrines 'beneath coverings of allegory, veils of myth, mathematical images, and obscure signs of fugitive meaning'. Ezekiel's chariot is treated by many commentators as just such a mathematical image, and it seems likely that Milton's reference to 'the throne and equipage of God's almightiness, and what he works' was directly prompted by his praise of the art of composition shown in the frequent songs in the Old Testament, the connecting link being the mathematical structure attributed to these songs as well as to the chariot. Milton redeemed his promise when he wrote *Paradise Lost*, since he based his description of the chariot of paternal deity on Ezekiel, and this chariot is certainly a symbol of 'God's almightiness, and what he works' (*Paradise Lost*, vi. 710–79). Although Milton's indebtedness to Ezekiel is a matter of common knowledge, no one seems to have been interested in studying what 'the common gloss of theologians' (*Paradise Lost* v. 435f.) may have been concerning this vision. One reason for this omission is surely that the role of the chariot in Milton's epic has not been properly understood, but the importance of this role and its direct relevance to the epic theme will be grasped on considering some traditional interpretations of Ezekiel's vision.

Gregory the Great is perhaps the most authoritative source for the view that the vision shows Christ seated in the middle, so that it anticipates and confirms the vision of St John of the Son of Man placed in the middle of the 7 candlesticks (Revelation, i. 12–13). Moreover, the chariot, like the candlesticks, symbolizes the created universe, so that both visions reveal the supreme truth that Christ

is always *in the middle*. That the chariot has 4 wheels within wheels
proves the thesis that the New Testament is contained in the Old,
through types, while the 4 winged creatures are taken as a
prophecy of the 4 evangelists.[38]

A splendid drawing of Ezekiel's vision adorns the frontispiece
of Antonius Fernandius' *Commentarii in visiones Veteris Testamenti*
(Loudun, 1617), and the text itself shows that Fernandius considered this vision as one of the most important of all Old
Testament prophecies about Christ. The drawing shows the
main body of the chariot as a globe studded with stars, and on top
of this sphere of the universe Christ is shown seated at rest on a
throne placed in the middle. The various interpretations summarized by the author collaborate to create a strong impression that
the vision shows Christ triumphant over evil, and Christ as ruler
of heaven and earth. The many occurrences of the number 4
(the 4 wheels within wheels, the 4 winged creatures and the 4
faces possessed by each) explain why the vision is taken as a
symbol both of the created universe and of the scheme of redemption. As Fernandius explains, these represent all the 4s of
the created universe – the 4 winds, the 4 elements, and the circle
of the 4 seasons of the year (*quatuor anni temporum circulum*).
Since 4 also relates to the 4 corners of the world, this shows that
the 4 gospels will be taken to these 4 corners. But the number
shows, above all, that it is Christ the Creator and Redeemer who
creates *concentus* and *concordia* in the world through the imposition
of this number at all levels of existence, spiritual as well as
physical. (This is, of course, a clear reference to the Pythagorean
*tetraktus* formula for harmony.)

The comments that follow present Christ in his traditional role
as the representative of Justice combined with Mercy. The elevation of the throne from the earth is said to represent *exactam iustitiae
rationem*, and the fact that Christ is seated indicates that he alone
is at rest. As St Bernard had explained, *tranquillus Deus tranquillat
omnia*. The 4 angelic shapes are given a gloss fetched from St
Jerome's commentary on Job xxv: by their free will all the angels
turn themselves towards the love of God and are made as it were
immobile because they persist in the truth. Their faces are always

turned towards God in contemplation of him, and their four-fold shape (each has 4 faces and 4 wings) makes them a fit symbol of constancy: *forma vero quadrata immobilitatis, et constantiae symbolum est.*

That there is a strong admixture here of Pythagorean ideas is quite obvious, and one is amused to find that Gasparius Sanctius, who published a commentary on Ezekiel in 1619, explicitly scouts the notion that there should have been any connection between Ezekiel and Pythagoras: Ezekiel was *not* to the Hebrews what Pythagoras was to the Greeks, let alone the same person. And what could be more insane than to believe that the soul had trans-migrated from the one to the other? The denial shows that such claims must have been made in order to account for the seeming similarity. It is perhaps even more amusing to discover that Sanctius, after his denial of any association between the two, calmly goes on to explain the vision in terms of Pythagorean ideas: the 4 wheels teach us that nature is made of 4, and it is through this number that unity is imposed upon multitude.

Both Fernandius and Sanctius interpret Ezekiel's vision as a revelation of the way in which the created universe achieves union with God through *obedience*. Several marginal glosses in Sanctius state that the chariot is a type of obedience, and Fern-andius makes the same point when he writes that the chariot represents *concordia creaturarum obedientia erga Deum*, so that all created things enjoy communion and concord (*omnia communiter, et concorditer – nulla contradictione*). And he adds that the vision is a prophecy of the incarnation of Christ and hence of the defeat of all evil spirits.

All of this is in complete agreement with the use that Milton made of Ezekiel's chariot in his epic, and the chariot, therefore, is the plainest possible clue to the presence, in the epic, of meaning-ful structures of the kind attributed to the Bible. As a type of obedience the chariot is directly relevant to an epic the theme of which is disobedience. As Gunnar Qvarnström was the first to discover,[39] Milton placed his description of the ascent of Christ in the chariot of paternal deity (the event which defeats Satan and his hosts for ever) at the exact mid-point of his epic, but, unlike

Qvarnström, I would explain this structural phenomenon not in terms of Cabalistic influence, but quite simply as evidence of Milton's familiarity with the 'common gloss of theologians'. We can leave Jewish mysticism alone and yet obtain, from the theologians, all we need to understand the role of the chariot within the epic and why it shows us Christ in the middle.

Christopher Ricks is surely voicing a general feeling when he writes that it is 'all very well to claim that we must disapprove of Adam [for choosing Eve, rather than God] because we know that on certain occasions there are higher claims. What has to be shown is that here, in the poem itself, there is a convincing embodiment of those higher claims.'[40] But the embodiment is right there, at the heart of the epic, when Christ, seated in that chariot which represents perfect union with God through obedience freely given, first defeats Satan and then creates the universe. And the embodiment is there, in our direct sensuous experience, in Books iv and v, of what a harmonious universe is like, and in the intellectual description and discussion of this universe in Books vii and viii. In between falls the war in heaven, a kind of anti-masque of disorder concluded when Christ, the embodiment of order, ascends the chariot on the command of God, the ascension being a prophecy of his incarnation. The fact that Milton preserved the traditional symbolic import of Ezekiel's vision when he adapted it to suit his epic purpose, argues strongly in favour of the importance which he attached to it. Certainly there could be no plainer embodiment of the state of obedience which is a state of harmony, and it is our ignorance of Biblical exegesis combined with our failure to connect the moral issue of obedience with the classically inspired concept of harmony that has prevented our recognition of the fact.[41]

Milton's evocation of Ezekiel's vision no longer tells us that the scheme of redemption, like the scheme of the universe, is based on the number 4, and that all levels of existence are harmonized and achieve union through this number which connects Biblical with classical number symbolism in such a striking manner. Yet Milton certainly tells us plainly enough that the violation of the law of obedience is a violation of the harmonious structure of the universe, including the microcosmos of man with his 4 humours and his 4 passions. We have failed to observe all this because we have forgotten the multi-faceted concept of world harmony which the Renaissance inherited from antiquity,[42] and so we no longer see that this concept inspired most of the details in Milton's picture of the prelapsarian world. The same concept inspired Milton's conduct of the war in heaven, the purpose of which is to show that all power and hence all harmony derive from God as the creative monad, and that multitude without unity is chaos and utter loss of power, physical as well as spiritual.[43]

There is, then, a solid foundation, in Biblical exegesis, for the use of meaningful structures by religious poets. If we accept Pico's argument that 'the scripture of Moses is the exact image of the world', then to imitate nature would mean to reproduce the kind of structure attributed to Holy Writ. *The Shepheardes Calender* as well as *Paradise Lost* show that symmetrical, or Christocentric, structures were particularly appealing. This was only to be expected as the thesis that Christ is always in the middle was nothing less than an obsession with some theologians, while it was universally accepted that Christ holds the middle of both Testaments (in the Old Testament through types). The view that Christ appeared *in medio annorum* must also be characterized as a theological commonplace closely connected with the concept of human history as a 'week' reflecting the events of the Mosaic week of creation.

The theologian Sardo, writing in 1614,[44] drew up a long list of examples showing Christ seated in the middle. Thus Christ is the central figure in the Trinity, placed between God the Father and the Holy Ghost, and Christ was born *in medio nocte* in the middle of Palestine, which in its turn is the centre of the world – Jerusalem being the *umbilicus terrae*. Furthermore, Christ was presented in the Temple *in medio doctorum* and crucified in the middle hanging between earth and heaven, all of which leads to the grand conclusion *Est itaque Christus, utriusque Testamenti centrum*. Francesco Giorgio pursues the same line of reasoning in his

*Problemata*, where he aligns the mid-point of the Heavenly Jerusalem with the mid-point of the earth, so that a plumbline dropped from the middle of the heavenly city (where stands the Tree of Life) would hit the roof of the Temple right above the Mercy Seat.[45]

Once the basic principles have been grasped, the patterns traced by theologians through the two books of God – the universe and the Bible – are fairly simple. There is certainly no need to attribute particular learning to poets who may have preferred to adopt the numerical technique of composition attributed to the deity.[46] A university background is indicated, and a mind drawn towards the syncretistic approach so admirably illustrated by St Augustine, but that is all. The presupposition is simply a thorough familiarity with Biblical exegesis of a kind that has been completely forgotten during the last two centuries or so. To this mantle of forgetfulness must be attributed the fact that so many tend to dismiss number symbolism out of hand as esoteric nonsense, or, at best, as evidence of a philosophic bias incompatible with true Christian piety.

To the Renaissance mind, however, the fourfold nature of the world and of the divine scheme of redemption was a *datum*, an absolute truth contained in the Bible as interpreted by all the great authorities. For this reason the fourfold structure of Lamentations was a prophecy of the 4 gospels to come. That Milton should have used this number for structural purposes, therefore,[47] would have lifted no critical eyebrows in 1667. Indeed, on coming across the centrally placed episode of the ascent in the chariot, readers would have been reminded of Christ's position in the middle and of the way in which he imposes harmony through the number 4. And their familiarity with the meaningful structures attributed to the Bible might easily have prompted a quest for similar 'technical felicities' in an epic based on the Bible. And if we turn to Spenser's scheme of a calendar, this scheme would have provoked associations with Christ as the sun/son of God whose circle encompasses us about on all sides, particularly since the preface proclaims that the cycle commences with January in order to celebrate the birth of Christ. The tempering effected by

63

the 4 of the seasons, the 4 of the passions and the humours, and the 4 of the gospels would have presented itself as a theme obviously connected with such a calendar, and the claim of the envoy that the calendar comprises all of time would seem reasonable to all who remembered St Augustine's alignment of the 4 ages of man and the 4 seasons with the ages in the universal history of man. Readers would have looked for further evidence of order in Spenser's poetic cosmos, perhaps connecting the concept of order with certain numbers featured in the Bible as well as in Plato or Pythagoras, and with the idea of a structure balanced symmetrically around the figure of Christ, who necessarily must appear *in medio annorum*. And Christ, placed at the centre as at the beginning and the end, would have represented the tranquillity of order, the haven of rest for our wearied hearts propelled like St Augustine's towards God, because of their own unrest. *Tranquillus Deus tranquillat omnia.*

It will be realized that the knowledge derived from a study of Biblical exegesis of the kind considered here, serves to elucidate themes as well as structures and that the former may be more important, on occasion, than the latter. That Milton should have placed the ascent in the chariot at the centre is less important than the thematic significance of the episode, but our perception of this significance is directly dependent on our awareness of the placing. That there should be an embodiment of what Christopher Ricks calls 'higher values' in *Paradise Lost*, is all-important, and if my view of this embodiment is accepted, then our response to it will depend on our familiarity with the kind of thinking illustrated by the commentaries on Ezekiel's vision or the Psalms of David. A quest for meaningful structures, therefore, may lead to sudden insight into major themes for the simple reason that these structures embody these themes. If a major poet has imitated the technique of creation so often attributed to the Deity – if he has devised a pattern in his mind before setting pen on paper – then inevitably a study of this pattern will take us right to the heart of his poetic vision. The pattern, so far from constituting a straitjacket, will be a virtually inexhaustible fountain of inspiration. Whenever structure is seen as prophecy, this must needs be so.

1 Pico della Mirandola, *On the Dignity of Man. On Being and the One.*
 *Heptaplus* (New York, 1965), p. 79. Paul J. W. Miller's introduction
 to this useful volume reveals, with startling clarity, our present-day
 attitude to the syncretistic bias of the Renaissance. Pico's belief in
 the one truth that can be found in Greek philosophy as well as in
 sacred writ is characterized as very curious, and it is noted, with
 some surprise, that 'Pico even had some misinformation on the
 "Egyptian" source of Greek thought' (p. ix). The syncretistic
 vision is reduced to a matter of a 'tolerant eclecticism' (p. x), a
 phrase which is utterly absurd, applied to men such as Pico or
 Ficino. The failure to grasp the rational core of this vision is indicated by the statement that 'Even such presumably clear-thinking
 rational philosophers as Plato and Aristotle were seen as initiates
 in a secret tradition of sacred truth' (p. x). To the Renaissance, as
 to antiquity, only the few were capable and worthy of being
 initiated into the cult of highest reason. What we have forgotten,
 today, is the simple point that the Renaissance associated the pro-
 foundest 'mysteries' with man's highest rational powers.
2 English translations appeared in 1586, 1589, 1594, 1602–5, and 1618.
 *The French Academie* is deeply indebted to the dialogues of Pontus
 de Tyard, and these in their turn to Pico, Giorgio, and Leone
 Ebreo.
3 Plato's numerical formula for the harmony of the universe is
 given in the *Timaeus*. Although Pierre de la Primaudaye adopts
 the orthodox view of creation *ex nihilo*, he combines it with the
 Platonic theory of creation according to a preconceived numerical
 pattern, referring, in so doing, to St Augustine. See the first few
 chapters of *The French Academie*, Book III, particularly Chapters
 i and xii. Chapter i explains the *lambda* formula (see the 1618
 edition, p. 638) and identifies it with the 7 'days' in the Mosaic
 week of creation. 'That all things consisted in numbers, and that
 there was neede of the knowledge of them to conceave the sacred
 misteries of God and nature' has been 'laboriously taught' not only
 by Pythagoras and Plato, but by the great doctors of the Church,
 and notably St Augustine. Francesco Giorgio's *De harmonia mundi*

(Venice, 1525 and 1536, and Paris, 1545) gives the most detailed Renaissance exposition of the *lambda* formula and its relevance to the Mosaic account of creation. That this syncretistic interpretation of Genesis influenced the theory of artistic creation is made perfectly plain in the preface, written by the French poet Guy le Fèvre de la Boderie, to the one-volume French translation of Pico's *Heptaplus* and Giorgio's *L'Harmonie du Monde* (1579).

Frances A. Yates, *The French Academies of the Sixteenth Century* (1947), points out that Mersenne placed his account of de Vaïf's Academy, founded in 1570, in his commentary on Genesis simply because it was assumed that the Mosaic story of creation agrees perfectly with that given by Plato in the *Timaeus*, and the purpose of the Academy was to popularize the 'musical' philosophy derived from Plato and Pythagoras and attributed to Moses as the true source.

4 Fabius Paulinus, *Hebdomades* (1589), V, i; p. 232. Paulinus is no doubt indebted to Pico, *On the Dignity of Man* and *Heptaplus* (see the *ed. cit.*, pp. 33 and 68f.). Similar statements can be found in Henry Reynold's *Mythomystes* (1632) where Pico's influence is patent.

5 P. 368. There are as many hymns by Orpheus as there are numbers by means of which the threefold God created the world in the form of the Pythagorean *quaternarius*.

6 Bk v, ch. v; p. 272.

7 St Augustine had organized the *De Civ. Dei* in 22 books (the number of letters in the Hebrew alphabet), and, as he explains himself, the book should be bound in two volumes: one containing 10 books of refutation (in imitation of the Decalogue), the second containing the last 12 books of positive doctrines (in imitation of the Apostolic evangelization of the world). See also *De Civ. Dei* VI. iii–iv for St Augustine's comments on the meaningfulness of the form given by Varro to his treatise of *Antiquities*. St Augustine used symbolic numbers for structural purposes also when he enumerated the false doctrines of one Vincentius; these were listed under 11 headings, since 11 was the number of sin by virtue of the fact that it goes beyond, or transgresses, the 10 of the law. St Augustine's works are full of passages on the meaningfulness of the numbers found in the Bible.

8 *Nec est aliud numerus quam ratio explicata.* Nicholas of Cusa, *De coniecturis*, in *Philosophisch-theologische Schriften*, ii (Wien, 1966),

66

p. 8. This may be somewhat freely translated: 'Number is nothing but reason in action.' The German translation reads: '*Die Zahl ist nichts anderes als der entfaltete Verstand.*'

9 See p. 108 of the 1587 edition. The syncretistic vision of the one truth was gradually discredited in the course of the seventeenth century, and with it the belief in meaningful form. Swift mocks the tradition in *A Tale of a Tub*, and a direct attack is found in *A Treatise Of The Sibyls . . . Written Originally by David Blondel; Englished by J.D.* (1661). St Augustine is said to have been much too credulous when he believed the claims made on behalf of Hermes Trismegistus (*De Civ. Dei* XVIII. xxiii), and so was the Emperor Constantine who accepted the view that the Erythrean Sibyl, Daphne, uttered 33 verses in a state of divine inspiration, verses that form an acrostic stating that Jesus Christ is Saviour. The sum total of lines, 33, was another 'proof' of the validity of this interpretation that Blondel was unable to accept. Acrostics, so he argues, are never written in a divine fury, but by crafty invention out of a design to cheat (p. 31). And that Virgil's fourth eclogue should contain a prophecy of the birth of Christ is utter nonsense; Constantine 'read in his *Poem*, what indeed is not in it, out of such an Imagination, as those have, who, looking up to the Clouds, think they see such and such Figures therein'. (P. 45.) Although the author refers to the 'seeming Novelty' of his sentiment, his views were destined to prevail.

10 *De Civ. Dei* XVII. xiv.

11 The numbering of the Psalms in the Authorized Version differs from that of the Vulgate. The numbers cited here will be those of the Bible used by the theologian in question.

12 For St Augustine's sermons on Psalms i–xxxvii the best English translation is that of Dame Scholastica Hebgin and Dame Felicitas Corrigan, *St Augustine on the Psalms*, in *Ancient Christian Writers* xxix and xxx (1960 and 1961). For the remaining psalms the best available English translation is the 6-volume edition published by John Henry Parker of Oxford from 1847 to 1857.

13 All quotations from Cassiodorus are from his *Expositio Psalmorum* in *Corpus Christianorum*, xcvii–xcviii (Turnholti, 1958).

14 *Mystical* is used by theologians to indicate a spiritual level of meaning over and above the purely literal level. Bede, in his commentary on the Psalms (*Opera* (1612) viii) defines *mysterium* as *spiritualem sensum*. Andrew Willet, *Hexapla in Exodum* (1608), p. 8, uses the

word in this sense when he writes that the 'mysticall number of twelve is used in Scripture, to describe the spirituall state of the Church under Christ' so that 'the new Jerusalem is set forth by twelve gates, and twelve foundations, Apoc. 21'. Pietro Bongo's *De numerorum mysteria* (1584–5 and many subsequent editions) is simply an encyclopedic survey of the symbolic meanings traditionally attached to the various numbers from one to multitude. It is interesting that Bongo considers the problem of editorial interference with the text; the Hebrews did not place the Psalms in any particular order, not even the first, the fiftieth, or the hundredth, it was Esdras who undertook the work, and later on the Seventy Elders. In this manner 'by a spiritual and celestial power, each of them was numbered and placed in the most perfect sequence'.

15 A number was considered perfect by mathematicians when it equalled the sum of its aliquot parts. Between 1 and 10, 6 is the only such number (the aliquot parts being 1, 2, and 3), 28 between 10 and 100. In all other cases the sum either falls short of, or exceeds, the number itself.

16 St Augustine, *De Trinitate*, IV. iv. 7–8 (*Numerus ternarius in Scripturis*). See *Oeuvres de Saint Augustin*, xv (Paris, 1955), pp. 356–61.

17 See particularly the *Prooemium* to his commentary on the psalms in *Opera*, xiii (Antwerp, 1612).

18 'Hence this number agrees with this psalm, which is concerned with the full remissions of sins.' See also Bede, *Opera* viii (Köln, 1612), cols 307f.: '*Constanter hic Psalmus, in quo est poenitentia anhelate, et peccatorum remissio postulatur, in ordine huius numeri collocatur.*'

19 See comments on the first Gradual Psalm (cxix). The symbolism of the 15 steps and the 15 Gradual Psalms conditions the division into 15 chapters of Cardinal Bellarmine's famous treatise on the ascent to God, as the preface explains. See *A Most Learned And Pious Treatise . . . framing a Ladder, Wherby Our Minds May Ascend to God, by the Stepps of his Creatures* (Douay, 1616), tr. by T. B. Gent, and *Iacob's Ladder consisting of fifteene Degrees or Ascents to the knowledge of God by Consideration of His Creatures and Attributes* (1638), by H. I.

20 Bede, *Opera* viii, cols 307–12 (the preface to the commentary on the Psalms).

21 Spenser, *Muiopotmus* (1590) and *Complaints* (1591). The same emblematic picture adorns the title-page also of Mornay's *A Woorke concerning the trewnesse of the Christian Religion* (1587), tr. Sir

Philip Sidney and Arthur Golding, a book whose bias is completely syncretistic.

22 See, for example, the commentary on Canticles, viii. 5 by Cornelius à Lapide, *Commentarii in Canticum Canticorum* (1637), p. 489: the God of Justice and Wisdom decreed that a tree should satisfy the sin committed by means of a tree, and that whence death came, life also should come (*ut in ligno satisfieret culpae in ligno commissae; ut Diabolus qui in ligno vincebat, in ligno quoque vinceretur; et unde mors oriebatur, inde vita resurgeret.*)

23 John Swan, *Speculum mundi* (1635 and 1644), p. 497 of the edition printed in 1644 (or 1643), writes that 'as man was formed the sixth day, and did eat of the tree the sixth hour: so Christ reforming man, and healing the fall, was fastened to the tree the sixth day and the sixth houre'. The day of the Fall, therefore, was Friday 22 April, 'the Sun then entring into Aries [*sic*], and giving beginning to the Spring, even as Christ was then promised for the quickening and reviving again of Mankind, who also about the same time of the yeare did actually shed his bloud, and thereby paid the price of Mans Redemption'.

Marcus Vigerius, 'Chorda Septima' *Rhetorica Divina de Oratione* (Nürnberg, 1517), gives numerous examples of *concentus ex dissonis*. 'Chorda Octava' associates both the Fall and the scheme of redemption with the number 40; the 'mystery' of 40 was introduced by the Fall, and Christ spent 40 days in the desert and was dead for 40 hours to annul the 40 days of the deluge and the 40 years of wandering in the desert. De la Haye's *Triumphus veritatis* (Antwerp, 1609), p. 157, in the same manner juxtaposes the Fall with Christ's 40 days in the desert. It seems reasonable to assume that Milton's choice of theme for *Paradise Regained* reflects this strong tradition.

Alexander Ross, *The First Booke Of Questions and Answers upon Genesis* (1620), p. 71, states that Adam fell the eighth day after his creation, so that resurrection on the eighth day serves to annul it. Cornelius à Lapide, *Commentaria in Pentateuchum Mosis* (1616), p. 54, as usual summarizes received opinions. Thus he refers to Pererius who believed there were 8 days between Adam's creation and his fall, while others argue in favour of 40 days, yet others 34 years for the reason that Christ lived into his thirty-fourth year, *et peccatum hoc expiavit*.

Alastair Fowler and Gunnar Qvarnström find that the chronological scheme of *Paradise Lost* comprises 33 days, the Fall occurring on the thirty-second day of the epic action and the sixth day of creation occurring on Day 19. This means that the Fall occurs on the fourteenth day after the creation of man, and 14 is associated with the Passion. See p. 49. At the centre of this chronological scheme (on Day 17) falls the creation of the sun, the traditional symbol of Christ, which means that the temporal scheme has a Christocentric structure, at the same time that the sum total of days (33) reflects the number of years spent by Christ on earth. See *The Poems of John Milton*, ed. John Carey and Alastair Fowler (1968), p. 445, and Gunnar Qvarnström, *The Enchanted Palace: Some Structural Aspects of Paradise Lost* (Stockholm, 1969).

24 See my article on the structure of *The Shepheardes Calender* in *Renaissance and Modern Studies* vol. xiii, pp. 49–75 (Nottingham, 1969).

25 See the detailed analysis of the chronological scheme in Qvarnström's study referred to above.

26 See St Thomas's comments on Psalm vi, where he follows St Augustine quite closely.

27 *In omnes Davidicos Psalmos . . . commentaria* (Rome, 1585).

28 This interpretation is not given in St Augustine's sermons on this Psalm, and I have been unable to locate the passage in his works. The commentary on the Psalms by the Jesuit Lorinus, *Commentarium in librum Psalmorum* (1611–16), iii. 479 explains that *sub similitudine arboris, quae in medio paradisi erat, Augustino hunc psalmum revelatum fuisse*.

29 See, for example, St Gregory, *Opera* (1674), i. 1174; Richard of St-Victor, *Opera* (1650), Ch. 3 on the Apocalypse, and A. Sardo, *De arcanis sacrae utriusque theologiae scholasticae* (Rome, 1614), p. 330. Sardo writes that the definition means that the nature of God is circular (*ipse est circulus*), and that the circle is a symbol of perfection. When Christ became man he did so in order that the circle connecting man with God should be complete. Sardo 'proves' the circular nature of the deity by referring to the fact that the numerical value of the letters in the name of God is respectively 5, 6, and 10, and that these are circular numbers. (A circular number reproduces itself in the last digit when multiplied with itself.) *Et sic Deus est veluti sphaera*. Much of this symbolism, by the way, is incorporated in the emblematic drawing, by William Marshall, adorning the title-page of John Swan's *Speculum mundi*.

30 *Problemata* III. i. 26 (fol. 140 v. of the 1574 edn).

31 This was a commonly accepted view. See John Colet, *Letters to Radulphus* (1876), pp. 23f.; Augustinus Eugubinus, *Cosmopoeia* (Loudun, 1535); Jean Bodin, *Universae naturae theatrum* (Loudun, 1596), pp. 18f.; Bartholomaeus Chassanaeus, *Catalogus gloriae mundi* (1617), p. 531, and Benedictus Fernandius, *Commentatiorum atque observationum moralium in Genesim* (Loudun, 1618), col. 106.

32 *Problemata* V. ii. 176 connects the interpretation of Job xxxviii with the concept of the *coeli concentus* (a harmony created by the orderly progression of things out of unity in the act of creation); it is of this order that the Prophet sings in Psalm cxviii. See also *Problemata* V. iv. 310.

33 M.-S. Røstvig, 'The Hidden Sense: Milton and the Neoplatonic Method of Numerical Composition'. *The Hidden Sense and Other Essays* (Oslo, 1963), pp. 1–112; M.-S. Røstvig, 'Milton and the Science of Numbers', in *English Studies Today* (Roma, 1966), pp. 267–88.

34 Bede, '*De computo dialogus*', *Opera* (1563), col. 111.

35 *Ibid.*

36 The dates of their commentaries are respectively 1621 and 1618.

37 Columbia edn of Milton's *Works*, Vol. III. i (1931), p. 237.

38 Gregory the Great, *Opera* (1674), I. 1174. See *The Poems of John Milton*, ed. John Carey and Alastair Fowler (1968), p. 761 n.

39 Gunnar Qvarnström, *Dikten och den nya vetenskapen* (Lund, 1961); the discussion of the enthronement of Christ in the chariot of paternal deity was revised and included in *The Enchanted Palace. Some Structural Aspects of Paradise Lost* (Stockholm, 1967).

40 See his review of three Milton studies in *The New York Review of Books*, 9 June 1966.

41 Don Cameron Allen, *The Harmonious Vision. Studies in Milton's Poetry* (Baltimore, 1954), p. 28, holds that Milton discriminated sharply between Christian and pagan philosophy on this point, although he admits that Christian thought had 'strong elements of pagan Pythagoreanism'. It is my impression that these elements had been so completely assimilated that they should not be referred to as 'pagan'. Further research is required before the extent of this assimilation can be properly assessed. An interesting study along these lines is S. K. Heninger's 'Some Renaissance Versions of the Pythagorean Tetrad', *Studies in the Renaissance*, viii, 7–33 (1961). See also Heninger's article on 'The Implications of Form for *The Shepheardes Calender*', *ibid.*, ix. 309–29 (1962).

42 Leo Spitzer, 'Classical and Christian Ideas of World Harmony', *Traditio*, ii (1944), 409–64 and iii (1945), 307–64. These important articles were published in book form (Baltimore, Md., 1963).

43 See, for example, St Augustine's *De vera religione*, xxxv (*Oeuvres de Saint Augustin*, vol. viii, pp. 118f.) and the sources cited in my article on 'Milton and the Science of Numbers', *English Studies Today* (Rome, 1966), pp. 267–88.

44 A. Sardo, *De Arcanis* (Rome, 1614), p. 391.

45 Giorgio, *Problemata*, VI. ix. 375.

46 K. K. Ruthven, 'Elizabethan Learned Poetry: An Introduction', *The Critical Survey*, iii (1967), 76, remarks *à propos* of Alastair Fowler's numerical analysis of Spenser's *The Faerie Queene* (*Spenser and the Numbers of Time*, 1964), that it 'leaves one in no doubt that numerology was among the more arcane accomplishments of medieval and Renaissance poets'. Although this is no doubt valid for more intricate numerical patterns connected with astronomy or astrology, it is important to bear in mind the pervasive presence of a fairly simple kind of half Biblical, half classical number-lore. The more intricate patterns presume the presence of simple patterns that would form a point of departure for more sophisticated poets.

47 This is argued by Gunnar Qvarnström in *The Enchanted Palace* (Stockholm, 1967).

# Theme and number in Chaucer's *Book of the Duchess*

RUSSELL A. PECK

Elegies normally move from turbulent emotion, embittered isolation and indolence, towards a renewed sense of community and acceptance of life. The *Book of the Duchess* differs from other elegies not so much in overall movement as in the philosophical consistency of its argument and the variety and indirectness of its rhetoric. The poem adheres to a cosmology of sympathetic correspondences. These correspondences are expressed largely through traditional analogues and numerological devices. My aim in this essay is to define the poem's themes within their cultural background and relate them to the poem's symmetrical form. The first section of my argument outlines relevant philosophical premises about man's mind and defines the poem's psychological plot. The second relates the plot to the idea of number and discusses symbolic numbers upon which the poem is built. The third considers number metaphors in the poem's diction.

## I

The *Book of the Duchess* is the drama of a soul overwhelmed by grief and struggling to reorient itself. Its general formula for mental restitution is Christian; its specific formula is Boethian. Let us begin by reviewing a fundamental question of medieval philosophy which has indirect bearing on the elegy. How can man, with his unstable and restless heart, hope to find happiness and repose in the mutable world? The traditional answer is paradoxical.[1] Man fulfils his nature and thus enjoys repose by loving God. But how does he love God? Since he can love only what he knows, he must know God. But how can man presume to know God? He may know God by knowing himself, for Scripture tells him that man was created in God's image. And how may he know himself? By evaluating his experiences and what history and Scripture tell him about himself – information he stores up in his memory, organizes in his intellect, and contemplates through love. This trinity of memory, intellect, and love enables him to perceive a likeness to God's triune Oneness.[2] While participating thus in divinity, he enjoys natural intention and finds repose.

Within this simplified Augustinian argument are several assumptions relevant to the *Book of the Duchess*. First, the argument assumes that an artist may be known by his work.[3] Man discovers God's thoughts in the pattern of creation. In Chaucer's elegy, recollection of the 'chef ensample' of Nature (l. 911), the 'goode faire White' (l. 948),[4] enables the bereaved to get beyond his grief to participate in something greater. Contiguous to this view is the idea that man, by assessing creation, becomes an artist in his own way. He allays the chaos of his passions with form. This explains the therapeutic benefit art has for Chaucer's 'poet' as he reads and writes himself out of his lethargy. St Augustine's argument also predicates that man's sense of being depends on the way he looks at things. The quest for mental composure places highest premium on the exploration of processes of intellection. It is a probing of memory, intellect, and love. In view of the prominence philosophers gave this consideration, no wonder dream vision became one of the most common genres of medieval literature. Finally, the argument affirms that one's sense of well-being is proportionate to one's sense of unity. Happiness is the focusing of one's life; sadness is its dispersal. Chaucer's friend John Gower summed up the matter succinctly when he observed that division is 'modor of confusioun'.[5]

Although these assumptions lurk behind Chaucer's fundamental conception of his poem, the more immediate model is Boethius' *De consolatione philosophiae*.[6] It is the obvious source to look to when a medieval writer deals with consolation and Fortune. In the *Book of the Duchess*, however, it is not simply philosophic assurance or scholastic logic that Chaucer gleans from Boethius. It is the plot.

The opening forty-three lines of the *Book of the Duchess*, like the First *metrum* of *Boece*, establish the poem's dilemma. The poet, overwhelmed by 'sorwful ymagynacioun' (l. 14), explains as best he can his grief and exhaustion. Mental frenzy has left him dazed and unable to sleep. He has lost his ability to differentiate experience (ll. 8–10) and is 'a mased thyng', 'felynge in nothyng' (ll. 11–12). Fearful of death (l. 24), haunted by fantasies (l. 28), he cannot get hold of himself. Sorrow has obliterated his sense of being, so that like Boece he cannot even tell what his trouble is (ll. 30–5).[7]

This opening description of the poet's confusion is not simply one of despair, however. There is more in his heart than sorrow. He may be confounded, but he has it in him to seek counsel in order to recover what he has lost. (Compare *Boece* V. *met.* iii, which explains man's confusion as simultaneous knowing and not-knowing.) Although trapped in a lethargy he does not comprehend, his analysis of its effects on his soul is astute. He knows his psychological disintegration is unnatural, 'agaynes kynde' (l. 16). Moreover, as he wonders 'be this lyght' (l. 1), he intuits the direction he must turn if he is to drive his dark spirit away. He also allows there is 'phisicien but oon' (l. 39) who may heal him of his sickness. The physician and sickness have puzzled critics, and indeed the allusion is cryptic (though deliberately so). Obviously the physician refers to one who heals; moreover, considering the illness, the healing must refer to the regaining of composure. Huppé and Robertson and, independently, J. Burke Severs have recently argued that the most likely association with 'phisicien but oon' would be God.[8] Certainly the tradition of Christ the healer is strong and offers an instant response in an elegiac context. In applying such a gloss, however, we must be careful not to obscure the subtlety of Chaucer's figuration. The poem is to some extent about revelation and discovery. Thus the physician metaphor must remain sufficiently flexible in our minds to apply to various manifestations of healing as they occur in the poem. The metaphor hovers throughout the poem in the Boethian archetype of counsellor-healer.[9] It is implicit in the well-intended genius of the poet as he studies clerks of 'olde tyme'; it is explicit in the recollection of 'goode faire White', the knight's 'lyves leche' (l. 920). It is manifest in 'Trouthe hymself' whom White embodies (l. 1003), and ultimately emanates from the vision 'be seynt Johan' of the homeward bound king, where Christ is indeed immanent. All these agencies of health are extensions of the same Christian archetype and apply differently at different stages in the distraught patient's search for tranquillity. Here at the outset of the poem he knows only the type, a matter 'good to kepe' (l. 43) until the rest is explained.

The plot gets actively under way when the poet calls for a book 'to rede, and drive the night away' (l. 49). Chaucer emphasizes the deliberateness of his act by giving him a real choice: he will read rather than play 'at ches or tables' (l. 51). The point seems to be that in his effort to re-order his mind, he intentionally disengages himself from Fortune's games, those diversions which obscure pain but do not cure the ailment. His decision to read is comparable to Boece's decision to write, an act of engagement which makes possible subsequent realization of 'sovereign good'.[10] Although the 'night' he hopes to drive away may be understood literally, it is also a figure for his heavy spirits. The success of his attempt is seen in the temperate, clear and cloudless morning of his dream.[11]

Reading is an apt emblem for taking counsel. (Consider the Middle English pun on 'rede'.) Boccaccio argues: 'Through fiction, it is well known, the mind that is slipping into inactivity is recalled to a state of better and more vigorous fruition.'[12] And such is true in the *Book of the Duchess*. The poet reads to free himself from his lethargy. Recall the Prologue to the *Legend of Good Women*, where we are told that men find in books 'olde thinges' to keep 'in mynde' which hold of 'remembraunce the keye' (F, ll. 17–28). The poet in the *Book of the Duchess* must think the same way, for he chooses his book with care, one written 'for to be in minde' (l. 55) by men who 'loved the lawe of kinde' (l. 56). It is suitable counsel for one who knows his behaviour is 'agaynes kynde'. Certainly its subject is appropriate. It is about 'quenes lives, and of kinges' (l. 58), that is to say, governance, which is precisely what he has lost.

The story of Alcyone exemplifies what happens to one who grieves too much. She is totally bereft when Seys dies. Trapped by sorrow, she alienates herself and unkindly wishes she were dead. Her grievous prayer is answered, but in her distraction she is unable to comprehend the answer. Seys appears as counsellor at the foot of her bed and offers the only advice open to men who face death in this world:

Awake! let be your sorwful lyf!
For in your sorwe there lyth no red.
For, certes, swete, I nam but ded;
Ye shul me never on lyve yse.
But, goode swete herte, that ye
Bury my body, for such a tyde
Ye mowe hyt fynde the see besyde;
And farewel, swete, my worldes blysse!
(ll. 202–9)

But Alcyone seems incapable of accepting the fact of death. She looks up after Seys observes compassionately, 'To lytel while oure blysse lasteth!' (l. 211), but she fails to understand. She 'saw noght' (l. 213). Instead of heeding his advice to arise, she dies.

To appreciate the counsel that this exemplum offers, we should consult the traditional version to see how Chaucer has altered it to his purposes.[13] About half of Ovid's tale concerns events prior to the shipwreck; this Chaucer condenses to a dozen lines. Clearly, for him Alcyone's grief is germane. But his most significant change is the conclusion. In Ovid, Ceyx advises Alcione to arise and mourn for her dead lord. She peers intently at the shade, then awakens to follow its advice. To mourn she goes to the shore where last she saw her husband, and there unexpectedly finds the body. As she runs towards it both are changed into birds. Chaucer reverses Ceyx's counsel and imposes specifically Christian attitudes on the conclusion. His Seys says Alcyone should mourn no more;

77

no counsel lies in sorrow (l. 203). He underplays death's significance, 'I nam but ded', and tells her where to find the body to
bury it. Unlike the Ovidian Alcione, Chaucer's sees 'noght'.
She ignores her counsellor's request to 'Awake' and 'bury my
body', and instead of arising, dies on the 'thridde morwe'. These
Christian attitudes which Chaucer adds to the story, namely, the
recognition of death as the end only of mortality, the need to
bury the body, and the allusion to the third morrow (traditional
time of Resurrection), define the futility of Alcyone's grief.[14]
She loses in effect, more kings than Seys: her grief drowns the
king of her soul.[15]

After reading the story, sad though it is, the poet shows a
remarkable renewal of spirits. His engagement in the art of
Nature's old clerks has been felicitous. Part of his rejuvenation
may be attributed to his diligence. He has been a model reader,
applying himself with industry to his work. He studies the text
closely, more than once, and wonders about its validity (ll. 231–3).
In doing so he begins to free himself from the lethargy of 'sorwful
ymaginacioun'. He becomes more objective, even playful. It is
as if some of the wit in the descriptions of shrewish Juno's
commands (ll. 136–52) and the messenger's descent to the cave of
sleep (ll. 179–87) has rubbed off on him. He decides to make a
game of sacrifice – to Morpheus, Juno, or someone else (it does
not seem to matter much with these pagan deities!) – in hope of
getting some sleep. Instead of relinquishing 'body, herte, and al'
(l. 116) to the false god as Alcyone had done (he knows 'god but
oon'), he sportingly offers a feather bed of pure white dove's
feathers, covered with imported black satin, and pillows encased
in 'clothe of Reynes' – all this and a chamber besides, decorated
with painted walls and tapestries. Surely such fees would please
Morpheus, and even Juno! His vow is a witty version of render-
ing to Caesar what is Caesar's, multiple fees to multiple gods.
What is more, it works. He lays his tired body to rest. As he
sleeps, head in book, he becomes the epitome of contemplation.

With the dream we enter the inner world of the mind. The
initial harmonious vision implies remembrance of 'kynde'.
The birds sing 'al of oon acord' (l. 305), a 'solempne servise'

(l. 302) like 'a thyng of heven' (l. 308). Their music is spontaneous and whole-hearted. Outside, the weather is bright and clear, and light streams through the windows. For the moment, at least, night has been driven away. This awakening into dream is not, however, ultimate recognition. It is more like an insight which provides a locus for the ensuing journey, a journey which will enable the poet to encompass what Boethius calls 'the longe moevynges of his thoughtes' (III. Met. xi. 6).[16] The glimpse of tranquillity holds focus for a moment, then is interrupted by the hunt. This interruption is the first of many which follow. The dream is filled with them. They stand as commentary on man's very existence in the mutable world where life is a progression of glimpses but never full vision.

The hart hunt is symbol of the poet's search for repose. Its meaning, like that of the physician, unfolds as the poem progresses. Huppé and Robertson suggest Christian traditions behind such hunts, the analogue being Christ's search for the soul.[17] In the *Book of the Duchess*, however, the essentially Christian character of the hunt is not made clear until the end of the hart-hunting, and even then it is perceived only through the dark glass of metaphor. Several critics have noted a pun on 'hert-huntyng' to imply 'soul-searching',[18] a gloss that labels appropriately the dialogue between Black Knight and dreamer. Perhaps we come closest to Chaucer's intention if we understand the hunting analogy as a search for *suffisance*. That is a term Chaucer uses several times in the poem, one which implies in addition to satisfaction, humanistic notions such as fulfillment of 'naturel entencioun', bliss, contentment, oneness of being, and true sense of domain, as well as philosophical notions such as Truth, Love, and Christ. It is a term which pertains both to what the soul needs and what the will desires.[19]

If we understand 'hert-huntyng' as search for *suffisance*, however, we should take care not to impose modern notions of psychology on the poem. The poem has nothing to do with analysis of personality. It probes, but not as our analyst would probe. Chaucer deals with a sequence of static and highly stylized surfaces. We move from a sick man, to a book, to a chamber, to a hunt, to woods, to a man in black, to a woman of white, to the veil of revelation itself. Each tableau brings the audience nearer the heart of the problem. (Compare the discovery of the wound in *Boece* I. *pr.* iv. 5–6.) The rhetoric of his mental search is distinctly different from the character exploration we expect in a modern novel. Martin Stevens is certainly right in insisting upon the static quality of the 'characters' in the *Book of the Duchess*.[20] (This does not mean that its plot is static.) Instead of psychological realism we get allusion and analogy. This is one reason why numerology plays so import a role in poetry of this kind. As we shall see, it helps keep analogues and referents straight.

The 'longe moevynges' of the poet's mind become polarized in the dialogue between dreamer and Black Knight. Their debate should come as no surprise, since we already encountered both implicitly in the opening monologue where the poet struggled to assuage his grief, at once forgetting and remembering. Chaucer's introduction of this inquest is carefully planned. The hunt's interruption brings with it a regrouping of metaphors. The dreamer enters a wood. This is the realm of 'kynde' with all her plenitude. It is also a realm of multiplicity, a place of many harts, does, fawns, and even squirrels besides, so many in fact that they exceed man's capacity to number them (l. 440). This is the realm of temporal nature. Here the eye of the beholder must distinguish, evaluate, and relate the beauty to himself if he is to enjoy it. The wood is potentially a paradise or a place in which to hide, depending on the 'entencioun' of the beholder. There, in the darkest place, we encounter the Black Knight, whose heart suffers the wound we are seeking to discover.

The knight has hidden away because he has lost his *suffisance*. His heart-cold grief has left him unable to share the common profits of nature. In fact, like Alcyone, he has rejected nature entirely, wishing he had never been born. The only gift he would gladly accept is death. Observing the unnaturalness of the knight's behavior (ll. 467–9), the dreamer assumes the stance of counsellor 'ryght at his fet' (l. 502). (Compare the stance of Seys as he appears to counsel Alcyone, or that of Philosophy at the 'uttereste corner' of Boece's bed.) What he sees is a man divided against himself, 'todrawen . . . diversely' by sorrow (to borrow Boethius' phrase).²¹ The knight argues with 'his owne thoght' (l. 504) as if he had 'wel nygh lost hys mynde' (l. 511); he complains 'withoute noote, withoute song,' the antithesis of the 'oon acord' of the harmonious chamber. Though his desperate mood is like that of Alcyone, he finally looks up to see his counsellor. The effect is immediately felicitous. He speaks courteously, 'as hit had be another wyght' (l. 530). Although the phrase underscores the knight's fragmented being, nevertheless his courtesy is a step in the right direction. It imposes some semblance of order, albeit artificial, on his spiritual anarchy and redirects his impulse towards community. Like Boece, he is being 'destroubled . . . out of . . . [his] thought' (l. 524).

What follows is an elaborate version of medieval psychotherapy. The dreamer, assuming the role of counsellor-physician, says he will do all in his power to make 'hool' this knight whose heart 'semeth ful sek' (l. 557) under his side. He gets the knight to talk through his grief three times. With each rehearsal the knight comes closer to the crux of his sadness, namely, the acceptance of death as a natural fact. The process of consolation, like that outlined in Boethius, is a combination of confession and recollection. The knight will both discover the wound he is trying to hide and at the same time reclaim truths his sorrow has obscured. He will, in effect, pull himself together through acts of memory, intellect and love.

The knight begins his shrift by lashing out against the very conditions of life. He cannot say 'no' to death, but he can at least say 'no' to life by choosing death:

> May noght make my sorwes slyde,
> Nought al the remedyes of Ovyde,
> Ne Orpheus, god of melodye,
> Ne Dedalus with his playes slye;
> Ne hele me may no phisicien,
> Noght Ypocras, ne Galyen;
> Me ys wo that I lyve houres twelve.
>
> (ll. 567–73)

Chaucer has contrived this catalogue of wilful negations to emphasize the degree of the knight's desire of self-annihilation. He will admit no Ovidian remedies, no Orphic music to draw him from his grievous hell, no Daedalean craft to free him from his 'mase', no physician, not even 'oon', to heal the sickness he calls life. Death has bereft him of his bliss (l. 577); now all – day and night – is hateful to him. Let it end. He would have death, not death him, and be free from life's Sisyphean hell (ll. 585–92). So greatly is he possessed by 'sorwful ymagynacioun' that he fancies himself the personification of sorrow: 'For y am sorwe, and sorwe ys y' (l. 597). (Recall Boethius's equation of sorrow and forgetfulness.)

The knight's insufficiency is the consequence of a mental trap into which he has fallen. What he had once thought to be so – that around which he had defined his order of being – now turns out not to be so. The words and their designated emotions with which he had measured his happiness, now define his sorrow: his former song is now his complaint, his glad thoughts now heaviness, his certainty now dread, his good now harm, his wit now folly, his day now night, his love now hate, his peace now war, and so on (ll. 599–615). His whole world has become falsely defined. *Suffisance* is not what he had thought. He sees himself victim of Fortune's 'pley of enchauntement / That semeth oon and ys not soo' (ll. 648–9). Was the oneness he felt in love only an illusion, another of Fortune's duplicities? There is much he must relearn and remember.

If the knight is to regain *suffisance* he must first come to see Fortune's game objectively. Thus his reorientation, like that of Boece, begins with a reassessment of Fortune.[22] This reassessment is not at first a conscious act. In fact, the knight begins by using Fortune as an excuse. He defensively contrives a highly artificial chess-fortune analogy, the convolution of his grief-stricken mind which is unable to redefine *suffisance* now that the semantic edifice of its identity has been reversed. Even so – despite the elaborate conceit – his talk leads him to a partial recognition: a step, albeit small, towards truth. He begins to recognize honestly the properties of Fortune: she blinds men, deceives them, and is

THEME AND NUMBER IN CHAUCER'S *Book of the Duchess*

always unstable. Though she defeated him so decisively that 'I kouthe no lenger pleye' (l. 656), having taken from him his 'fers' (keep in mind the possible pun on 'fers' as queen and 'fers' as counsellor), he admits that he must admire Fortune, despite his loss, and acknowledges that he would have made the same move had he had her power. This leap of mind towards objectivity not only helps him gain perspective on his grief. It also is an implied assertion of his queen's virtue. Formerly he had only been able to affirm his love by vehemently negating what was left after the loved one's death.

The immediate effect of his acknowledgment is, however, despair:

> allas! that I was born!
> For evermore, y trowe trewly,
> For al my wille, my lust holly
> Ys turned; but yet, what to doone?
> Be oure Lord, hyt ys to deye soone.
>     (ll. 686–90)

As he regresses, the compassionate dreamer interrupts:

> Have som pitee on your nature
> That formed yow to creature.
>     (ll. 715–16)

His appeal is like that of Philosophy to desperate Boece, who reminds him, 'Thow hast left for to knowen thyselve what thou art. . . . For thow art confunded with foryetynge of thiself' (I. Pr. vi. 67–72). Like Philosophy, the dreamer reminds his friend of the patience of Socrates (ll. 717–19), and challenges his thoughts on suicide, thoughts which will necessarily plague the knight until he redefines *suffisance*. The dreamer exposes the knight's defensive word-game by belittling what the knight circuitously claimed he had lost:

> But ther is no man alyve her
> Wolde for a fers make this woo!
>     (ll. 740–1)

It is a painful but necessary stroke. By taking the knight's chess conceit literally, the dreamer compels him to reveal what is beneath, forcing him to heal the gap between words and reality by re-explaining.

The knight objects to the dreamer's challenge with the couplet that becomes the poem's refrain:

> Thou wost ful lytel what thou menest;
> I have lost more than thow wenest.
>     (ll. 743–4; cf. 1137–8 and 1305–6)

This refrain sets off the three stages of soul-searching and accentuates the limitations of human understanding. It is true both literally and ironically. The knight is exasperated over failing to make himself clear. He is also exasperated over his own confusion. In the forgetfulness of his sorrow, he does not himself know what he means nor what he has lost.

Compared to the opening dialogue between the Black Knight and the dreamer (ll. 514–57), this next bit of dialogue (ll. 714–57) dramatically manifests the progress of the knight's therapy. The first exchange between knight and dreamer was marked by courtesy, which was in itself, as we have seen, a step towards coping. This second exchange goes beyond courtesy, however; it extends to true mutuality and implies the reshaping of community. The knight invites the dreamer to sit down and listen 'hooly' and with good intent as he tries again to come to grips with his sorrow. This single physical act of sitting together, amidst all the soul-searching, stands out like a stride before the mantel in a Henry James novel.

The second rehearsal of the knight's grief begins with oaths upon 'trouthe' (l. 753) and salvation (l. 755), oaths indicative not only of earnestness, but also of the direction of the quest. This time, speaking without pretence of conceit, the knight tells the history of his falling in love. The pattern of his courtship is in itself a commentary on the nature of human engagements. Never was he capable of understanding fully what was happening to

84

him. He first fell in love not with his lady, but with the idea of love. Moved by a vague desire, he became Love's thrall. He admits he was preoccupied with love, but acknowledges that there was nothing unnatural in his behavior (ll. 775–91). In his idleness (l. 798), with 'Yowthe' as his mistress (l. 797), he simply suffered the adolescent itch, his thoughts 'flytting' and 'varyinge' (ll. 801–4). Like Amant in *Roman de la Rose*, he was inquisitive and vulnerable.[23] He wandered vaguely in love, he knew not why, until he happened to find (l. 805) a suitable object on which to open the weir of his emotions. He was naïve. He compares himself to a white wall or a table, ready to receive 'al that men wil theryn make, / Whethir so men wil portreye or peynte' (ll. 780f.). The 'painter' who fixed indelibly her image on his mind turns out to be 'the goode faire White', the 'oon' (l. 818) among many who could bring his life into focus. Recollection of the fortuitousness of their meeting causes the knight to cry out against Fortune again (ll. 811–16), but recollection of the lady's beauty and 'measure' immediately restores his equanimity. Here, then, despite the fact that she is dead, the true felicity of her being begins to become manifest to the vacillating knight.

This second rehearsal dramatizes the processes of intellection. Chaucer explores both the way people get to know things and also the way they reknow and understand more fully. We discover that the erotic indulgence of the youth became an increasingly profound understanding. Enchanted by her physical beauty, the comely motion of her dancing, and so on, the amorphous youth began to discover the meaning of measure, harmony and proportion (ll. 848–1041). She taught him governance and brought form to his life. Moreover, the Black Knight, through his remembering of the past (see especially l. 945), is, in the very presence of the dreamer, reclaiming truths which he, in his grief, had forgotten. St Augustine observes in *Confessiones* that memory contains not only images stored there through the senses, but also laws of number, proportion, dimension and quality.[24] These higher properties are precisely what the knight is re-encompassing. He recalls the natural beauty of the 'goode faire White' and remembers that

> trewly she
> Was hir [Nature's] chef patron of beaute
> And chef ensample of al hir werk,
> And moustre; for be hyt never so derk,
> Me thynketh I se hir ever moo.
>
> (ll. 909–13)

So keen the recollection becomes, it is as if she were with him. His is a mental resurrection, it seems, as he swears twice by the 'roode' (ll. 924, 992) and again by the 'masse' (l. 928). He recalls that she was his 'lyves leche' (he is finding his physician in his own mind) and compares her to the resurrection bird, 'the soleyn fenix of Arabye' (l. 982). The more vivid she becomes, the more pious his praise:[25] the symmetries of her beauty hint of The Song of Songs; she has as much 'debonairte' as 'Hester in the Bible' (l. 987). In fact, she is so true, in no way counterfeit, that, like Mary,

> Trouthe hymself, over al and al
> Had chose hys maner principal
> In hir, that was his restyng place.
>
> (ll. 1003–5)

To the vagrant lover, this remarkable woman became the epitome of suffisance and self-possession ('No wyght myght do hir noo shame, / She loved so wel hir owne name', ll. 1017–18). Through recollection, she is making possible the transformation the vagrant knight had insisted could not take place. Unlike Alcyone who 'saw noght' after the incubus appeared to her mind, he peers intently.

The dreamer again interrupts to ask how one could have loved better. The question focuses the knight's commitment to love, but still he vacillates. He could not have loved better, he heatedly insists – a mood much in contrast to his previous cold and 'astonied' rejection of life, yet one that, as he elevates his love to 'goddesse' (l. 1040), still veers from true perspective. He boasts she excelled all virtuous women of pagan times (ll. 1052–

87). But such assertions lead only to the dead-end of the past. They offer no hope of consolation. Again the dreamer challenges: 'Me thynketh ye have such a chaunce / As shryfte wythoute repentaunce' (ll. 1113–14). The knight resoundingly denies he will repent of that love: 'I nyl foryete hir never moo' (l. 1125). The fact is, of course, that in his grief he has forgotten her in so far as she embodied patience, measure, governance and 'Trouthe', those virtues he is now recalling. The dreamer presses harder with his 'demandes': 'Telleth me eke what ye have lore' (l. 1135). The question is well-timed, and it is crucial. For if all that the 'goode faire White' embodied is lost, then Truth is mutable and Fortune reigns supreme. The knight balks again with the ambiguous refrain:

'Yee!' seyde he, 'thow nost what thow menest;
I have lost more than thou wenest.'

(ll. 1137–8)

But the dreamer is relentless:

Nyl she not love yow? ys hyt soo?
Or have ye oght doon amys,
That she hath left yow? ys hyt this?
For Goddes love, telle me al.

(ll. 1140–3)

Both questions are pertinent. In accepting the challenge, the knight will neither profane her love nor his own. 'Before God', he says, he will prove the validity of their love.

The last rehearsal of the knight's woe brings together various patterns of vacillation and interruption, particularly those of seeking, losing and finding. The knight recounts his marriage, telling how he wrote songs to his lady, declared himself to her, and then was refused. Little did he realize then that this was not the only loss he would know. In 'pure fere' he 'stal away' (l. 1251). (The phrase recalls line 381, where the hart 'stal away' and was lost.) After a year, the lady, of her own volition, returned to him, gave him a ring, and agreed to accept his love. The effect

was miraculous, like another resurrection: 'I was as blyve /
Reysed, as fro deth to lyve' (ll. 1277-8). Bound through stable
love, the two became one (ll. 1292-5), but not to live happily
ever after. For again there is an interruption – this time, death.
And again the knight has stolen hopelessly away. The first
refusal was but training for the second. 'Where is she now?' the
dreamer abruptly intrudes. The effect is overwhelming. As the
knight wavers before the truth, his lines harken back to the story
of desperate Alcyone: 'He wax as ded as stoon' (l. 1300; cf. 123)
and cries out, 'Allas, that I was bore!' (l. 1301; cf. 90, 686).
Then, insisting on the validity of what the 'goode faire White'
was ('ryght that was she!', l. 1307), he acknowledges the fact:
'She ys ded!' (l. 1309). The wound has been discovered, the word
games stopped. Death has been seen for what it is, but so has the
'goode faire White', whose virtue has been remembered.

The conclusion to the poem is perhaps its most remarkable
achievement. Acceptance of one truth makes possible the perception of another. With the knight's acknowledgment of death
and the dreamer's expression of compassion, the horn sounds the
end, at least 'for that tyme' (l. 1313), of the 'hert-huntyng'.
(The implication seems to be that hart hunts are an inevitable
part of mortal life and will continue.) Then, quite marvellously,
a third 'resurrection' occurs. The forest mysteriously disappears,
and the knight and dreamer see before them, only a little way off,
'a long castel with walles white, / Be seynt Johan! on a ryche hil'
(ll. 1318-19). To this castle the king rides 'homwardes' (l. 1315).
The castle bell 'smyten houres twelve' (l. 1323), and the dreamer
awakens. Huppé and Robertson have read the iconography of this
last description correctly in pointing out that it signifies the New
Jerusalem.[26] Such an emblem grows naturally from the plot and
is most appropriate to the elegy's conclusion. In Boethian
terminology, it is man's 'true country', the model of 'sovereign
good' that underlies and justifies man's feeble social analogies.
It is the 'maner principal' of Truth, the gracious answer to man's
acceptance of death. That the castle is near at hand suggests Acts,
xvii 27 ('He is not far from any one of us.'). To make the allusion
to Revelation more specific than Chaucer does would go against

the integrity of the poem, which does not conclude with a moral, but rather a glimpse and new orientation.

St Augustine observes that memory is man's means of moving from outward forms to inward forms in order to transcend to eternal forms.[27] So has Chaucer's plot moved. The poet who had suffered the anarchy of 'sorwful ymagynacioun' began re-ordering his mind by turning outside himself to read of kings and queens. Then, dreaming of the emperor's hunt, he turned within himself in search of *suffisance*. Now, as dreamer and knight (the 'longe moevynges' of his soul) stand before the transcendent vision, he beholds the king and domain whose *suffisance* bridges time and eternity and offers promise of marriage after which there are no more interruptions.

But the poem does not end with that vision. The success of the mind's journey is at best partial. Since man can perceive higher truth only through enigma, he is doomed to fail to achieve full understanding. Bells awaken the poet and the glimpse vanishes. What had seemed an end turns out to be only another beginning. The poet is still part of the mutable world, the world of Lancaster and Richmond, the world of analogy. Nevertheless, he becomes an active man and through his art gives form to his experience, even though his dream is 'queynt' and he does not understand it fully. By nature he is inevitably naïve. Yet, as St Augustine observed, 'Let no one think that he has discovered nothing if he has been able to discover how incomprehensible is the object of his search.'[28] 'Be processe of tyme', the poet will put 'this sweven in ryme / As I kan best, and that anoon' (ll. 1331–3). Blanche is 'but dead', and with his poem he buries her body. It stands as counsel for others who know not 'what is best to doo' (l. 29), to help them make an end – 'now hit ys doon' (l. 1334).

2

The plot of the *Book of the Duchess* concerns the mental reorienta-tion necessary to man confronted with death. Since hope for eternity is an essential part of the Christian answer to death, a medieval poet in treating the universal side of his elegiac theme, might predictably use cosmological numbers to join his time world sympathetically to the eternal. In Chaucer's poem, however, not only do symbolic numbers provide recognizable links with cosmic truths; indeed, the very idea of number pertains to its theme. Number signifies more than mere enumeration; it implies both form and order. Without number there would be chaos.[29] Arguing from Scripture, St Augustine insisted that the numbers that the Creator impressed on all things reflect Divine Wisdom itself.[30] So too St Bonaventura, who saw in number 'the outstanding exemplar in the mind of the Maker, and in things . . . the outstanding trace leading to wisdom'.[31] To read the numbers of creation is to appreciate its form and participate in the notes of divine harmony. St Isidore, proclaiming the importance of numbers to all areas of man's learning, argued: 'Through number we are instructed in order not to be confounded. Take number from all things, and all things perish.'[32] His maxim applies to states of mind as well as physical bodies. Death is the unnumbering of the body; despair the unnumbering of the soul. One need not stretch his ingenuity far to argue that the *Book of the Duchess*, with its movement from 'sorwful ymagynacioun' to 'measure', is a poem about number. Its plot is, in effect, the renumbering of the poet's spiritual chaos so that he might at least dream of heaven's music.[33]

Chaucer alludes to this process at the end of the poem when his poet composes experience into comprehensible form by putting his thoughts into 'rime'. In fact, as we examine the form closely, we discover that it is ordered with more than simple rhyme. By intricately balancing parts with each other Chaucer has rhymed ideas. Through analogy, allusion and juxtaposition, he sustains several themes simultaneously as each subplot magnifies the poem's overall movement. This interweaving of parts in itself suggests measure, proportion and harmony, the balance sought by the distracted poet prior to his reading, dreaming and writing. Yet the numbering of his experience involves more than balance and antithesis. His plot has been so carefully numbered that its very form assumes metaphoric significance.

The *Book of the Duchess* seems to be ordered around the number

3. It has 3 main parts, each set in a different dimension of time and reality: the poet's search for repose, conducted in the waking world of present time; the history of Alcyone's loss, told by clerks of past time; and the dream vision, moving freely about in time and in its conclusion prognosticating eternity. Each main part is in turn patterned by 3: (i) The waking poet's search consists of his account of his restlessness, his prayer for sleep after reading, and his awakening to record his dream. This part forms a frame, like a Chinese box, for the other 2 main parts so that the basic plan of the poem is in effect three-in-one. (ii) Alcyone's story consists of her grief over Sey's departure, the interlude with the gods, and then the return of Seys' body with counsel. (iii) The dream, with its 3 descriptive settings (chamber, wood, New Jerusalem, each a local commentary on the dreaming poet's relative state of mind), also consists of 3 plot segments: the awakening in the chamber; the hunt; the encounter with the Black Knight. These 3 segments are also trifurcated. (*a*) The chamber scene includes 3 related descriptions: the singing of birds outside; the walls and windows inside; the temperate sky above (the spatial arrangement here anticipating the outside-inside-above patterns in the subsequent dream). (*b*) The hunt, with its call, forloin, and end of hart-hunting, is also marked by 3. (*c*) Finally, the encounter with the knight consists of the triple rehearsal of his grief, each part being sharply demarcated by the refrain.

The structural beauty of the *Book of the Duchess* lies not simply in its triplicities as such, but in their interweaving. The frame pattern of the poet's waking moments is mirrored in the dream, where the hunt forms a sub-frame containing the encounter with the knight and his 3-part rehearsal of his life. This placing of 3s within 3s within 3s creates a sense of probing and discovery as the plot moves from one frame into another. The effect is comparable to that of a vision within a vision. This device is what makes the conclusion to the poem so stunning, as the Black Knight's story, the hunt and the dream all come together and end at once in the singular image of the New Jerusalem.

Chaucer might have chosen 3 as his structural number for various reasons. It is the first *real number* and thus is called the expressive form of 1.[34] It is the number of love and full vision, the number through which all things in nature are bound together.[35] Because of its traditional connotations of unity, harmony, realization, and expression, it is an appropriate measure for a poem concerned with realization and recovery of lost sense of being. Trinity is God's answer to death, the cosmic remedy of the division and dissolution of the dyad. For the poet it becomes mode and means for his quest.

In the *Book of the Duchess* Chaucer's 3s are not restricted to distribution of parts. They are imprinted on much of the poem's internal structure as well. We have spoken of the threefold pattern of *seeking-losing-finding* (or, in the mutable world, perhaps only *concluding* instead of *finding*), a pattern reflected in the hart hunt, in the Black Knight's courtship and in his recollection of love. The cosmic model behind the pattern is Christ's Passion and Resurrection, the historical circumstance when Trinity and Love's victory became manifest on the third day after men had sought and been disappointed. Chaucer alludes specifically to the model with his reference to the 'thridde morwe' in the story of Alcyone. Her death, as we have seen, reverses the model. In the poet's spiritual struggle, on the other hand, the model is implicitly fulfilled. In his confrontation with death at the beginning of the poem he says he cannot sleep 'day ne nyght' (l. 2), 'ne nyght ne morwe' (l. 22), until late this 'other night' (l. 45), that is, late this *second* night, when he reads his book and then dreams. Instead of dying as Alcyone did, the poet awakens within the third morrow and writes. Not only, then, are there parallel occurrences of seeking-losing-finding (concluding) in the dream, each being accompanied by allusions to resurrection; that pattern is implied in the poet's autobiography as well.

The number 3 is that of soul and mind,[36] since both bear the image of Trinity. In this regard it may be instructive to relate the patterns of intellection and perception in Chaucer's soul-searching poem to those worked out by medieval philosophers.[37] Virtually every scholastic argument on the Trinity hinges on an analogue in man's mind. Philosophers and theologians explored with greatest sublety the ways man's sense of self is measured by 3.

Not only is his mind a trinity (*memoria, intelligentia, voluntas*); his very perception follows a threefold rhythm.[38] One of the best-known treatises to draw on the Augustinian format of illumination through triplicities is St Bonaventura's treatise on meditation, *Itinerarium mentis in Deum*.[39] Similarities between threefold patterns of illumination described there and those of the *Book of the Duchess* are well worth considering. (My point is not to imply that the *Itinerarium* is a source for Chaucer's poem, but rather to demonstrate succinctly characteristic medieval attitudes towards the mind's workings.) St Bonaventura's analogues to perception may be summarized as follows: (i) *Apprehensio:* The soul turns from selfish preoccupation to explore outside itself. In creation it discovers *vestigia* of the Creator, which, though corporeal and temporal, provide the mind with an objective approach to divinity. This initial step is made in darkness and ignorance. It is the evening of the soul and likened to life outside grace under the Old Law.[40] (ii) *Oblectatio:* The mind, responding to the senses' discourse with nature, moves into itself to discover further patterns of the Creator. These patterns are the surest *vestigia* of creation since they reflect his very image. This meditative stage is the morning of the soul; the mind goes beyond sense to higher truths such as form, power, operation and measure, and is likened to life under the New Law.[41] (iii) *Diiudicatio:* The mind, now in contemplation, passes above itself towards the eternal. This is the noon of the soul when soul realizes proportion and number and through love participates in divine illumination. This stage is likened to insight of Revelation.[42]

The reorientation of Chaucer's grieving poet occurs through patterns similar to those of St Bonaventura's mental journey. He begins in darkness and confusion, goes outside himself to the book, and there discovers traces of 'kynde' that help him to a more objective perspective. Then, as in St Bonaventura, the second stage of intellection is inward. In his 'ynly swete . . . sweven' (l. 276) the time is morning. His sorrow is tempered by delight in nature's well-regulated domain. The 3 chamber descriptions having anti-cipated the outward-inward-above pattern, the ensuing dialogue between dreamer and knight (the 'longe moevynges' of the poet's thought) dramatizes the process of moving beyond senses to discover measure, harmony, proportion and beauty. The outward-inward (dark to light) pattern is repeated in the knight's rehearsal as he tells how he turned outside self to love Blanche, and now, after her death, turns inside self to rediscover her impression. The third stage of the journey occurs at 'houres twelve', the noontime of the poet's awakening,[43] as dreamer and knight look up to contemplate the White Castle above them. The transcendent castle, consequence of love, is emblem of revelation, judgment, and eternity. Parallels such as these indicate how ingrained the threefold pattern of intellection was throughout medieval thought.

A final numerological curiosity in the *Book of the Duchess* that pertains to the threefold journey towards revelation may be seen in Chaucer's naming of the 'goode faire White'. Editors have been puzzled by the two long lines (905, 942) which both have an extra foot and contain the word 'whyt'. Attempts have been made to emend the lines to scan, but it seems likely to me that the extra foot in each is designed to anticipate and heighten the metaphysical import of 'White' when she is actually named in line 948. Twice her name is enigmatically hinted at in the long lines on her beauty, then it is made manifest. At least one early reader (presumably John Stow) understood the riddle and thrice noted 'Blanche' in the margins of the Fairfax manuscript alongside each of the lines.

Although numerological composition is readily apparent in the inner and outer architecture of the *Book of the Duchess*, it does not, so far as I can determine, play a significant role in regulating the number of verses allotted individual segments of the poem.[44] Two notable exceptions, however, may be found in the songs of the Black Knight. The first, a complaint to death, which the dreamer says is 'withoute noote, withoute song', is 11 lines long (475–86).[45] Chaucer has called attention to its length by suggesting it is 'ten or twelve' verses. (Possible significances of those numbers we shall consider in a moment.) The number 11 is universally glossed as one of both excess and deficiency, a number beyond law (signified in 10) and short of revelation and grace (signified in 12).[46] The knight's complaint exhibits both an excess of sorrow and deficiency of perspective. Chaucer has heightened the idea of disharmony by breaking the complaint into uneven stanzas after the fifth verse, the central and discordant line (the line which breaks the couplet pattern) being 'Allas, deth, what ayleth the' (481). The knight's second song (ll. 1175–80), on the other hand, is 6 lines long. It occurs in the third rehearsal of his sorrow and is part of his declaration of love prior to winning the 'goode faire White'. The number 6 is that of perfection and fruitful marriage.[47] In its 6 verses this song describes the joy which sight of his lady brings the knight. It thus anticipates the bliss he later achieves. The knight calls attention to its craft by discussing Pythagoras and Tubal, the alleged founders of the art. He has artfully divided his verses into 3 couplets, the third rhyming with the first.

The whole of the *Book of the Duchess* is 1333 lines, that number, with its single 1 and triple 3s, which add to 10, being in all ways a sign of unity.[48] But if there are other instances of symbolic disposition of verses in the poem the case for them must be tenuous indeed. Chaucer's practice of disposing material according to number seems generally to be confined to symbolic organization of larger units.

## 3

The most obvious and in some ways the most interesting number symbolism in Chaucer's poetry occurs in the diction itself. One of his principal devices for linking theme to higher reality is the weaving of number metaphors into the poem's texture.[49] Such numbers individually seem inconspicuous, though cumulatively, through traditional associations, they monitor our understanding of a good deal of the poem's wisdom. The most significant number metaphors in the *Book of the Duchess* are 1, 8 and 12. All have complementary connotations of harmony, fulfilment, regeneration, and revelation – ideas which define the end sought in the psychological plot. Moreover, they all share properties in common with 3, the poem's structural number.[50] The poem contains other number metaphors also, though they are more incidental and may be discussed in conjunction with the more prominent numbers. (Not every number mentioned in the poem is symbolic, of course.) Let us begin with Chaucer's use of the monad.[51]

In our discussion of the poem's plot we have seen that the bereaved narrator is a man who, in his grief, is divided against 'kynde' and himself. The plot is his attempt to regain a sense of oneness with self and community. (Compare Boethius' equation of one and good, III. Pr. xi. 45.) This aspect of his search is emphasized repeatedly in the dream through allusions to divided self and puns on the word 'hool'.[52] If the knight is to be made 'hool' he must tell 'hooly' his grief. His is a search for at-one-ment through confession of grief and recollection of the 'goode faire White'. Throughout the poem Chaucer has set out this aspect of the plot with number metaphors. In every instance in which the protagonist seeks guidance, Chaucer subtly uses the figure 1. First the poet acknowledges that 'phisicien but oon' may heal him. Then, as he tries to get hold of himself, he receives a book from 'oon' who suddenly appears in his company. After he reads he acknowledges 'god but oon', placates the multiple gods with multiple gifts and is released from his many distractions to dream. At first, he sees with singularity of vision: the birds sing as one, 'al of oon acord' (l. 305), 'att oo word' (l. 306), a song of heaven. That singularity does not last, however. The hunt calls him. Even so, he still seems to have 'oon' near to help when he needs. 'Oon, ladde a lymere' (l. 365) appears to explain that Octovyen is the huntsman. Individually these 1s are incidental. Cumulatively they become a reminder that the persona, despite his fragmentation, is part of a community whose nature becomes clear only towards the end of the poem.

The dream progresses into the dual realm of Flora and Zephirus, 'they two that make floures growe' (l. 403). Theirs is, as we have noted, the realm of nature whose bounty exceeds man's ability to 'rekene and noumbre, / And telle of every thing the noumbre' (ll. 439–40). In their world, Fortune has prerogative to play her games. She is by nature the adversary of at-one-ment. She has divided vision,[53] 'ever laughynge / With oon eye, and that other wepynge' (ll. 633–4). She knows how to manipulate the mutable world of 'swiche seven' (l. 408) and with her duplicities has blinded 'many oon' (l. 647). 'She ys pley of enchauntement, / That semeth oon and ys not soo' (ll. 648–9). With her 'false draughtes dyvers' (l. 653) she captured the one 'fers' that mattered to the Black Knight, the one in which his suffisance resided, then left him trapped in the mental disjunction we spoke of earlier. When the dreamer meets her victim he finds him divided, arguing with himself.

It should come as no surprise to us that Chaucer presents the 'goode faire White' in terms of 1. She is first introduced as 'oon / That was lyk noon of the route' (ll. 818–19). Later she is described as unique among 10,000 (l. 972)[54] and compared to the 'soleyn fenix of Arabye; / For ther livyth never but oon' (ll. 982–3). Nor are we allowed to believe that her beauty is mere 'pley of enchantment'. Though many men try to impose their fantasies on her, she plays a game opposite to Fortune's, tempers their judgment, and through moderate behaviour teaches them 'mesure'. In her composure she is epitome of beauty and harmony, complete in herself, in no way counterfeit. Her mind is wholly inclined towards good; she is the 'ensample' of nature, and 'maner *principal*' of 'Trouthe'. Because of her oneness others are able to define themselves and move towards oneness also.[55] Notice the emphasis Chaucer gives the concept of union as the knight recalls life with Blanche once she gave him 'al hooly' her gift of mercy:

Therwyth she was *alway* so trewe,
Our joye was ever *ylyche* newe;
Oure hertes wern so *evene a payre*
That *never has that oon contrayre*
*To that other*, for no woo.
For sothe, *ylyche* they suffred thoo
*Oo* blysse, and eke *oo* sorwe *bothe*;
*Ylyche* they were *bothe* glad and wrothe;
*Al was us oon, withoute were.*

        (ll. 1287–95; italics mine)

At this precise moment, as the knight recalls their union of hearts, the dreamer interrupts the last time to precipitate plain recognition of death: 'Where is she now?'

The mere honest confrontation of death does not, of course, restore that union which the knight had known. It does allow for higher vision, however. As the ambiguous 'they' begin to 'strake forth' and the king rides 'homwardes', one guide is still before them. The forest of multiplicities has disappeared. Knight and dreamer gaze as one at the hill 'which was from *us* but a lyte'. Theirs is a communal glimpse of the singular city, domain of sovereign good and their atonement.

Closely related to the 1s in the *Book of the Duchess* are the 8s, 8 being a number of new beginnings and thus naturally akin to 1.[56] Like the 1s, the 8s coordinate the motion of the plot with cosmic rhythms that man is privileged to participate in. The 2 occurrences of 8 (the 8-year sickness and the Emperour Octovyen) have been explained by Huppé and Robertson with what seems to me the right idea though perhaps not the right example.[57] They suggest the 8-year sickness and the healing physician may be a 'specific reflection of an 8 years' malady found in the New Testament, that of Aeneas in the Acts of the Apostles'.[58] In light of patristic glosses on Aeneas' illness they conclude that the 8 in conjunction with the physician in Chaucer's poem might be understood as a figure for Christ who brings about a cure for the languor of earthly delight. That Aeneas' malady might hover in the background of Chaucer's 8-year sickness is an intriguing possibility, though it seems somewhat remote to me. More likely, Chaucer simply had in mind the commonplace overtones of the number, the same overtones that led glossators to read Acts as they did. The octad is one of the most comprehensible numbers in medieval numerology. From earliest times it was held to be a sign of new beginning and stability beyond mutability. Thus in Christian lore 8 became the number of Christ, Baptism, Resurrection, Justice and the New Jerusalem.[59]

In his poem it seems likely to me that Chaucer intends the 8, with its specific Christian connotations, to anticipate the regenerative action of the poem's plot. The passage reads as follows:

I holde hit be a sicknesse
That I have suffred this eight yeer,
And yet my boote is never the ner;
For there is phisicien but oon
That may me hele; but that is don.

(ll. 36–40)

I would suggest 'eight yeer' sickness for two reasons. First, in death, the 'goode faire White' has entered the eighth epoch of her life (eternal reward, her 'boote' beyond sevenfold mutability), while the poet, who measures his life by her, remains part of the bootless, hectic time-world. Second, as the poet remarks with anxiety that his reward is no nearer (presumably one expects justice in an eighth year), he anticipates the new beginning to which analysis of grief will lead him. The number comments on his expectations as well as his disappointment. Like the allusion to the 1 physician, his thoughts on 'kynde' and his oath to light, the 8 helps define his circumstance and aspiration as he begins the elegy.

It is worth comparing Chaucer's use of the number with that of Thomas Usk in *Testament of Love*, a work also dealing with soul-searching organized upon a Boethian analogy. In the *Testament* the aggrieved narrator also prays for comfort in an eighth year. Moreover, he explains what the figure means:

Now than I pray that to me [come] sone fredom and grace in this eight[eth] yere; this eighteth mowe to me bothe be kinrest and masseday, after the seven werkedays of travayle, to folowe the Christen lawe; and, what ever ye do els, that thilke Margaryte be holden so, lady, in your privy chambre, that she in this case to none other person be committed.[60]

Usk seems to be using the number 8 precisely as Chaucer uses it in his elegy, to suggest new beginning, grace, peace of mind, and reward. He may very well, in fact, be imitating the *Book of the Duchess*, in which case his treatment of 8 stands as a fourteenth-century gloss on Chaucer's.

Our analysis of the metaphor gains strength with the appearance of the Emperour Octovyen in the dream. Here Huppé and Robertson's explication is excellent. They gloss 'Octovyen' as a pun, 'eight (Christ) coming',[61] and suggest that the king's return to the castle at the conclusion is an emblem of Christ's return to the Holy City at Vespers, 'time of reward for the just in the heavenly kingdom'.[62] In applying such an analysis to the poem, however, emphasis must fall on the enigmatic character of the vision. It does not imply allegory, only analogy.

The poem's 8s thus seem to function in conjunction with the 1s as symbols of those cosmic truths which enable Christian man to cope with death's overwhelming isolation. So do the 12s. All the poem's 12s occur within the dream itself,[63] and appropriately so, for 12 is traditionally a sign of Revelation, Resurrection, Grace, regeneration and fulfilment.[64] It carries strong associations with Apocalypse, and thus is especially pertinent to elegies. Of the 6 occurrences of 12 in the *Book of the Duchess*, the references to 'houres twelve' (ll. 573, 1323)[65] are outstanding in that Chaucer uses them, like the 8s, to measure beginnings and endings of main sections of his plot. As the dreamer begins to engage the knight in conversation, the knight says he is woeful to live 'houres twelve' (l. 573). By juxtaposing the apocalyptic number with the knight's death-wish, Chaucer creates an effect comparable to Alcyone's dying on the third morrow and the poet's sickness in the eighth year. In each instance the numbers, with their strong overtones of Christian regeneration, heighten our awareness of the aggrieved one's despair and at the same time remind us of the universal answer to his dilemma. The second 'houres twelve' (l. 1323) creates a strikingly opposite effect, however, and in that regard is comparable to Octovyen's homeward journey and the poet's awakening on the third morrow. This time, instead of setting off self-condemnation and despair, 'houres twelve' marks the achievement of discovery. Instead of rebelling the knight accepts death. By coupling the beginning of his quest with its end Chaucer measures the distance his knight has come. He who was 'withoute note, withoute song,' now finds his tune in the bells' music. If there had been any doubt as to the meaning of the white castle on the hill, there can be none once the 12 bells sound. They provide conclusive evidence of the vision's meaning.

The other 12s in the dream are less suggestive than 'houres twelve', though none the less important as part of the dream's texture. In lines 831–2 the knight, having recalled the first time he saw his lady, spontaneously cries:

By God, and by his halwes twelve,
Hyt was my swete, ryght as hirselve.

Here the oath to God and the 12 apostles enhances nicely the dramatic event taking place in the poem. The patristic explanation of Christ's choice of 12 may be pertinent in this regard. They were to be his messengers, spreading news of the Trinity to the four corners of the earth.[66] Their 3 × 4 signifies their mission, that being revelation of grace. In light of so familiar a gloss, to swear by God and the 12 saints is to swear by revelation itself. The oath is apt at this moment in the poem since it is through reknowing of 'goode faire White', whom the knight has just recalled meeting, that he will, as we have seen, master his despair.

Similarly, when the dreamer says of the knight's sorrow that even though he 'lost the ferses twelve' (l. 723) he would have no reason for suicide, the 12 could suggest revelation, though mainly it implies totality. The implication may be that even if all counsellors or graces were lost and man completely blinded by Fortune, he should not give up hope. Or, perhaps we should follow W. H. French's suggestion that 'fers' simply means 'queen' and that the dreamer is showing surprise by exaggerating, saying in effect, 'Even if you'd lost a dozen queens there would be no cause for such sorrow.'[67] Either way the 12 suggests the inclusive and echoes other 12s in the dream to help fill out the perfect 6.

The other 2 instances of 12 are the first in the dream. Both occur in similar idiomatic phrases meaning 'a few'. We learn that the trees of the wood where the knight sits are 'ten foot or twelve' apart (l. 420). Later, the knight makes complaint in 'ten vers or twelve' (l. 463). That 'ten or twelve' was common idiom for 'a few' or 'many' we may be sure.[68] Nevertheless, in their particular contexts and in collocation with other 12s in the poem, these 2 instances stand out as something more than simple idiom. We have already noted in our discussion of symbolic verse structure that the actual verse number (11) of the knight's complaint seems contrived for symbolic effect. Perhaps the 'ten or twelve' has special point too, especially since it repeats the figure Chaucer has just used to describe the trees. (As one becomes familiar with Chaucer's use of number metaphors he discovers that Chaucer regularly repeats them in close proximity when a particular point is implied.) Let us examine more carefully the first occurrence of the number (l. 420).

The spacing of trees in the Black Knight's wood apparently goes back to the *Roman de la Rose* on which this portion of Chaucer's poem seems to be modelled. In the *Roman*, however, the trees are said to be apart *plus de cinc toises ou de sis* (which the Middle English *Romaunt* translates as 'fyve fadome or sixe').[69] Why should Chaucer alter numbers in his *Book of the Duchess* where he saw no need to do so in his translation of the *Roman* (assuming that that part of the *Romaunt* is his)? And why then would he add that the trees were 'fourty or fifty fadme lengthe' (l. 422)? Perhaps he simply changed the first formula to get another 12 into his poem. But why then the additional formula on height which introduces new numbers altogether?

It is possible that Chaucer may be following the common practice of reading numbers in relation to each other. (See Hugh of St-Victor's third rule, *secundum modum porrectionis*, whereby 10 in relation to 12 would signify motion towards revelation since 10 in such a combination is associated with the Old Law and negative justice and 12 with the New Law and positive justice once the two commandments of love have been added.)[70] The idea of justice and motion towards revelation through love is apt gloss for both 'ten or twelve' phrases in the poem since they introduce the dream-plot which moves from the forest of potentiality towards Truth embodied in the White Castle. What is more, a comparable gloss pertains to 40 in relation to 50. The number of exile – 40, and 50, sign of Whitsuntide (Pentecost), conjoin to signify motion from exile towards the blessing of Love

(Holy Spirit).[71] It is conceivable then, that Chaucer, in measuring the forest of potentiality, means to anticipate through number metaphors the direction of the dream's resolution. Such metaphors would be in keeping not only with other 12s in the poem but with the movement of the plot in general. The fact that the phrases are formulaic does not rule out the possibility that Chaucer might use the formula for his own purposes.

As postscript to this discussion of number metaphors in Chaucer's elegy, a word should be said regarding the puzzling reference to the Black Knight's age. Since John of Gaunt was actually 29 at the time of Blanche's death, attempts have been made to emend the line which says the knight is 'foure and twenty' (l. 455) to read 'nyne and twenty'.[72] More recently, Beryl Rowland, accepting the notion that the Black Knight need not be identified with Gaunt, suggests that 'foure and twenty yer' reflects the age of Chaucer himself.[73] It seems more likely to me that Chaucer deliberately chose the number, as he chose other numbers in the poem, to enhance through metaphor the poem's theme. The number 24 is a sign of fullness and bounty, mainly because of the number of hours in a full day, but also because it is a multiple of the superabundant 12.[74] In the poem's context it implies the knight is in fullness of life, like the scene of plenitude around him, and thus restresses the unnaturalness of his grievous mood. Also, since the number has apocalyptical overtones, it may be understood in conjunction with the 12s as one more sign of impending revelation.

In conclusion we see that Chaucer has relied extensively on traditional numerology both in the external architecture and in the setting out of his elegy's theme of consolation. Since the poem explores the mind's journey from the darkness of 'sorwful ymagynacioun' to the revelation of Love and Truth, Chaucer chose numbers – particularly 1, 3, 8 and 12 – which relate to medieval concepts of mind, revelation, harmony and repose. These numbers are more than mere rhetorical decorations. They provide links between the poem and its cosmic background. They are, in fact, Chaucer's means of justly representing Nature as God created it. We must remind ourselves that for Chaucer 8 (for example) *is* the eternal number. It does in truth define the sphere of the fixed stars, mark the beginning of the new week, designate the establishment of the New Jerusalem. Indeed, Chaucer's own life received new beginning from the octagonal baptismal font. This he knew on the authority of Scripture, the theologians, the philosophers, the scientists, the ancients, and, more obviously, from his own experience. He needed only to look around him. For Chaucer as poet to use number in his poetry was simply to accord the best of his ideas with the Best Ideas, those of the Creator Himself. Number is a crucial part of his imitation of life as it is, whether that life be a parody of truth or a fulfilment. It provides his readers as well as himself with the means of discovering essential analogies between individual natures and Absolute Nature. With his 1s and 3s he explores the mind in its innermost workings, and with his 8s and 12s he discovers the end whereby the mind realizes and fulfils its 'naturel entencioun'. The aesthetic of his poem becomes that of Nature itself, a realism of sympathetic correspondences.

## NOTES

1 My summary of man's search for God is based on St Augustine's *De Trinitate*, a work of enormous influence throughout the Middle Ages (e.g., Hugh of St-Victor, *De arca Noe morali*, and St Bonaventura, *Itinerarium mentis in Deum*). See esp. *De Trin.*, VIII. iv. 7–VIII. vi. 9 and XIV. xiv. 20, on love and knowledge; VIII. vi. 9 and IX. iii. 3, on man as God's image. For a summary of the *De Trinitate*'s pertinence to medieval theories of secular love see Frederick Goldin, *The Mirror of Narcissus in the Courtly Love Lyric* (Ithaca, N.Y., 1967), pp. 207–58.

2 E.g., *De Trin.*, X, on Memory, Intellect and Love, the trinity through which man comes to higher knowledge. Cf. *Confessiones*, X, with its discussion of the storehouse of Memory. *De Trin.*, XIV. iii. 5–XIV. xiv. 20, summarises the process of intellection and explains the analogy between man's mind and God.

3 St Augustine's analogy between God and artist, so prominent in the *De Trinitate*, the *De vera religione* and his sermons on the Gospel of

St John, became the standard way of explaining God's thoughts. E.g., St Anselm, *Prosologion*, II, and *Monologion*, Xff.; Hugh of St-Victor, *Eruditionis didascaliae liber septimus* (*PL*, clxxvi, col. 814); St Bonaventura, *Breviloquium*, ii. 11 and throughout *Itinerarium mentis in Deum*; and St Thomas Aquinas, *Summa theologica*, I. qu. i. arts 9–10. Scriptural basis for the idea is Romans i. 18–20. For our purpose the idea's prevalence is best manifested in the commonplace treatment afforded by Chaucer's contemporary Thomas Usk: 'The crafte of a werkman is shewed in the werke' (*Testament of Love*, i. Prol. 69, ed. Skeat, *Works of Chaucer*, 6 vols and supplement [Oxford, 1894–7] vii. 3). Usk's point is that by study of earthly models we approach higher truth:

> Now, principally, the mene to bringe in knowleging and loving his creatour is the consideracion of thinges made by the creatour, wherthrough, by thilke thinges that ben made understonding to our wittes, arn the unsene privitees of god made to us sightful and knowing, in our contemplacion and understonding. These thinges than, forsoth, moche bringen us to the ful knowleging [of] sothe, and to the parfit love of the maker of hevenly thinges (*ibid.*, i. Prol. 54–61).

4 All my references to Chaucer's works come from F. N. Robinson, *Works of Geoffrey Chaucer*, 2nd edn (1957). Quotations from Boethius are in Chaucer's translation.

5 *Confessio Amantis*, Prol. 852, ed. G. C. Macaulay, *Works of Gower* 4 vols (Oxford, 1899–1902), ii, 28. See *Boece*, III. Pr. xi and Dante, *De monarchia*, i. 1–16, for more extended discussions of oneness as good, division as evil. The idea is Platonic with pre-Socratic origins.

6 In 1369, the year of Blanche's death, Chaucer unquestionably knew Boethius through Machaut, whose *Confort d'Ami* presents Boethius as a counsellor, and through Jean de Meun, who relies on Boethius for nearly all philosophical matter in *Roman de la Rose*. But I see no reason to believe, as Skeat did (*Works of Geoffrey Chaucer*, i. 483), that Chaucer would not have known Boethius at first hand so early. Study of Boethius would have been part of his schooling. (See D. W. Robertson, Jr, 'The Historical Setting of Chaucer's *Book of the Duchess*', *Mediaeval Studies in Honor of Urban Tigner Holmes, Jr.* [Chapel Hill, N.C., 1965], pp. 175ff.) Although the *Book of the Duchess* does not offer numerous lines taken directly

from the *Consolatio*, as the poems of the 1380s do, that simply indicates that Chaucer was not yet in the midst of translating it. Parallels in theme and plotting devices are too numerous to be coincidental. Chaucer must surely have known the treatise intimately before writing his elegy.

7 Philosophy, says Boece, 'is fallen into a litargye, which that is a comune seknesse to hertes that been desceyved. He hath a litel foryeten hymselve' (I. *pr.* ii. 19–22). See *Boece*, I. *pr.* vi, for Philosophy's discussion of sorrow as cause of lost sense of identity; also I. *pr.* v (on lost domain) and III. *pr.* xii.

8 Bernard F. Huppé and D. W. Robertson, Jr., *Fruyt and Chaf* (Princeton, N.J., 1963), pp. 32–4, and J. Burke Severs, 'Chaucer's Self-Portrait in the *Book of the Duchess*', *PQ*, xliii (1964), 32–33.

9 *Boece*, I. *pr.* iii. 2ff., though physician and medicinal metaphors run throughout the teatise.

10 See I. *pr.* i. 2–3, where in a cause and effect relationship Philosophy appears as Boece ponders and writes. Philosophy immediately casts out the 'mermaydenes' of Fortune who would lull Boece with forgetfulness and calls upon her own muses, who are, in effect, the music of 'kynde'. Discussions of 'sovereign good' are too pervasive to cite. (The phrase occurs over fifty times in Chaucer's translation.) 'Sovereign good' is ultimately equated with 'sovereign god', though it is explored in terms of 'sovereign blisfulnesse', 'sovereign suffisaunce', 'sovereign power', 'sovereign reverence', 'sovereign clernesse', and 'sovereign delyt', all of which dimensions of man's being depend upon his awareness of 'sovereign good'. See esp. Bk III. These are also the terms explored and end sought by the poet in the *Book of the Duchess*.

11 Although metaphors of night, clouds, tempest, drowning and grief, in contrast to those of light, fair weather, clearness, stability and temperance, are commonplace in medieval literature, they are especially pronounced in Boethius, with which use Chaucer holds strict accord. (See esp. *Boece*, I *met.* ii. and I. *met.* iii.)

12 *Genealogia deorum gentilium*, XIV. ix; tr. C. G. Osgood, *Boccaccio on Poetry* (Princeton, N. J., 1930), p. 51. Compare Richard de Bury, *Philobiblon*, tr. E. C. Thomas (1925), pp. 7, 12, 93, 99, who argues on behalf of books as good counsellors.

13 The story occurs in Ovid, *Met.*, xi. 410ff. Chaucer knew it also from Machaut's *La Fonteinne Amoureuse*, 539ff., a version which also concentrates on events after the shipwreck, though Machaut's

concern is with Morpheus rather than Alcyone. Though some details of phrasing in *Book of the Duchess* seem to be influenced by Machaut's narrative, Chaucer evidently worked directly from Ovid or perhaps a moralized version.

14 The moral implications of Chaucer's version are similar to those made explicit in *Ovide Moralisé*, ed. De Boer (Amsterdam, 1936), IV. x-xiii, where Alcyone's excessive grief, which leaves her totally at Fortune's mercy, is compared to storms at sea tossing her soul like a ship without sailors, since her senses have stopped guiding her properly. But where the Old French clerk makes the moral by glossing the principal story, Chaucer alters the story and dispenses with the gloss.

15 An appropriate gloss on Alycone's death might be taken from Gower's *Confessio Amantis*, where Genius advises Amans: For conseil passeth alle thing / To him which thenkth to ben a king; / And every man for his partie / A kingdom hath to justefie, / That is to sein his oghne dom. / If he misreule that kingdom, / He lest himself, and that is more / Than if he loste Schip and Ore / And al the worldes good withal: / For what man that in special / Hath noght himself, he hath noght elles, / Nomor the perles than the schelles' (viii. 2109-20).

16 Labels of 'ego' and 'alter-ego' have sometimes been applied to the Black Knight and dreamer. Those terms work well enough to convey the psychological nature of the debate, though 'longe moevynges' of thought is more apt in that it embodies Chaucer's own words from a context out of which he conceived of mental behavior. Philosophy explains how man may regain his sense of sovereign good by entering the depths of his mind, there to 'rollen and trenden withynne hymself the lyght of his ynwarde sighte; and . . . gaderyn ayein, enclynynge into a compas, the longe moevynges of his thoughtes; and . . . techyn his corage that he hath enclosid and hid in his tresors, al that he compasseth or secheth fro withoute' (III. *met*. xi. 3-9). In the *Book of the Duchess* the dreamer and knight represent divergent tendencies in the poet's distraught soul, which ultimately come to rest in the compass of the White Castle.

17 *Fruyt and Chaf*, p. 49, esp. n. 21, which lists sources for allegorizing God as hunter-king pursuing the soul. The difficulty of applying their gloss to Chaucer is the fact that in the *Book of the Duchess* man seems to be the seeker, Octovyen the guide.

18 Donald C. Baker, 'Imagery and Structure in Chaucer's *Book of the Duchess*', *SN*, xxx (1958), 23; Georgia Ronan Crampton, 'Transitions and Meaning in the *Book of the Duchess*', *JEGP*, lxii (1963), 486ff.; Huppé and Robertson, *Fruyt and Chaf*, pp. 49ff. Joseph E. Grennen, 'Hert-Huntyng in the *Book of the Duchess*', *MLQ*, xxv (1964), 131–9, takes exception to seeing metaphysical overtones in the hunt. By exploring medieval medical documents he concludes that since Chaucer's description of the knight's malady is 'scientifically accurate' (though detailed 'with some freedom, to be sure', p. 134), it is folly to look for 'spiritual meaning' in the hunt.

19 See *Boece*, III. *pr.* ix, for Philosophy's explication of 'suffisaunce'. She equates it with reverence and power, 'thre tynges . . . al o thyng' (l. 43), to which she adds other names as well, such as 'noblesse' and 'gladnesse', insisting, of course, that though of various names, their 'substaunce hath no diversite' (ll. 83–4).

20 'Narrative Focus in the *Book of the Duchess*: A Critical Revaluation', *Annuale Mediaevale*, vii (1966), 18–24.

21 *Boece* I. *pr.* v. 70. See III. *pr.* xi–*pr.* xii, for discussion of God's oneness and its importance to man's mind. For pertinent observations on fulfilling of 'naturel entencioun' in the quest for wholeness of being see III. *pr.* iii. 1ff.; III. *pr.* xi. 149–87; IV. *pr.* ii. 132ff.; V. *pr.* iv. 215.

22 Fortune is defined and discussed throughout Bk II of *Boece*. In II. *pr.* iv. 38 Philosophy uses a chess metaphor to describe one overcome by grief at Fortune's hands.

23 Compare the first sensations of love in *Le Roman de la Rose*, ll. 1301ff., ed. E. Langlois (Paris, 1920), ii. 67ff., where the lover wanders through the exotic garden towards the well of Narcissus while the bothersome Deus d'Amors follows in the distance, his bow strung, waiting for the lover to locate the object of his already present desire.

24 'Item continet memoria numerorum dimensionumque rationes et leges innumerabiles . . . Sensi etiam numeros omnibus corporis sensibus, quos numeramus: sed illi alii sunt quibus numeramus, nec imagines istorum sunt et ideo valde sunt' (*Confessiones*, X. xii. 19 [*PL*, xxxii, col. 787]). See also *Confessiones*, X. xi. 18.

25 For a complete study of Chaucer's use of religious metaphors in his portrayal of the 'goode faire White', see James I. Wimsatt, 'The Apotheosis of Blanche in *The Book of the Duchess*', *JEGP*, lxvi (1967), 26–44.

26 *Fruyt and Chaf*, pp. 91–2.

27 The idea occurs in various places in the *De Trinitate*, esp. XIV. vii.
10 (*PL*, xlii, cols 1043–4) and XV. iii. 5 (*PL*, xlii, cols 1060–1),
where St Augustine summarizes earlier arguments. The idea is
also implicit in the exuberant outburst in praise of memory in *Confessiones*, X. xvii. 26 (*PL*, xxxii, cols 790–1). Cf. *De vera religione*,
xxix. 72 (*PL*, xxxiv, col. 154).

28 F. Goldin, from Moignt's edn of the *De Trinitate* (*Mirror of Narcissus*
Ithaca, N.Y., 1967, pp. 249ff.). Cf. *De Trin.*, XV. viii. 14ff. and St
Anselm, *Monologion*, lxv.

29 Recall the argument of Conscience to the friars in *Piers Plowman*
(B Text xx. 266–8, ed. Skeat): 'Kynde witte me telleth, / It is wikked
to wage yow ye wexeth out of noumbre! / Heuene hath euene
noumbre and helle is with-out noumbre.' Cf. the Parson's observations to the Canterbury pilgrims (X (I) 217–18): 'Job seith that in
helle is noon ordre of rule. / And al be it so that God hath creat
alle thynges in right ordre, and no thyng withouten ordre, but
alle thynges been ordeyned and nombred; yet, nathelees, they that
been dampned been nothyng in ordre, ne holden noon ordre,'
where 'ordre' and 'nombre' are synonymous. St Augustine argued
that form is dependent upon number. Without number things
cease to exist (*De libero arbitrio* II. xvi.).

30 *De libero arbitrio*, II. xvi. 41–4 (*PL*, xxxii, cols 1263–5); so too in art,
where all makers organize their work by number. See also *De
vera religione* xviii. 36; xxvi. 49; xxix. 52; xl. 75; xlii. 79–xliii. 81
(*PL*, xxxiv, cols 137, 143, 145, 155–9), and *De musica*, vi (*PL*, xxxii,
cols 1161ff.), where St Augustine discusses the importance of form
and how through number God may be seen in all things. For
Scriptural authority, see Wisdom xi. 21.

31 *Itinerarium mentis ad Deum*, ii. 10, tr. George Boas (Indianapolis,
Ind. 1953), p. 20.

32 *Etymologiae*, III. iv. 3 (*PL*, lxxxii, col. 156): *Per numerum siquidem, ne
confundamur, instruimur. Tolle numerum rebus omnibus, et omnia
pereunt.*

33 Cf. Boethius' attitude towards music as a curative for disordered
man (I. *pr.* i. 70; II. *pr.* i. 44; II. *pr.* iii. 10; III. *pr.* i; and III. *met* xii).
See III *pr.* xi. 50–70, on death as breach of number concord. Music
is by definition harmonious numbers.

34 1 and 2 are unreal numbers in that they represent point and line but
not space. The first number to designate a realizable area is 3. See

Vincent Foster Hopper, *Medieval Number Symbolism* (New York, 1938), p. 99.

35 The number 3 is that of love, vision and realization because God is love, God is light and God is manifest as Trinity. Love is the Third Person which binds First and Second together in a bond of peace (St Bernard, *De diligendo Deo*, xii; St Anselm, *Monologion*, xlix–liii). Similarly, Love which binds the Trinity also binds creation (St Augustine, *De Trin.*, IX). St Augustine argues that love itself is a 3 in that it consists of him who loves, that which is loved, and the act of loving (*De Trin.*, VIII. x. 14); in fact man's awareness of being is a 3, consisting of mind (*mens*), the knowledge with which mind knows itself (*notitia*), and love (*amor*) whereby mind loves self and knowledge.

36 E.g., St Cecile's argument in the *Second Nun's Tale* (VIII (G) 332–41). Plato, *Republic*, 580 D–E, and Plotinus, *Enneads*, V. i. 10, call 3 the number of the soul; so too Macrobius, *In somnium Scipionis*, I. vi. 42. In addition to St Augustine's discussions of 3 and soul cited in n. 35, see St Anselm, *Monologion*, lix; St Thomas Aquinas, *Summa theologica*, I. qu. xlv., art. 7; and St Bonaventura, *Itinerarium mentis in Deum*, iii. 1–7.

37 For an outline of several threefold patterns of ascent towards God, all of which are ultimately derived from St Augustine's discussion of the Trinity, see Charles Singleton, *An Essay on the Vita Nuova* (Cambridge, 1949), pp. 105–9.

38 St Augustine devotes most of *De Trin.* XI to considerations of threefold processes of seeing and perceiving (esp. XI. ii. 2–5; XI. v. 8–9; XI. vii. 11–12). He notes that there is an object perceived, a vision which did not exist before the perception, and an image of the object which resides in the mind. So too in recollection, where memory provides the image stored there until thought recalls it, which is then discerned in the mind once recalled, and which thus exists there so discerned because will recalled it. Thus external and internal vision are both threefold.

39 *Opera Omnia S. Bonaventurae*, ed. Franciscans of Quaracchi, 10 vols (Rome 1882-1902), v. 293–316. Although St Bonaventura defines his journey in 6 stages (6 being, he says, but 2 modes of three), his argument advances by juxtaposition of analogous 3s, since that is number of mind and the natural reflection of divinity.

40 *Itinerarium* ii. 4. See also i. 2–4 and v. 1–5.

41 *Itinerarium* ii. 5.

42 *Itinerarium* ii. 6–9.

43 Huppé and Robertson regard 'houres twelve' as a sign of vespers rather than noon:

> As he [the dreamer] sees the vision of Christ returning to the Heavenly City, the castle bell tolls twelve, the vesper hour which signifies the time of reward for the just in the heavenly kingdom. The sound is a promise of comfort in loss and of hope of future joy. Moreover, it brings the dream to a rounded conclusion, since the dream itself began in the 'dawenynge'. That is, it began with Lauds . . . the promise of the Resurrection, and ends with Vespers, the promise of the reward of the just. (p. 92)

The ambiguity of the phrase allows for both interpretations in that the vespers of the poet's dreaming, with its religious vision (thus Church time), becomes the noon of his awakening into the secular, world with its 'process of time'. For a comparable manipulation of religious and secular time in Chaucer, see my discussion in 'Number Symbolism in the Prologue to Chaucer' *Parson's Tale*', *English Studies*, xlviii (Amsterdam, 1967), 205–15.

44 In this regard Chaucer differs from Dante or subsequent Renaissance poets such as Spenser and Milton, who use symbolic verse count extensively. On Dante, see Hopper, *Medieval Number Symbolism*; Charles S. Singleton, 'The Poet's Number at the Center', *MLN*, lxxx(1965), 1–10; and Frederick W. Locke, 'Dante's Miraculous Enneads', *Dante Studies*, i (1968), 59–70. On Spenser and Milton, see Alastair Fowler, *Spenser and the Numbers of Time* (1964); A. Kent Hieatt, *Short Time's Endless Monument* (New York, 1960); Maren-Sofie Röstvig, 'The Hidden Sense', in *The Hidden Sense and Other Essays* (Oslo, 1963); and Gunnar Qvarnström, *The Enchanted Palace* (Stockholm, 1967).

45 The discrepancy between actual verse count of 11 lines and editorial verse count of 12 (i.e. 475–86) may be traced back to Thynne's addition of 'line 480' ('And thus in sorowe lefte me alone'). Skeat rightly pointed out that the line is spurious (it is found in none of the 3 MSS), but he maintained Thynne's line numbering nevertheless. Subsequent editors have done likewise, so that in Robinson's edition, e.g., l. 479 is followed by l. 481. Some editor needs to be brave enough to observe that the Black Knight's song, unlike the rest of the poem, is not composed in couplets but rather stanzas rhymed *aabba, ccdccd* (Baugh, *Chaucer's Major Poetry* [New York,

1963] is to be commended in this regard), then forget about the 'missing line' and restore the correct line numbering (which Baugh does not do).

46 For characteristic discussions of 11 in relation to 10 and 12, see St Augustine, *De Civ. Dei* xv. 20; *On the Gospel of St John*, Tractate xxvii. 10; Sermon i. 34 and Sermon xxxiii. See also *Catena Aurea*, tr. J.H.N. (1870), ii. 640, where St Thomas Aquinas cites St Augustine and Origen to the same effect. Cf. Hugh of St-Victor, *Exegetica* xv (*PL*, clxxv, col. 22), where by manner of extension, 11 is said to indicate transgression outside measure.

47 The number 6 is perfect since it equals the sum of its aliquot parts $(1 + 2 + 3 = 6)$ and the fruitful marriage number because it is the product of the first male and female numbers $(2 \times 3 = 6)$. E.g., Nichomachus, *Theologumena Arithmeticae*, tr. D'Ooge (Ann Arbor, Mich., 1938), pp. 96, 106, 109; St Augustine, *De Civ. Dei*, xi. 30; Macrobius, *In somn. Scip.*, I. vi. 12–17; St Isidore, *Etymologiae* III. v. 11; *Timaeus* 55; and Philo Judaeus, *On the Creation of the World*, ii (tr. Yonge, *Works*, i, 3–4). It is notable that Chaucer uses both 6 and 11 in conjunction with each other with implications comparable to those discussed here in the Parson's Prologue. See my 'Number Symbolism in the Prologue to Chaucer's *Parson's Tale*', 212–14.

48 Robinson's edn runs to 1334 lines, of course, since it has no line 480. See n. 45 above.

49 For discussion of symbolic numbers elsewhere in Chaucer's diction, see my consideration of 2s in 'Sovereignty and the Two Worlds of the *Franklin's Tale*', *Chaucer Review*, i (1967), 255–6; 3s and 1s in 'The Ideas of Translation and "Entente" in the *Second Nun's Tale*', *Annuale Mediaevale*, viii (1967), 28–33; and 6, 10, 11 and 29 in 'Number Symbolism in the Parson's Prologue', pp. 212ff.

50 The numbers 1 and 3 are both signs of unity, 3 being the expressive form of 1 (see n. 35). The number 8 pertains to Trinity in that it too is an expression of unity, justice, Christ and eternal life (see n. 56). And 12 is a sign of revelation and totality because of its 3 (Trinity) which multiplied by 4 (number of earth) marks the spreading of the good news everywhere (see nn. 66 and 70).

51 Macrobius offers one of the most eloquent celebrations of the monad (*In somn. Scip.* I. vi. 7ff.): it is the beginning and end, measure of all numbers, the number of the supreme God, and thus the

number of mind which sprang from God. Cf. St Augustine, *De Trin*. IV. vii. 11, on 1 as number of God; *Confessiones* II. i. 1, *De Trin*. VI. vi. 8 and VI. x. 12, on 1 as stability; *Boece* III. *pr*. xi, on *oneness* as good, *division* as death and destruction; Dante, *De Monarchia* i. 1–16, on man's need for oneness and peace; and *Boece* III. *pr*. ix, on the frustration of trying to divide that which may not be divided.

52 Ll. 553, 554, 746, 751, 756; 504, 511, 530.

53 A recurrent concern throughout Chaucer's poetry is the dilemmas which 2-eyed men with their divided vision get themselves into. Often in Chaucer 'eyen two' becomes a metaphor for the limitations of man's perspective in the face of Fortune and mutability.

54 St Jerome, *Adversus Jovinianum*, i. 22, notes that 10,000 is a number of Godliness. (See Hugh of St-Victor, *Exegetica*, xv [*PL*, clxxv, col. 22], for an explanation.) While it is easy to find 10,000s in medieval literature which have nothing to do with godliness, in this instance it is precisely the effect Chaucer seeks.

55 Macrobius, *In somn. Scip*. I. vi. 7ff., is useful here in realizing the implications of White's oneness: just as all numbers find their definition in the monad, so men, through her oneness, perceive their own.

56 For explanations of 8 as a return to unity see Macrobius, *In somn. Scip*., I. v. 17; St Basil, *De Spiritu Sancto*, xxvii. 66; St Gregory Nazianzen, *Oration* xli; and St Augustine, *Exposition on Psalm vi*. On 8 as sign of immortality, the New Jerusalem, eternity, Resurrection and Easter, see Hugh of St-Victor, *De arca Noe morali*, i. 16; and St Augustine, *Contra Faustum*, xvi. 29; *Civ. Dei*, xv. 20; and Epistle lv. The number 8 is of baptism and circumcision (sign of purification). It numbers the survivors after the deluge, a story that prefigures the Last Judgment and baptism, and, since the eighth beatitude repeats the first, it implies blessedness (St Jerome, *Adversus Jovinianum*, i. 37–40, and Berchorius, *Reductorium morale*, XIII. xxviii). For additional discussion and patristic references, see Alastair Fowler, *Spenser and the Numbers of Time*, p. 53, and Huppé and Robertson, *Fruyt and Chaf*, pp. 49–50.

57 I arrived independently at a comparable reading of these numbers in an essay presented in 1962 at the University of Rochester and later included in my *Number Symbolism and the Idea of Order in the Works of Geoffrey Chaucer* (Indiana University Doctoral Dissertation, 1962, unpub.)

58 *Fruyt and Chaf,* p. 33.

59 See n. 56.

60 *Testament of Love* I. v. 101ff. 'Margaryte', to whom he hopes to be committed, is Usk's figure for the soul, grace, learning, wisdom, Holy Church, etc.

61 *Fruyt and Chaf,* pp. 49–50.

62 *Ibid,* p. 92.

63 Ll. 420, 463, 573, 723, 831, 1323.

64 The basis for such traditions, as far as the Middle Ages is concerned, is Revelation. Like 8, 12 is glossed with great consistency. See nn. 46 above and 66 and 70 below.

65 Bertrand Bronson, 'Concerning "Houres Twelve"', *MLN* lxviii (1953), 515–21, was first to comment on the importance of 12s in the poem. He suggests that they are repeated for emphasis and that they suggest fulfilment, completion, and finality, since medieval clocks ran on a 12-hour cycle.

66 E.g., St Augustine, *On the Gospel of St John* xxvii. 10 and xlix. 8; and St Thomas Aquinas, *Expositio in Apocalypsim* iv.

67 'Medieval Chess and the *Book of the Duchess*', *MLN*, lxiv (1949), 261–4.

68 The idiom occurs in *Canterbury Tales,* I (A) 4141; V (F) 383, VIII (G) 675 and *Romaunt of the Rose,* 7593; *Piers Plowman,* B v. 214; *Confessio amantis,* Prol. 526, ii. 52, ii. 2063, iii. 1049, v. 2456, v. 3738, v. 4403, viii. 1426; and the Judgment Play of the Townley Cycle (*EETS,* e.s. cxxi), p. 367, l. 9. In all but 3 instances (*Cant. Tales,* VIII (G) 675; *Confessio amantis,* v. 2456; and *Piers,* v. 214), the twelve rhymes with *selve,* clearly suggesting a rhyming device. *Dix o douze* appears only occasionally in O.F. literature (e.g., once in *Le Roman de la Rose,* though never in Machaut), so almost certainly the idiom is native, not a borrowed literary convention.

69 *Le Roman de la Rose,* ed. Langlois, l. 1368; see M.E. *Romaunt of the Rose,* l. 1393.

70 *Exegetica,* xl (*PL,* clxxv, cols 22–3). For 10 as unenlightened justice, see *Catena Aurea,* with its glosses by St Augustine, Bede, and St Ambrose on Luke xix. 11–27 and Mark v. 42. Cf. St Augustine, *On the Gospel of St John,* Tractates vii, xvii, xxiv, and cxxii, on 10 as number of the Decalogue and 2 the precepts of Love.

71 E.g., St Augustine, *Sermon,* i. 32 (*Nicene and Post Nicene Christian Fathers,* ed. Schaff, 1st ser., 8 vols [New York, 1887–92], vi. 258) for a typical gloss on 40, and *On the Gospel of St John,* Tractate

cxxii. 8, for typical commentary on 50 as a sign of jubilee and Pentecost. Or, see *De doctrina christiana*, II. xvi. 25, for discussion of both. Cf. Maurice H. Farbridge, *Studies in Biblical and Semitic Symbolism* (1923), pp. 142ff., for extensive discussion of 40 to signify an ill-fated period, trial, exile, or denial.

72 See Robinson's note to l. 445, *Works*, p. 775. Samuel Schoenbaum, 'Chaucer's Black Knight', *MLN*, lxviii (1953), 121–2, argues against emendation on grounds that 24 suggests a young man and that 'bereavement in youth is even more touching than separation in later life.' Charles Nault, ' "Foure and Twenty Yer" Again', *MLN*, lxxi (1956), 319–21, answers that 30 was considered young by medieval standards and that there is probably a scribal error after all, xxviiij being intended rather than xxiiij.

73 'Chaucer's "Mistake": *The Book of the Duchess*, line 455', *American Notes and Queries*, iv (1966), 99–100. Langhans, *Untersuchungen zu Chaucer* (Halle, 1918), pp. 281ff., offers a similar suggestion. But see Robertson, 'Historical Setting of Chaucer's *Book of the Duchess*', p. 179ff., for a convincing explanation why neither Gaunt nor Chaucer should be identified with the Black Knight.

74 See Hopper, *Medieval Number Symbolism*, pp. 128–9.

# Sir Gawain: pentangle, *luf-lace,* numerical structure

A. KENT HIEATT

Whatever else *Sir Gawain and the Green Knight* may signify, it is certainly about keeping troth. Two novel pieces of evidence for this aspect of the poem are presented here. They possess general and methodological interest in addition to the light that they shed on *Sir Gawain.*

The distinction which J. A. Burrow, in his recent admirable study, draws between the symbolic qualities of the pentangle, or symbol of *trawþe* in this work, and of the *luf-lace,* the girdle of contrary signification, is germane here although the present article opposes it: 'Unlike the pentangle, the belt is not, so far as the poem is concerned, a "natural" symbol. It does not, that is, have any particular symbolic value on the strength simply of its intrinsic natural properties. So while the pentangle is necessarily a token of "trawþe" and could not possibly, in the poet's view, be otherwise, the belt is a token of untruth only because it happened to play the part it did in Gawain's adventure.'[1] Elsewhere, Burrow assigns these two symbols respectively to the *impositio secundum naturam* and the *impositio ad placitum* or *impositio iuxta arbitrium humanae voluntatis* of fourteenth-century speculative grammarians.[2]

In fact, however, the *Gawain*-poet gives grounds for regarding the *lace* as a natural, not an arbitrary, symbol of imperfection. Its symbolic qualities oppose, but belong to the same class as, those singled out in the pentangle; and the relationship of these two objects is that of a balanced, two-part symbolic structure rather than that of an isolated construct (the pentangle) to a mere narrative motif (the *lace*) to which significance has been arbitrarily attached. That this two-part symbolic structure is likely to be the creation of an author writing a poem about troth is the implication of the first part of this article. The point of the second part is that the author almost surely built a numerical connection between the pentangle as a symbol of troth and important structural features of his poem. It may be that the same holds true for the *lace*. There is all the more reason, then, to think that the poem is mainly about keeping troth.

The explicit use made in *Gawain* of the intrinsic qualities of the pentangle is well known.[3] In the first place, this figure is a sign that 'Salamon set sumquyle / In bytoknyng of trawþe' (ll. 625–6) because each line in it immovably 'umbelappez and loukez in oþer' so that each angle braces all the others and so that the line defining the pentangle is 'endelez' (l. 629) in a sense well known to American school-children, who are taught to draw the five-pointed star of the national flag using only straight lines and never lifting the pencil from the paper. In fact it is called the 'endeles knot' (l. 630). In the same way, Gawain's excellences are said to fit together in an irrefragable and immutable pattern. This pattern had never failed. There had been no point in it to show a special juncture different from the rest ('ne samned neuer', l. 659). It had never broken. Like the pentangle, it had been without end at any angle or point ('noke') (ll. 657–61). In the second place, the pentangle has 5 points, and Gawain had 5 kinds of fivefold excellences, making a total of 25. For these two reasons, the pentangle appears on Gawain's shield in this romance, in red gold upon a red background (ll. 618–20, 662–3), and upon his coat-armour (ll. 637, 2026) against a background of red (l. 2036).

The *luf-lace* is similarly well known. It is a girdle worked in green and gold (l. 1832), with pendants (ll. 2038, 2431). It is a sign of *vntrawþe* (l. 2509) – disloyalty and inconstancy – and also, in Gawain's opinion, of an ensuing train of peccancy (ll. 2374–5, 2379–83, 2508). Going to his assignation with the Green Knight, he wears it bound twice about him, over the red of the coat-armour with its pentangle. When informed of its true significance, he undoes it and throws it from him, but subsequently wears it back to court, as a baldric, over his right shoulder and knotted under his left arm:

Abelef as a bauderyk bounden bi his syde,
Loken vnder his lyfte arme, þe lace, with a knot,
In tokenyng he watz tane in tech of a faute.

(ll. 2486–8)

Subsequently, the rest of the court adopt this device.

It has often been suggested, of course, that the color green in this *lace* has associations that make it naturally suitable for the principle associated with the Green Knight, or for Gawain's fault. In fact, Burrow himself very properly and subtly takes up the idea at several points.[4] Perhaps the most obvious secular association of green for the fourteenth century was disloyalty in love.[5] The liturgical connection with hope, however, and the other connections with the natural world, with vigor, with the Green Man, or with the recurrence of spring cannot be excluded. Yet none of these associations would justify classing the *lace* as a symbol arising from the *impositio secundum naturam* in the strong sense which holds for the pentangle. There is nevertheless another, more substantial association that makes the *lace* a natural symbol for Gawain's shortcoming.

One important meaning of *lace* (Chaucer's *las*, *laas*) is the *OED's Lace* 1: 'a net, noose, snare', corresponding to Old French *laz*, Italian *laccio*, and Spanish-American *lasso*, ultimately from Latin *laqueus*, of which the principal meaning is 'noose'.[6] The word is often used figuratively with the general meaning 'snare' or with one of the more specific meanings, in medieval and later verse. Typically, a personified principle or a divinity spreads a *lace* to catch the unsuspecting. Of Venus, for instance, 'Lo, alle thise folk so caught were in hire las, / Til they for wo ful often sayde "allas!"' ('Knight's Tale', *Canterbury Tales*, I, 1951–2); 'But Love had broght this man in swich a rage, / And him so narwe bounden in his las' (*Legend of Good Women*, ll. 599–600); 'Women the haveth in hire las' (*King Alisaundre*, l. 7698); 'him þat bound is in loues lace';[7] the *OED's* quotation for 1491: 'the laces and temptacyons of the deuyll'. The *laz* laid by the Love God beside the Fountain Perilous in the *Roman de la Rose* may be nets (as used to entangle birds) rather than nooses: 'Cupido' sowed here 'd'Amors la graine' (ll. 1588–9) and

> fist ses laz environ tendre,
> E ses engins i mist, por prendre
> Damoiseles e damoisiaus,
> Qu'Amors ne viaut autres oisiaus.[8]
>
> (ll. 1588–94)

But specifically a noose (i.e., with some kind of knot, usually a running one) is often intended, as in the meaning of the original Latin word. In Italian, the primary meanings of *laccio* are 'noose', 'slip knot', 'thong', 'lace'.[9] The *Gawain*-poet's contemporary Petrarch, however, usually means 'noose' in using this word figuratively.[10] Remembering Laura, for instance, he says that Time now braids her hair in firmer knots so as to compress his heart with so powerful a noose that only Death can undo it:

> torsele il tempo poi in piú saldi nodi,
> e strinse 'l cor d'un laccio sí possente
> Che Morte sola fia ch' indi lo snodi.[11]

Conceivably he may sometimes mean a net, as in this use of the diminutive, 'Non volendomi Amor perdere ancóra / Ebbe un altro lacciuol fra l'erba teso' (cclxxi); but he more often means something like a lasso.

The *Gawain*-poet seems to have had two things in mind in using, or accepting, the concept and word *lace* for the device by which Gawain is successfully tempted. In the first place, he capitalizes on the habitual and general figurative meaning 'snare', 'trap', because snaring Gawain is what Bertilak's wife (in the first instance) is trying to do: the association is almost unavoidable when recognized. In the same connection, the association of *lace* with the catching of wild animals is supported by (and supports) the analogy between Bertilak's hunting and his wife's attempts to seduce Gawain on three successive days; and most readers seem to have accepted this analogy, even when they cannot follow Dr

H. L. Savage into all of the detailed correspondences which he has enumerated between the hunting scenes and the doings of Gawain and the wife of Bertilak.[12]

In the second place, however, the poet seems to wish to convey a signification directly contrary to that of the pentangle when he has Gawain knot the *lace* around his body (it will be remembered that the meaning 'noose' necessarily involves a knot). When Gawain attires himself to undergo his trial at the Green Chapel, he doubles the *lace* about himself, over his red coat armour (ll. 2033–6). Apparently he knots it, for when in his chagrin he takes it off to fling it to Bertilak, the operation is described thus: 'Þenne he kaȝt to þe knot, and þe kest lawsez' (l. 2376), although the meaning of *kest* ('fastening'?) is uncertain. Later the physical situation is completely clear. As he returns to the court, the *lace* is tied (*loken*) around him under his left arm 'with a knot' (l. 2487).

The 'endeles knot', or pentangle, is perfect because it is all of a piece: each line 'umbellappez and loukez in oþer / And ayquere it is endelez'. Like Gawain's former continuum of virtues, it 'ne samned neuer in no syde, ne sundered nouþer, / Withouten ende at any noke aiquere'. For this reason, mainly,

> Hit is a syngne þat Salamon set sumquyle
> In bytoknyng of trawþe.

In direct contrast (and with a partial verbal repetition) one reads on the subject of the *lace*:

> þe blykkande belt he bere þeraboute
> Abelef as a bauderyk bounden bi his syde,
> Loken vnder his lyfte arme, þe lace, with a knot,
> In tokenyng he watz tane in tech of a faute.

A now natural reading of these lines is that this 'token of vntrawþe' (l. 2509) opposes naturally the token of 'trawþe', not by authorial fiat, but because the *lace* is not endless. Its ends must be tied together; and its very visible knot shows where, in its imperfection, this frail and pliable object must be 'samned' together in order to make an enclosure, unlike the pentangle and, for instance, unlike the pearl which is 'endeleʒ rounde' (*Pearl,* ll. 738), being 'wemleʒ, clene, and clere' (l. 737).

In this connection, Gawain's statement about the knotted earnest of his fault, 'Þer it onez is tachched twynne wil hit neuer' (l. 2512), takes on more weight as emphasizing the snare-like qualities of the *lace* and perhaps the significance of the knot itself. Equally in accord with this interpretation is the lady's specifying that the *lace* should be fixed around the body (ll. 1851-2), not simply carried. It should be noted as well that the similar green, tasseled *lace* wrapped around the shaft of the axe with which Bertilak arrives at Arthur's court, 'louked' (l. 217) ('was attached', presumably 'was knotted') at the head of the shaft and was fastened ('halched ful ofte') at many points along the shaft – again, presumably, by knots.[13] The lengthy passage (ll. 187-95), in the same scene, on the horse's ornamentally knotted mane (green and gold, like the *luf-lace*) and the forelock and tail, both bound with a green band and the latter decorated with an intricate knot, may accord with this symbolism.

The *luf-lace*, then, like the pentangle, has traditional associations, which are most likely to have rendered its choice as a symbol in *Sir Gawain* an *impositio secundum naturam*. Its vividly scandalous character may be played down when it becomes the mark of an order of knighthood, but its geometrical imperfection in needing to be knotted and its character as a noose (as well as its no doubt startling *enker* green) are always there. Just as much as in the case of the pentangle, the *lace* seems to be the *Gawain*-poet's calculated symbolic device and not a chance narrative motif, whether inherited or not from other material. Further, the conceptually fixed, symmetrical, apparently calculated symbolic opposition (endlessness – incompleteness; knotlessness–knottedness; rigidity-pliability; protected area–trap) between these two most important symbols in the romance suggests that what they stand for – troth and untroth – are what *Sir Gawain* is about.

This discussion of pentangle and *luf-lace* in terms of their symbolic relationship now moves to certain structural considerations.

As J. P. Oakden points out, the *Gawain* stanza, in combining an indefinite number of unrhymed alliterative long lines with a bob and wheel, is a 'daring experiment'.[14] It is unprecedented in the extant verse from the Alliterative Revival. The experiment is, of course, hugely successful, partly because of the element of flexibility: the bob and wheel may be introduced *ad lib.*, within certain wide limits. But what I wish to show here is that the poet had an additional reason for desiring flexibility in stanza length.

As has often been noted, the number of stanzas in each of the poet's two *chefs-d'oeuvre* is 101. Presumably he was aiming at this total in both *Pearl* and *Sir Gawain*, for he would scarcely have hit it twice by chance.[15] Further, the echoing (and concluding) line in *Pearl* – the one which repeats elements of the first line – is No. 1212. The number 12, drawn from *Revelation*, is undoubtedly the most important one in the narrative of the poem: the Heavenly Jerusalem is built upon manifold units of 12s (length, breadth, foundations, trees, etc.) and the procession of virgins and innocents numbers 144,000. Duplication of a number in the fashion of '1212' is known elsewhere in medieval number symbolism.[16] It cannot, however, be automatically assumed that the total number 1212 was intended to have symbolic significance, for that total would inevitably follow, given a desire for 101 stanzas and a prior choice of an invariable stanza length of 12 lines (even though that choice in itself may have symbolic significance).

Nevertheless the echoing line in *Sir Gawain* also occurs at a point to which a parallel meaning may be attached: it is No. 2525. The number 25 is a highly significant number in the romance, for Gawain has 5 times 5 ('fyue and sere fyue syþes', l. 632) excellences. That is why he bears the pentangle. Moreover, since the length of the *Gawain* stanza is variable, the line number 2525 does not automatically arise from the stanza total of 101, as the number 1212 does in *Pearl*. Either one is faced with an extraordinary coincidence, or the poet wished to memorialize a significant number in the total number of lines up to and through the echoing one in both *Pearl* and *Sir Gawain*, at the same time that he wished to maintain a total of 101 stanzas in each.[17] If in fact he did this, then his way of doing it in *Sir Gawain* was curiously like that of Edmund Spenser in *Epithalamion* and may bear witness to a more general practice: in *Epithalamion,* according to my now widely accepted demonstration, Spenser's desire for a significant total of 365 lines in 24 stanzas led him to use stanzas of irregular length, as he does not do elsewhere.[18]

In versifying an action-filled, eventful narrative (unlike *Pearl,* for instance), a poet would find it much easier to reach a fixed number of lines in a fixed number of stanzas if he could vary the number of lines per stanza. But in the case of *Sir Gawain* a device would be needed to create a stanzaic impression, since the long, unrhymed, alliterative lines of this poem would in themselves seem no more stanzaic than, say, the alliterative *Morte Arthure.* A concluding, rhyming bob and wheel would provide the necessary punctuation, and in fact the 101 bobs and wheels of *Sir Gawain* are the only aural evidence for the 101 stanzas (a small, invariable marginal mark generally indicates to the eye the beginning of each stanza in the manuscript).

The echoing line 2525 in *Sir Gawain* is not the concluding one but is followed by the last, 5-line bob and wheel. But apparently the echo, not the concluding line, was the critical point for the author. In any case, within the stanzaic framework of *Sir Gawain* he could not have made his last line the echoing one even if he had wanted to. His choice of a stanza would have embarrassed him, since it is apparently impossible to repeat even the essentials (e.g., 'After segge sesed at Troye') of his long alliterative line 1 in the short line of any of his wheels.

In sum, the identity in number of stanzas, and the significant numbers 1212 and 2525 in the totals of lines through the echoing lines in *Pearl* and *Sir Gawain,* establish a very strong likelihood that their author intended the observed numerical patterns to have significance. They also provide a likely reason for the choice of an unprecedented stanzaic pattern in *Sir Gawain.* Possibly they provide the same for the choice of stanza in *Pearl,* in the sense that, arithmetically, 12-line stanzas form the most elegant means for arriving at the desired multiple of 12. All of these matters are of interest in the history of numerical composition in late medieval times. Above all, however, in the case of *Sir Gawain,* the apparent reference to the symbolism of the pentangle in the numerical structure of the poem is further evidence that the poet was composing a poem about troth, because that is what the pentangle represents.

I now come to a further set of structural patterns in *Sir Gawain* which are themselves of much interest but for which I am unable to offer a fully satisfactory explanation. They may be related to the motif of the imperfection of the *lace*. Before any discussion of them, the traditional division of the romance into 4 fitts, or parts, which has been called into question, must be rehabilitated. (This has, in fact, been recently and strongly done, but in somewhat different terms, as I shall point out.)

This division, corresponding to the 4 largest illuminated initial capitals in the part of the manuscript devoted to *Sir Gawain*, was introduced by Sir Frederic Madden in the first printed edition, for the Bannatyne Club in 1839. It has been continued in every other printed version since. Nevertheless Mrs L. L. Hill contended in 1946, 'It has become evident that there is no absolute fourfold division of *Gawain*. Such a division exists only in printed tradition and cannot be supported by any attentive examination of *Cotton Nero A. x.* or of the poem itself.'[19] While admitting that Madden's divisions corresponded with the positions of some of the illuminated capitals, she pointed out that he failed to introduce such divisions at the no less than 5 other illuminated capitals in the manuscript text of *Gawain*. In her opinion, Madden had been led to make his divisions largely by another feature of the manuscript: 3 series of thin lines running across the page in each case at the same place in the text where the illuminated capital separates each of 'Madden's' fitts from the following one. But, she says, in the total manuscript (containing *Pearl*, *Purity*, and *Patience*, as well as *Gawain*) there are only 4 such 2-line elements. Of these, 3 occur in *Gawain*, as already stated, and the fourth occurs in *Purity* at line 1157, at the beginning of what Gollancz designated as Part iii. It follows that if the criterion of horizontal lines were applied in order to make divisions in the manuscript as a whole, then there should be only 'a twofold division of *Purity* despite the fact that the poet has said, "Þus vpon þrynne wyses I haf yow þro schewed," line 1805; and the same standard would leave *Patience* and *Pearl* with no divisions at all.'[20] The importance of Mrs Hill's thesis was enhanced when it was supported by Professor Morton W. Bloomfield in his review of *Gawain* studies: 'There is a good case for dividing the work into nine divisions. . . . It is surprising that this suggestion has not been taken up by literary critics.'[21]

There is reason, nevertheless, to believe that Mrs Hill somewhat overstated the case; in fact, the primacy of the 4 divisions has recently been reasserted by both Donald R. Howard and James W. Tuttleton.[22] The initials at the so-called fitt divisions are larger than the other 5 in *Sir Gawain*[23] and, unlike those 5, have at their heads, running across the page, horizontal blanks in the text.[24] More importantly, the inked lines running across the page at the fitt divisions are a more significant divisive feature than Mrs Hill recognized. She neglected to note 2 further cases of such lines. At the beginning of *Purity* (Folio 57a), and separating this poem from the preceding *Pearl* the first poem in the manuscript), 3 such lines run from the top of the illuminated initial across the page. Similarly, at the beginning of *Patience* (Folio 83a) 3 lines running across the page from the initial separate that poem from the preceding *Purity*. (*Gawain*, the final poem, is in its turn separated from *Patience* by a large space at the top of its first page – about half the length of the text on that page.) As Mrs Hill says 2 horizontal lines (in appearance similar to the 3-line divisions which I have enumerated) separate each fitt from the other in *Gawain*. The only other horizontal division in the manuscript is the one in *Purity* (Folio 73a) that she mentions; but, as far as can be determined from the facsimile, it is a single line, not double like the ones in *Gawain*. It occurs at the beginning of the relation of the last episode in *Purity*, universally admitted to be one of the 2 main divisions of the poem. Each of these 6 units of horizontal lines in the manuscript occupies an otherwise blank horizontal strip, at least 1 line high, created by the initial's rising higher than the top line of text which it faces. There are places at the tops of pages in the manuscript text of *Pearl* – Folios 44a, 46b, 49a, 52b – where in each case there is room for such horizontal lines next to one of the initials which begin each of the 5-stanza units of *Pearl*, but the scribe has not added lines here, because (as I would claim) he or the scribe of the exemplar did not feel that this was a division important enough to merit that visual device for separating major portions of the poem. The case thus stands that there are 6 horizontal dividers in the manuscript – 2 of 3 lines each, 3 of 2 lines each, and 1 of 1 line. The first 2 dividers separate poems from each other; the last, of only 1 line, is at a main division. Where the scribe had space for such lines next to an initial, but where there is not a prime logical division of the poem, he does not add lines. The 2-line divisions in *Gawain*, then, would seem to be of prime divisive importance in the scribe's or his exemplar's system, particularly as they are associated with the largest initials in the poem, exclusive of the opening one. It cannot be excluded, of course, that the smaller initials may correspond to subdivisions valuable for an interpretation of the poem (of which more later); but the case for 4 main divisions in *Gawain* seems secure.

If, then, the validity of the traditional fourfold division as it appears in all printed editions of *Gawain* is assumed, two series of numerical parallelisms are discernible in the poem. The first has to do with Fitt i (the first half of the Beheading Test) and Fitt iv (the second half of the Beheading Test). (A) In Stanza 10 of Fitt i, the first axe and its *lace* make their appearance (ll. 208ff.). (B) In Stanza 20 of Fitt i, Bertilak as the Green Knight departs:

Halled out at þe hal dor, his hed in his hande,
Þat þe fyr of þe flynt flaȝe fro fole houes.
To quat kyth he becom knwe non þere,
Neuer more þen þay wyste from queþen he watz wonnen.
(ll. 458–61)

(C) In Stanza 21, the axe, undoubtedly with its green *lace*, reaches its ultimate destination. It is hung against the wall-tapestry above the dais in Arthur's hall. That is the end of Fitt i. (A) In Stanza 10 of Fitt iv (the second half or the Beheading Test), an axe, with yet another gleaming *lace*, again appears (ll. 2222–6). (B) In Stanza 20 of this fitt, Bertilak again departs:

Þe knyȝt in þe enker grene
Whiderwarde-so-euer he wolde.
(ll. 2477–8)

(C) In Stanza 21 of the same fitt, the *luf-lace* (knotted this time around a man, not an axe) reaches its ultimate destination in the poem. Wearing it over the pentangle and the red cloth of his coat-armor (ll. 2485ff.), Gawain reaches Arthur's court (l. 2489). This, however, is not the end of Fitt iv. An additional, 22nd stanza – the one-hundredth and first of the poem – goes beyond the natural arc of the parallelism with Fitt i, in order to relate the reaction to Gawain's shame, the founding of the order of the *lace*.

The second series of numerical parallelisms occurs in Fitt iii, the 3 days of the Temptation (see Table). In Stanza 11 (ll. 1402ff.) of this fitt, Gawain and Bertilak make an agreement – a *forward* or *couenaunt* – and the company of Bertilak's castle go to bed. In stanza 22 (ll. 1668ff.), after a succession of events corresponding precisely to the succession in the first sequence of 11 stanzas, another agreement in terms of *trawþe* is made, and the company go to bed. In Stanza 33 (ll. 1952ff.), after the same succession, a third promise 'in god fayþe' is made, and it is said to be time for the company to go to bed. As at the end of the other series, however, this is not the end of the fitt. A thirty-fourth stanza follows, in which Gawain makes his farewells to the inhabitants of the castle (ll. 1979–88). Except that Gawain goes to bed, the events of this stanza go beyond the natural arc of parallelism with the action of the other 2 series of 11 stanzas.

The promises which form the most important articulating points of the second numerical series are of paramount importance, although it is the cream of the jest that Gawain should not know this. Like the pentangle and the *luf-lace*, they concern *Sir Gawain's* great themes, *trawþe* and *vntrawþe*. In this second series at the end of the first sequence in Fitt iii, Bertilak and Gawain again agree to exchange what they gain on the following day, as they had done first at the end of Fitt ii, and they jocularly drink on the *couenauntez*:

## Fitt III, The Three Sequences

(l., ll. = line or lines; s., ss. = stanza or stanzas.)

|  | FIRST DAY | SECOND DAY | THIRD DAY |
|---|---|---|---|
| I First stages of hunt | 1126–78 (53 l.) 2 ss.+1 l. | 1421–68 (48 ll.) 2 ss.−7 ll. | 1690–1730 (41 ll.) 1 s.+12 ll. |
| II The happenings in Gawain's bed chamber to departure of lady | 1179–1308 (130 ll.) 1 s.−1 l.+ 3 ss., +1 s.− 10 ll. (4 ss.+ 18 ll.) | 1469–1557 (89 ll.) 7 ll.+3 ss. | 1731–1871 (141 ll.) 1 s.−12 ll., +5 ss.,+2 ll. (6 ss.−10 ll.) |
| III Gawain's rising, religious observance, recreation with the two ladies of the castle | 1309–18 (10 ll.) | 1558–60 (3 ll.) | 1872–93 (22 ll.) 1 s.−2 ll.,+ 1 l. |
| IV Conclusion of hunt; dressing or skinning of deer, boar, fox; return to castle | 1319–69 (51 ll.) 2 ss.−2 ll. | 1561–1620 (60 ll.) 1 s.−3 ll.,+ 1 s.,+1 s.− 2 ll. (3 ss.− 5 ll.) | 1894–1923 (30 ll.) 1 s.−1 l.+ 2 ll. |
| V Events of the evening: exchange of what has been gained during the day, entertainment; in 11th s. of each series: mention (1) of retirement of company for night; (2) of early activities of next morning; (3) of pledge(s) | 1370–1420 (51 ll.) 2 ll.+2 ss. | 1621–89 (69 ll.) 3 ss.+2 ll. | 1924–78 (55 ll.) 1 s.−2 ll.+ 1 s. |
| TOTALS | 11 ss. (295 ll.) Average stanza is 27−ll. | 11 ss. (269 ll.) Average stanza is 24+ll. | 11 ss.(289 ll.) Average stanza is 26+ll.) supernumerary 1979–97 (19 ll.) 1 s. |

And efte in her bourdyng þay bayþen in þe morn
To fylle þe same forwardez þat þay byfore maden:
Wat chaunce so bytydez hor cheuysaunce to chaunge,
What nwez so þay nome, at naȝt quen þay metten.
Þay acorded of þe couenauntz byfore þe court alle;
Þe beuerage watz broȝt forth in bourde at þat tyme.

(ll. 1404–9)

At the end of the second sequence of 11 stanzas, they make the same agreement:

Ande þer þay dronken, and dalten, and demed eft nwe
To norne on þe same note on Nwe ȝerez euen,

(ll. 1668–9)

and at the same time Bertilak makes a second promise, in solemn form, although Gawain cannot know the gravity of Bertilak's involvement:

'as I am trwe segge, I siker my trawþe
Þou schal cheue to þe grene chapel þy charres to make
Leude, on Nw ȝerez lyȝt, longe bifore pryme.'

(ll. 1673–5)

At the end of the third sequence of 11 stanzas, Bertilak repeats the promise in due form:

'In god fayþe,' quoþ þe godmon, 'wyth a goud wylle
Al þat euer I yow hyȝt halde schal I redé.'

(ll. 1969–70)

The sting in its tail is sharpened by the parallel form of Bertilak's assurance when, metamorphosed into the Green Knight, he meets Gawain at the Green Chapel, apparently to cut off his head: 'And þou schal haf al in hast þat I þe hyȝt ones' (l. 2218).

One point worthy of note in the first series – the one having to do with the Beheading Test – is that the *lace* (the third in the narrative) which accompanies the second axe in the tenth stanza of the

129

Fourth Fitt seems to have no function in the text unless it is there to fulfill the numerical parallelism with Stanza 10 of Fitt i, containing the first *lace*. The third *lace* is thus slipped in with its axe:

A denez ax nwe dyȝt, þe dynt with to ȝelde,
With a borelych bytte bende by þe halme,
Fyled in a fylor, fowre fote large –
Hit watz no lasse bi þat lace þat lemed ful bryȝt –.
(ll. 2223–6)

If this means what it seems to mean, it is *ignotum per ignotius* – the length of an axe ratified by the unknown length of its *lace*. This *lace* then disappears from the story, its place in the arithmetical series taken (as I claim) by the *luf-lace*.

The 2 arithmetical series which I have posited – the 2 sequences of the Beheading Test and the 3 sequences of the Temptation – are unlikely to be coincidental, because their constituent parts differ greatly in length and in other respects. In the 2 halves of the Beheading Test there is, it is true, a rough episodic parallelism. The 2 antagonists go each to the other's abode and expose themselves to beheadings. But the 2 sequences of episodes differ so greatly in other respects as to suggest that the parallels of the tenth, twentieth, and twenty-first stanzas in the 2 fitts are the results of calculation. In the Temptation, the episodic parallelism is much closer among the 3 sequences, but the amounts of text devoted to parallel episodes differ quite enough to throw off the overall numerical parallelism if it were not the result of calculation. The exchange of gifts, for instance, arrives in the ninth stanza in the second sequence, in the tenth stanza in the first and third sequences. The reason for this is that the events of the bed chamber on the second day, being largely a repetition of those on the first, take up less space – 3 stanzas plus 7 lines (ll. 1469–1557) – than the first day's 4 stanzas plus 18 lines (ll. 1179–1308). On the third day, on the other hand, the events in the bed chamber are quite involved, taking up more than $5\frac{1}{2}$ stanzas, and the details of Gawain's confession and absolution take up almost 1 stanza (ll. 1876–84). Each of these discrepancies (as I call them) is compensated for so as to arrive at the assertion or reassertion of a promise in the eleventh stanza. On the second day, that is, the author allows himself a much fuller description of the evening's activities (ll. 1621–85) than on the other 2 days, which makes up for his brief bedroom scene; on the third day, however, the preliminary and concluding accounts of the hunt and the account of the evening's activities amount to less, stanzaically (about $4\frac{1}{2}$ stanzas), than they do on the first day (6 stanzas) and the second day ($7\frac{1}{2}$ stanzas), and compensate for the other lengthy episodes. It is true that the more varied evening activities of the third day down through the eleventh stanza of this sequence actually occupy more lines than those of the first day (55 against 51), but the author has allowed considerably more lines in his eleventh stanza on the third day than on the first (27 against 19) so that the scheme still works, stanzaically. This is apparently an instance of his capitalization on his initial choice of an unprecedentedly flexible stanza.

What the poet may have intended by this ordering is very much in question. It may have been simply his way of going to work: so many stanzas arbitrarily allotted for this part of the story, so many for that, particularly if he intended to arrive at a fixed total of 101 stanzas. At the same time, one notes that the number of stanzas in each of the series here considered is a multiple of 5, plus 1: 101 stanzas, 21 stanzas and 11 stanzas.[25] I see no way of proving that the author's intention here was to build a numerical conception of the *lace* into the work as I believe he built into it the concept of the pentangle. Still, the idea is worth pursuing for a moment.

What such an arithmetical conceit would signify is that, as the *luf-lace,* with its knot, adds an element which ruins the perfection signified by the knotless pentangle, so 5 plus 1, or a multiple of 5 to which 1 unit is added, signifies imperfection.[26] A way of carrying out this system in the remaining fitt, the second, is to divide the fitt into 4 units of 6 stanzas each (5 + 1). At 2 points, this division corresponds in a sense to smaller illuminated capitals in the manuscript. In stanza 6 (ll. 619ff.) of this fitt – a stanza beginning with an illuminated capital – there appears for the first time the pentangle, highly significant as a symbol but destined to be overcome. In stanza 12, which also begins with an illuminated capital, there appears the castle, apparently by a miracle in answer to Gawain's prayer but also to be the stage for his undoing. In stanza 18, Gawain celebrates, for the first time after his prayer, what he had prayed for so urgently – 'þe servyse of that syre' – in the chapel at evensong, but he also meets there his ultimate undoers, Bertilak's wife and Morgan la Fay (ll. 928–69). In the twenty-fourth stanza of this fitt, Bertilak induces Gawain to undertake the first of the apparently jocular but in fact solemn promises of the Temptation: 'Swete, swap we so, sware with trawþe' (l. 1108). Further such promises, jocular according to Gawain's estimate but grave in formula and fact, define the divisions which I have posited in Fitt iii.

As I have just shown, of the 5 smaller illuminated initials, which do not introduce fitts, 2 correspond to sequences which I propose in Fitt ii. The significance of the other 3 smaller ones may be touched on now.[27] One, at line 1421, corresponds to the beginning of the second of the sequences I propose for the Temptation, in Fitt iii. The other 2 do not correspond to any of the units here proposed, but are of some independent interest. One (l. 1893) introduces the stanza in which Bertilak strikes at the fox, who draws aside from the blow but is immediately caught by one of Bertilak's dogs. The other (l. 2259) introduces the stanza in which Bertilak, as the Green Knight, strikes his first blow at Gawain, and Gawain winces aside. Possibly the author wished to introduce these 2 remaining capitals in order to call attention to the parallel, which goes into some detail. Bertilak

> watz war of þe wylde, and warly abides,
> And braydez out þe bryȝt bronde, and at þe best castez.
> And he schunt for þe scharp, and schulde haf arered;
> A rach rapes hym to, ryȝt er he myȝt,
> And ryȝt bifore þe hors fete þay fel on hym alle,
> And woried me þis wyly with a wroth noyse.
>
> (ll. 1900–5)

On the other hand, as the Danish axe descends toward his neck Gawain

schranke a lytel with þe schulderes for þe scharp yrne.
Þat oþer schalk wyth a schunt þe schene wythaldez,
And þenne repreued he þe prynce with mony prowde wordez.

(ll. 2267-9)

Gawain's answer begins, 'I schunt onez, / And so wyl I no more' (ll. 2280-1). It goes without saying that there is the possibility of a parallelism between the fox's and Gawain's wincing aside, and, lightly touched, between the fox's and Gawain's alternative escape-routes, foredoomed because of the efficiency of Bertilak's creatures (his dog, his wife, his *lace*). There is also the verbal agreement of 'schunt' (ll. 1903, 2268, 2280) and 'scharp' (ll. 1902, 2267), and the canine and churlish surquidry (ll. 1905, 2269).

In the matter, then, of the 9 initials in the manuscript text of *Gawain*, 7 (4 beginning the fitts, and 3 others) correspond to either the initial or final stanzas of sequences which I have suggested, and the remaining 2 initials point to a parallelism of a kind well known in the romance, mainly through the work of H. L. Savage. But 3 of the sequences that I suggest (the last 2 in Fitt ii, the last 1 in Fitt iii) have no illuminated capital initially or finally.

It must be said finally and regretfully that the overall numerical scheme proposed here for the fitts is so complicated as to be un-satisfactory, not because the *Gawain*-poet may not have followed it (I believe that he did, at least in Fitts i, iii, and iv), but because I see no way of demonstrating it fully. The sequences of stanzas, as noted, run like this: Fitt i, 21; Fitt ii, 6+6+6+6; Fitt iii, 11+11+11+1; Fitt iv, 21+1. I have included this scheme here only in the hope that someone else may see further than I do.

One other feature of the poem strongly suggests numerical calculation. In the later Middle Ages, the traditional life-span of Christ is 33 years, or 33 and a fraction years, or (perhaps more commonly) 32 and a fraction years.[28] One of these numbers is often a part of the numerological structure of medieval poems.[29] In *Sir Gawain*, the most extensive references to Christ – both to his birth and to his cross – appear in stanza 32. Gawain rides on Christmas Eve,

Carande for his costes, lest he ne keuer schulde
To se þe seruyse of þat syre, þat on þat self nyȝt
Of a burde watz borne oure baret to quelle;
And þefore sykyng he sayde, 'I beseche þe, lorde,
And Mary, þat is myldest moder so dere,
Of sum herber þer heȝly I myȝt here masse,
Ande þy matynez to-morne, mekely I ask,
And þerto prestly I pray my pater and aue
   and crede.'
He rode in hys prayere,
And cryed for his mysdede,
He sayned hym in syþes sere,
And sayde 'Cros Kryst me spede!'

(ll. 750–62)

Stanza 33 begins immediately thereafter, with an illuminated capital: 'Nade he sayned hymself segge, bot þrye' (l. 762). Apparently as Gawain crosses himself for the third time, he sees the castle within which he can accomplish his desire. The occurrence of the threefold action in Stanza 33 seems to be another example of duplication, as with lines 1212 and 2525. And the appearance of these references to Christ in Stanzas 32–3 is likely to be, as in other poems making use of the number 33, a gesture in the direction of a numerological concept.[30]

Speaking generally, the extent to which numerical structure and numerology are to become factors in the study of Old and Middle English literature remains a matter of guesswork. Important as instances of these practices may be in establishing some idea of a possible tradition, each instance must as yet be judged in comparative isolation. At a minimum, given the likelihood of the numerical ordering outlined here, it is obvious that an important new shaping factor in the amounts of material devoted to the several parts of the *Gawain* narrative has to be taken into account. Even if considerable adjustment were initially available to the author (conceivably other multiples or powers of 5 than 2525 for the total of lines), the limitations as the plan progressed would increase, until for the articulation of succesive episodes of the 3 days of the

Temptation it is not a great exaggeration to find an analogy in the simultaneous articulation of space in fourteenth-century vaulting, where the complicated pattern of rib and boss in one bay is given by that in all of the others.

Such methodological considerations are of less significance here, however, than the production of strong evidence for the theme of *Sir Gawain* itself, and two such pieces of evidence have been brought forward. It is true that, like other classics, this poem can be usefully looked at in an extraordinary number of ways. Urbanity and courtesy, for instance, and their opposites, are certainly preoccupations of the fourteenth-century author and his hero. It is entirely within the realm of possibility, also, that the author sees certain historical figures behind his characters. He seems to be concerned with the historical destiny of Britain. Certainly a seasonal myth is somewhere in the folkloristic origins of the plot. The alternations of nature and civilization in the work are as plain as the difference between the hunters' quarry-strewn landscape and the life of the castle. The faultiness of many women and the perfection of the Virgin obviously strike him as notable truisms. But it seems wilful to say that the principal theme of *Sir Gawain* is anything but the consistent maintenance of explicitly and implicitly undertaken covenants with others. This remains true whether it is maintained that the author's particular set is towards glorifying a remarkable approximation of this theme taken as an ideal, or examining the baneful or beneficial consequences of falling short of it, or describing the common limitation upon the common human potential for it. The architectonic balance between the rigid, endless, and seamless pentangle of troth and the apparently yielding, incomplete noose of untroth with its ends knotted together is one of the pieces of evidence produced here for this theme; the other is the set of numerical structural considerations of which the most obvious is the signification of the pentangular excellences in the echoing line 2525. Just as strong evidence for this theme exists, in the present writer's opinion, in the tissue of expressed and implied promises which lie on the surface of the poem at first reading. This latter evidence, however, has not proved sufficient to convince a number of critics.[31]

# NOTES

1 *A Reading of Sir Gawain and the Green Knight* (1965), p. 158. Donald R. Howard takes an apparently opposite position (with which also I partly disagree) on the symbolic status of the pentangle. See his 'Structure and Symmetry in Sir Gawain', *Speculum*, xxxix (1964), 426: 'The pentangle has an *assigned* symbolic value; it is put into the poem to stand for an abstraction. . . . The shield and girdle, however, take their symbolic meaning from the situation.' As will appear, the disagreements here are mainly semantic.

2 P. 187.

3 All quotations from *Sir Gawain* follow *Sir Gawain and the Green Knight*, ed. J. R. R. Tolkien and E. V. Gordon, 2nd edn, rev., ed. Norman Davis (Oxford, 1968).

4 E.g., pp. 14–17.

5 For the association of green with love, see, for instance, 'The Squire's Tale', *Canterbury Tales*, V. 646–7; the ballade 'Against Women Unconstant' ('Madame, for your newfangelnesse'), attributed to Chaucer in the *Works*, ed. F. N. Robinson, 2nd edn (1957), p. 540; and J. Huizinga, *De Herfsttij der Middeleeuwen*, 2nd edn (Haarlem, 1928), pp. 397–8. See also the English translation, *The Waning of the Middle Ages* (New York, 1954), p. 120, which, however, omits all footnote citations.

6 See *OED* and Walther von Wartburg, *Französisches etymologisches Wörterbuch* (Basel, 1950), 180 (*laqueus*, 'schlinge'). For purposes of this article, Wartburg's citation of Norman *mettre dans le là*, 'tromper', and Jersey *sous vos lâs*, 'sous votre puissance', are interesting. See also, in connection with 'love-lace', his Middle French, Modern French *lacs d'amour*, 'cordons repliés sur eux-mêmes de manière à former un 8 couché'. See also the *OED*'s citations for *Lace* v. 1. 'to catch in, or as in, a noose or snare'.

7 *Secular Lyrics of the XIVth and XVth Centuries*, ed. R. H. Robbins (Oxford, 1955), No. clxxvii, l. 82.

8 Ed. E. Langlois, *Publications de la Société des Anciens Textes Français*, No. ccxii, Vol. ii (Paris, 1920).

9 *Cambridge Italian Dictionary*, ed. Barbara Reynolds (Cambridge, 1962).

10 See Kenneth McKenzie, *Concordanza delle Rime di Francesco Petrarca* (Oxford, 1912), *laccio*, *lacciuolo*.

11 *Rime sparse,* cxcvi, in *Le Rime sparse e I Trionfi,* ed. E Chiòrboli, Scrittori d'Italia, cxxvi (Bari, 1930).

12 *The Gawain Poet: Studies in His Personality and Background* (Chapel Hill, N.C., 1956). See also introduction to *The Complete Works of the Gawain-Poet,* ed. John Gardner (Chicago, 1965), pp. 76–8; F. L. Utley, 'Folklore, Myth and Ritual', in *Critical Approaches in Medieval Literature,* ed. Dorothy Bethurum (New York, 1960), p. 90.

13 Larry D. Benson, *Art and Tradition in Sir Gawain and the Green Knight* (New Brunswick, N.J., 1965), p. 40, notes the parallelism between the *lace* on the axe and the *luf-lace.* Incidentally, the suggestions in Benson's passage here concerning the origin of the *luf-lace* in other magical tokens share one point with all other such suggestions with which I am acquainted: for this token, only the *Gawain*-poet uses the word *lace.*

14 *Alliterative Poetry in Middle English,* i (Manchester, 1935) 218.

15 For 'significant' stanza totals or line totals in poems, see E. R. Curtius's appendix on arithmetical composition in his *Europäische Literatur und lateinisches Mittelalter* (Bern, 1963); an earlier edn was translated by Willard Trask as *European Literature and the Latin Middle Ages* (New York, 1953). 100 stanzas or lines make a more frequent total than 101. See 2 examples of the former in Samuel Singer (ed.), *Die Religiöse Lyrik des Mittelalters* (Bern, 1933), p. 43 and another in G. G. Perry (ed.), *Religious Pieces in Prose and Verse,* EETS, O.S., 26 (1867 and 1914), No. ix (2 6-line stanzas plus 11 8-line stanzas). Others: Christine de Pisan's *Cent balades* and *Cent balades d'amant et de dame* (a continuous narrative), Jean Le Seneschal's *Livre des cent balades* (a continuous narrative), and Alain Chartier's *La belle dame sans merci* in 100 stanzas. But Christine de Pisan's *Proverbes mouraulx* contains 101 units. Chaucer's *Parliament of Fowls,* contains 99, 100, or 101 stanzas, depending on how the triolet near the end is counted, and may have been intended to contain 700 lines (by maximum allowable repetition of the refrain in the triolet).

16 See V. F. Hopper, *Medieval Number Symbolism* (New York, 1938), p. 9.

17 In the light of this poet's structural use of units of 5 in *Pearl* and his preoccupation with 5 in *Sir Gawain,* the structure of Jean de Castel's *Le Pin* is of some interest: 55 quatrains, each 5 being connected by rhyme.

18 *Short Time's Endless Monument* (New York, 1960), pp. 8–15.

It should perhaps be pointed out that a likely numerical structure has now been ascribed to the most famous alliterative poem in English. MLA Scholars' Conference 16, on the topic 'The Structure of *Beowulf*', 27 Dec. 1968, received from Thomas E. Hart a paper, '*Ellen:* Some Tectonic Relationships in *Beowulf*', containing such a scheme. A description of the resemblances between the 'modular' units proposed in that paper and those proposed below for *Sir Gawain* awaits the publication of Professor Hart's results.

19 'Madden's Divisions of *Sir Gawain* and the "Large Initial Capitals" of *Cotton Nero A. X*', *Speculum*, xxi (1946), 67–71; quotation, p. 71.

20 *Ibid.*, p. 69.

21 '*Sir Gawain and the Green Knight:* An Appraisal', *PMLA*, lxxvi (1961), 7–19; quotation, p. 17.

22 See Howard, as cited above (n. 1), pp. 429–33. For Tuttleton, see 'The Manuscript Divisions of *Sir Gawain and the Green Knight*', *Speculum*, xli (1966), 304–10, esp. p. 305.

23 See *Pearl, Cleanness, Patience and Sir Gawain, Reproduced in Facsimile from the Unique MS. Cotton Nero A. X. in the British Museum, with Introduction by Sir I. Gollancz*, EETS, o.s., clxii (1923). In 2 cases the initials at the fitt divisions are twice as large and in a third case even larger: the letter for Fitt i is 8 lines tall; for Fitt ii, 4 lines; for Fitts iii and iv, 6 lines. The other 5 are 3 lines high.

24 As Howard, p. 433, points out.

25 Of course 5 is the number of the pentangle, and all but 1 of the stanza groups in *Pearl* contain 5 stanzas each. Perhaps the initial choice of the number 5 for *Sir Gawain* depended upon its well-known medieval association with the Virgin. There are 5 letters each in *Maria, virgo, mater*. Mary is often said to know 5 joys. In the Christmas service, the two antiphons *Ad Laudes*, namely '*Quem vidistis*' and '*Genuit puerpera*', have each $5 \times 5 \times 5 = 125$ letters, as is pointed out in an important book which I have drawn on elsewhere in this article: J. A. Huisman, *Neue Wege zur dichterischen und musikalischen Technik Walthers von der Vogelweide, mit einem Exkurs über die symmetrische Zahlenkomposition im Mittelalter*, Studia Litteraria Rheno-Traiectina, i (Utrecht, 1950), 95–6, n. For the antiphons, *see Liber usualis Missae et officii pro dominicis festis et festis I, vel II, classis, cum cantu gregoriano, ex editione vaticana adamussim excerpto* (Paris, Turin, Rome, 1932), pp. 361–2. See also the 'Song of the Five Joys', *Religious Lyrics of the XIVth Century*,

ed. Carleton Brown (Oxford, 1967), pp. 44–6, in 5-line stanzas; the 'Orison of the Five Joys', *ibid.*, pp. 29–31, in 5-line stanzas if the refrain is included; 'A Prayer to the Five Joys', *English Lyrics of the XIIIth Century*, ed. Carleton Brown (Oxford, 1932), pp. 27–8, in 5 stanzas; and a fifteenth-century carol of the 5 joys, in 5 stanzas, *Ancient Christmas Carols*, ed. Edith Rickert (London, 1928), p. 205.

Gawain's chief fealty seems to be to the Virgin. Her image appears on one side of his shield; the pentangle, the symbol of 5 in the poem, appears on the other. One of his 5 classes of excellences has to do with the 5 joys of Mary (646–7). She apparently helps him in his most need when Bertilak's wife is closest to seducing him (ll. 1768–9). In the matter of the connection of 5 with *Pearl*, the daughter in that poem, a queen in heaven as Mary is Heaven's Queen, honors the Virgin highly (*Pearl*, ll. 433–44).

26 The notion that perfection is ruined by adding 1 unit is known to medieval number symbolism in the number 11, going 1 beyond the 10 commandments, and in 13, going 1 beyond the 12 apostles. See Hopper, pp. 87 (St Augustine), 101, 152 (Dante), 131.

27 Howard suggests that the smaller capitals are probably significant, but less so than the 4 large ones (pp. 429–31). The former 'were probably placed in accord with the author's – or scribe's – sense of dramatic rhythm' (p. 433). It should be noted that Professor Howard's analysis of the structure of *Sir Gawain* is a very interesting one, too complex to be summarized here.

28 Cf. *The Pricke of Conscience*, ed. R. Morris (Berlin, 1863), v, 4987–8: 'þan was he of threty yhere elde, and twa, / And of thre monethes ar–with alswa.' Lucifer in *Piers Plowman* gives Christ 32 winters; see the three-text edition, ed. W. W. Skeat (Oxford, 1886), I, Passus xviii, 296 (B-Text); Passus xxi, 334 (C-Text).

29 Aside from the obvious example in the *Commedia*, see E. W. Bulatkin, 'The Arithmetic Structure of the Old French *Vie de Saint Alexis*', *PMLA*, lxxiv (1959), 495–502, where the tradition of 33 and a fraction is followed. A number of similar examples are cited in Fritz Tschirch, 'Schüsselzahlen', in *Beiträge zur deutschen und nordischen Literatur, Festgabe fur Leopold Magon* (Berlin, 1958), pp. 32–5.

30 A close parallel to the practice in *Sir Gawain* is cited in Tschirch, p. 37: in Stanza 33 of the South-German *Annolied* (c. 1080–1110) Cologne is said to have been converted by 3 missionaries, and then to have had 33 bishops up to Anno himself.

A. KENT HIEATT

31 Professor Rudolf Willard resigned to me his interests in numerical
structure in *Gawain* long ago, and Professor Helaine Newstead
helped me to present a paper on the subject at an early stage before
the Arthurian Section of MLA. Professor Talbot Donaldson
kindly helped me with final additions. I am greateful to all three but
wish to implicate none.

# Placement 'in the middest' in *The Faerie Queene*

MICHAEL BAYBAK, PAUL DELANY
A. KENT HIEATT

I

In an essay such as this one, concerned with centre-points in *The Faerie Queene*, it is only fair to point out that the idea of investigating arithmetical centre-points of this poem seem to have originated in Alastair Fowler's *Spenser and the Numbers of Time*.[1] Where we have so far found it difficult to follow him is in the matter of entertaining, simultaneously, 3 alternative systems of stanza-counting (cantos alone, cantos + proems, and cantos + proems + arguments). Applied consistently, our system (cantos only) works in Books I, II, and III, and fails to do so in our opinion in IV, V, and VI. The conclusion that we draw below seems to us the most likely one, or at least that one which is susceptible of demonstration. We therefore hold out for the view that Spenser regards the 12 cantos of each book of *The Faerie Queene* as, metaphorically, that book's substance, to which the proem is, metaphorically, a curtain-opener (e.g. I. Proem. 4. 9: 'The which to heare, vouchsafe, O dearest dred a-while.'), and that the arguments are, theoretically, summaries.

Against this must be said, however, that Fowler's total of 1800 lines (page 40) in the 3 books of the 1590 edition of *The Faerie Queene* is striking, and yet depends upon counting cantos, proems, and arguments (the last counted as 2 fourteeners each, not as 4 lines each). It may also be significant that, as with our results, this pattern does not work for Books IV, V, and VI. It must be admitted, in addition, that one of the authors of the present essay argued, in *Short Time's Endless Monument: the Symbolism of the Numbers in 'Epithalamion'*,[2] for two systems of counting in that

141

poem: the total number of long lines – 365 – was claimed to be significant, but so also was the total of long lines excluding the envoy or *tornata*, for this total – 359 – was supposed to signify the degrees covered by the sun while the starry heaven was making a full daily circle, the discrepancy being the assurance of the seasons and the year. The *tornata* here addresses the rest of the poem as though it were a finished product in much the same way that a proem looks forward to a book of *The Faerie Queene* as though the book were not yet begun. Something may therefore be said on both sides of the question, and with that understanding we may ring up our own curtain.

It is now a commonplace of criticism that Spenser describes the 'stately mount' rising in the middle of the Garden of Adonis (*FQ* III. vi. 43) in terms which identify it with the anatomical *mons Veneris*.[3] But most critics have simply noted the correspondence, and passed on. As we shall show, however, Spenser introduced this anatomically central elevation in the arithmetically central stanza of Book III. We maintain that the mount is central both to the thought and to the narrative structure of its book. Moreover, Spenser used similar narrative devices and settings in the central passages of Books I and II. All 3 books, as originally published, turn upon passages that are central by both arithmetic and significance. In addition, all 3 passages are signalled by the phrase 'in the middest' or a variant; in 2 of the passages the phrase occurs in the central stanzas and in the other it immediately precedes.

2

As Renaissance Platonism valued circles, so it necessarily valued centres. Castiglione reminds us: 'Beauty cometh of God, and is like a circle, the goodness whereof is the centre.'[4] Donne, parodying the commonplace, brought the circles to a different centre:

Although wee see celestiall bodies move
Above the earth, the earth we till and love:
So we her ayres contemplate, word and hart
And vertues; But we love the Centrique part.[5]

He was not alone in fixing man's centre at the pudenda; the human body was often shown as circumscribed by a circle which the outstretched hands and feet touched at 4 points, and whose centre was the pubis.[6] The mount in Spenser's garden represents, then, the centre of the little world of man as well as the fruitful and generative centre of the poem's external world.[7] And Spenser reinforced this position of double centrality by a device that has apparently not been noticed before: Stanza 43 of Canto vi, whose first line is 'Right in the middest of that Paradise', occupies, in the 1590 text, the exact mid-point of Book III as the 340th of 679 stanzas.[8]

The Mount's central position in Book III is appropriate in many ways. On its 'round top' Venus and Adonis create the forms which populate the world outside the garden. We may find it paradoxical that a 'Legend of Chastitie' should enact its rich pageant of diverse loves (cf. III. v. I) around the central and dominant landmark of the *mons Veneris*; yet such an apotheosis of the generative organs is typical of the peculiar combination of mysticism and forthrightness in Spenser's conception of sexuality. In particular, the timeless union of Venus and Adonis on the mount finds its historical counterpart in the great end which Book III looks toward: the union of its heroine, Britomart, with Arthegall. This supreme work of the 'sacred fire' of Love will bring together a couple whose intercourse will inaugurate Britain's historical mission:

From whose two loynes thou [Love] afterwards did rayse
Most famous fruits of matrimoniall bowre,
Which through the earth have spred their living prayse,
That fame in trompe of gold eternally displayes.[9]

(III. iii. 3)

One aspect of the sexuality of the Mount, as well as of the Garden, is thus fertility. Another is sexual pleasure perfected. Venus' and Adonis' enjoyment of each other is explicitly anatomical: it occurs within the 'pleasant arbour' within the myrtle grove on the summit of the *mons*. This sensual bliss is an implicit criticism of love's aberrations in the rest of Book III. A. C. Hamilton[10] has drawn attention to the several permutations of the Venus and Adonis myth in Book III; for our present purpose we may single out the myth's relevance to what might be called the theme of 'enemies of Love'. In Spenser's world, these are, especially, the forms of sexuality which are facile, violent, or unnatural, and which sometimes masquerade under the conventions of Courtly Love. In contrast to the central bower, for instance, the bower of Venus and Adonis depicted on the arras of Malecasta's castle (III. i. 34–8) sadly travesties the lovers' relationship. This scene shows us love as it exists at the *circumference* of the circle whose *centre* is the idyllic mount. Here, at the beginning of the Book, Adonis is destroyed by the malignant forces which thwart love in the fallen world:

> he lyeth languishing,
> Deadly engored of a great wild Bore,
> And by his side the Goddesse groveling
> Makes for him endlesse mone, and evermore
> With her soft garment wipes away the gore,
> Which staines his snowy skin.
>
> (III. i. 38)

With their elaborate yet base rituals, the abode of Malecasta, and that of Busirane in Cantos xi, xii, at the other end of the Book, show how the instinct of sexual love can be perverted. They serve as foils to the innocent, paradisal naturalism of the Garden of Adonis. In both castles, and only there, Britomart is wounded; her hurts are superficial, but it is not until she sees her own blood that she is roused to use her full strength in overpowering the guardians of the two dwellings.[11] Since her chastity includes, potentially at least, the chaste sexuality of married love, her adventures should aim at an ideal condition in which she could lay aside her weapons and no longer fear the assaults of corrupt and worldly love. She does not achieve this state in Book III, but we do find its symbolic equivalent in the safe and 'eternall blis' enjoyed by Adonis in his central bower:

Ne feareth he henceforth that foe of his,
Which with his cruell tuske him deadly cloyd:
For that wilde Bore, the which him once annoyd,
She firmely hath emprisoned for ay,
That her sweet love his malice mote avoyd.

(III. vi. 48)

In the cantos furthest away from the centre of Book III, then, we find two powerful visions of sexuality perverted, degraded, or tortured. Britomart may be imagined as questing through the area of lust and violence which surrounds the central paradise of the Book; eventually, by her union with Arthegall, she will reconcile chastity and sexuality, and make her womb the fountain of a great race of faerie kings and queens who will continue her battle against the outer anarchy. We therefore suggest that both the central mount and the idea of a central harmony contrasted with a peripheral disorder provide a keystone for the structure of Book III, in contrast to the more linear narrative of the first 2 books.

3

Although Book III may lack the narrative coherence of a novel, it is rich in a kind of form and symmetry of which Spenser is the peculiar master in English literature. The arithmetic symmetry already pointed out we take to be simply Spenser's way of reinforcing the book's structure. Furthermore, Books I and II provide corroborative evidence for this practice: Spenser appears to have paid particular attention to the mid-points of all the three books of *The Faerie Queene* that appeared in 1590.[12]

Each of the first two books follows the career of a dominant hero to a decisive outcome. In Book I the Red Cross Knight both kills the Dragon and espouses Una in the last canto, although his progress to this final success has not been smooth and unhampered. As others have pointed out,[13] it is pivotal in Spenser's scheme that Redcross should falter halfway through his quest and have to be redeemed by Arthur, an instrument of Grace (I. vii). In his account of this episode, Spenser draws an implicit parallel with another malingerer, the nymph who lives in the fountain from which Redcross drinks:

> one day when *Phoebe* fayre
> With all her band was following the chace,
> This Nymph, quite tyr'd with heat of scorching ayre
> Sat downe to rest in middest of the race.
>
> (I. VII. 5)

As Robert Kellogg and Oliver Steele note,[14] she 'is apparently an invention of Spenser's designed as a mythological emblem of Red Cross' sitting "down to rest *in middest* of the race" ' (our italics). Her fane is a *locus amoenus*, and as such parallels the settings of the central passages of Books II and III, as we shall note. We hear of a 'breathing wind', 'trembling leaves', 'chereful birds' chanting 'sweet musick' (vii. 3), a 'bubbling wave' (vii. 4).

This part of the episode, containing the significant phrase 'in middest', does not, however, occupy the arithmetical centre of Book I; that centre, 7 stanzas further along, is reserved for the downfall of Redcross himself, which the Nymph's action prefigures. After drinking from the Nymph's fountain, and while remaining in her fane, he is so weakened that when the giant Orgoglio appears and aims a huge blow at him he cannot resist. He sidesteps the blow itself, but the force of it is so great 'That with the wind it did him overthrow, / And all his sences stound, that still he lay full low' (vii. 12). The stanza in which he is thus felled, and the following one containing a simile on his condition, mark the precise mid-point of Book I in the 1590 text.[15] Orgoglio then throws him into a dungeon, where he languishes until released by Arthur. That the downfall of the hero of Book I occurs at precisely this point would seem to be more than mere coincidence.

In Book II, the numerical mid-point in the edition of 1590 falls within the episode of Mammon's final temptation of Guyon in the Garden of Proserpina. This passage exhibits the devices which we have already indicated. The three stanzas (II. viii. 53–5) that describe Proserpina's silver seat and the golden apples growing nearby form this mid-point, and in the first of these stanzas the familiar catch-phrase recurs: 'The Garden of Proserpina this hight; / And in the midst thereof a silver seat' (II. vii. 53).[16] Further, the Garden itself is a *locus amoenus* in reverse: it is 'goodly garnished / With hearbs and fruits' (vii. 51), but of a 'direful deadly blacke, both leafe and bloom'; there is 'a thicke Arber' (vii. 53), as in the deeply protected abode of Venus and Adonis; there are 'golden apples' (vii. 53); and there is a 'blacke flood' (vii. 56) instead of the bubbling wave (I. vii. 4) of the Nymph's retreat where Redcross met his doom.[17]

The structural centrality of this episode helps to corroborate what others have already maintained concerning the central importance of this temptation to Spenser's concerns in Book II. As Frank Kermode has pointed out,[18] there is considerable agreement that the ordeal in the cave is the crisis of Guyon's quest. Kermode's interpretation, to which we in part subscribe, is that the temptation by Mammon, like that of Christ in the Wilderness, is a nearly total one (excluding concupiscence, the subject of the Bower of Bliss), and that the climactic temptation, that in the Garden of Proserpina, is towards mental intemperance, indulgence in vain learning. Whether or not the aim of the temptation is precisely this, it seems fitting that the Book of Temperance should have at its centre golden apples – symbols of both classical and Biblical temptations – which the hero in exercising his peculiar virtue *refuses* to pluck. The apple of Genesis is not explicitly mentioned; but, like Milton,[19] we cannot help contrasting Guyon's abstention with Eve's seduction by the fruit.[20]

At the numerical centre of Book I, to conclude, we find a symbolic action – the Red Cross Knight's swoon – and at the numerical centres of Books II and III symbolic objects: the silver seat and golden apples and the *mons Veneris*. The arithmetical calculation is sufficiently precise to make coincidence very unlikely: the 'numerical centres' here are the central stanza of III, the 2 central stanzas of I, and the 3 central stazas of II, in terms of the total number of 9-line *Faerie Queene*-stanzas in all 12 cantos of each book of the first edition. Furthermore, the phrase 'in [the] middest [midst]', construed by us as a kind of covert signal, occurs in these stanzas in II and III, and 7 stanzas earlier in I where an event prefigures the immediately ensuing central one. The locales of all 3 central events have a certain similarity within differences: in III, a grove of trees making a pleasant central arbour; in I, a grove surrounding an apparently pleasant fountain of covertly malign effect; in II, an arbour sheltering a central seat of which the temptations are obviously malign.

The fact that Spenser disturbed 2 of these numerical symmetries by changes in the edition of 1596 seems to us of less importance than the points that we feel have been almost surely demonstrated: his interest in numerical composition was strong enough during the process of original composition for him to have built significant numerical mid-points into all of the books of the first edition, and the very existence of these mid-points is sufficient evidence that the episodes embodying them are of overriding importance in the books in which they occur.[21] Analysis of these landmarks can tell us much about Spenser's notions of poetic structure, and about his general concept of poetic art.

NOTES

1 1964, *passim*. Gunnar Qvarnström had previously found significance
in the centre-point of *Paradise Lost*, first edn, where, at vi. 762
in modern editions, Christ, now wearing the sacred urim, mounts
his chariot with Victory at his right hand to do battle with Satan.
See Qvarnström's *Dikten och den nya vetenscapten. Det astronautiska
motivet* (Lund, 1961): now in modified English version, *Poetry and
Numbers*, Scripta minora Regiae Societatis Humaniorum Litterarum Lundensis, 1964–5 (Lund, 1966), pp. 93ff.

A centre-point in a very different kind of literary work of the
Renaissance should be noted: it is to be found in Bk I of the *Essais*
of Montaigne. As he says in the 28th essay of that Book, he had
planned to place a work of his great friend Etienne de la Boétie
in the centre of Bk I. In the event Montaigne located at the precise
arithmetical centre of this Book, as the 29th of 57 items, 29 sonnets
by de la Boétie. As Michel Butor points out in an introduction
(Montaigne, *Essais*, ed. Andrée Lhéritier [Paris, 1964, 1965], I, liv)
the number of available sonnets apparently controlled the number of
essays which Montaigne included in his Bk I, since the conceit here
obviously is connected not only with the central placement of the
sonnets, but also with the fact that an item containing 29 parts is in
turn the 29th item in a larger series, necessarily preceded by 28
essays and followed by a like number.

2 A. Kent Hieatt, *Short Time's Endless Monument* (New York, 1960).
It now seems fairly sure to him that Spenser included a significant
centre-point, of the kind discussed here, in *Epithalamion*. L. 217
reads 'The which do *endlesse* Matrimony make' (Hieatt's italics). In
this numerical celebration of time and of the victory over it of both
generation and poetry, these words of the central line seemed to be
keyed to the last line, 'And for short time an *endlesse* moniment'
(the only other occurrence of the word *endless* in the poem) and
even by contrast to the first, 'Ye learned sisters which have *often-
times*'. In the numerical complexities which have already been
widely accepted as phenomena of this poem, it is possible to believe
as well that a further symmetry is significant here: the centre-point
is also the twelfth long line of the twelfth of 24 stanzas. It is not,

however, the centre-point of the 365 *long* lines of the poem; it is the 182nd long line, which is the one immediately preceding the central long line. Spenser may have taken comfort here in a further extension of the meanings assigned (*Short Time's Endless Monument*, pp. 47–59) to the line reproaching the poem in the *tornata* or twenty-fourth stanza: 'Ye would not stay your dew time to expect'. (The words *due* and *duly* are also used only in the twelfth and twenty-fourth stanzas of the poem.)

3 See William Nelson, *The Poetry of Edmund Spenser* (New York, 1963), p. 209, and additional citations in his corresponding footnote 4.

4 *The Book of the Courtier*, tr. Thomas Hoby, ed. W. H. D. Rouse (London and New York, 1959), pp. 308–9.

5 *John Donne: The Elegies and The Songs and Sonnets*, ed. Helen Gardner (Oxford, 1965), 'Loves Progress' (Elegy xviii) ll. 33–6.

6 Less often it was the navel. For contemporary illustrations and references see Rudolf Wittkower, *Architectural Principles in the Age of Humanism* (third edn, 1962), Pls 2–4, pp. 14ff., 22ff., 101ff.; and Fowler, pp. 260–8.

7 Cf. Adonis' reproductive function: 'For him the Father of all formes they call; / Therefore needs mote he live, that living gives to all' (III, vii, 47).

8 This count, and those for Bks I and II below, include only the 12 cantos of each book, not its proem and not the four-line 'arguments' prefaced to each canto. Furthermore, in Bk III the changes at the end in the 1596 text move the centre-point 1 stanza back. See n. 21 below.

9 Spenser is quoted from *The Works . . . A Variorum Edition*, ed. Greenlaw *et al.* (Baltimore, 1932–57).

10 *The Structure of Allegory in 'The Faerie Queene'* (Oxford, 1961), Ch. 4.

11 These are the 6 knights led by Gardante in Canto i, and Busirane alone in Canto xii. Verbal parallels between the episodes are close. Compare i. 65–6 with xii. 33–4.

12 Fowler (p. 72) already considers the arithmetically central point of Bk I significant, but his location of it at I. vii. 5 is not precisely correct by any count.

13 E.g., Hamilton, pp. 71ff.; Robert Kellogg and Oliver Steele (eds), *Books I and II of 'The Faerie Queene'* (New York, 1965), p. 30.

14 P. 152, n. The point had already been implied in Fowler, p. 72.

15 Leaving out, as we did with Book III, the 4 prefatory stanzas. See n. 8 above. The addition of I. xi. 3 in the 1596 text again throws the pattern off.

16 Stanza 54 is the middle one of Book II, omitting the prefatory stanzas. We think that this stanza should be taken with the stanza preceding and the one following as a single unit of description. In any case, stanza 54 describes the apples that offer the culminating temptation.

The phrase 'in the midst' or 'in the middest' is fairly often used by Spenser – some 18 times in *The Faerie Queene* – and not only at or near the middle points of books.

17 A further resemblance between the conditions of the heroes at the mid-points of Bks I and II has been pointed out to us: as Redcross, lolling on the greensward with Duessa, is weakened by drinking from the fountain, so Guyon is also weakened by his temptation. But because Guyon resists, Providence helps him more directly than it does Redcross, with an angelic intervention.

18 'The Cave of Mammon', in *Stratford-upon-Avon Studies 2: Elizabethan Poetry* (1960), p. 158.

19 See the famous passage on Spenser in *Areopagitica* (*Complete Poems and Major Prose*, ed. M. Y. Hughes [New York, 1957], pp. 728–29).

20 The temptation of Guyon may lead towards overweening infringement upon the divine (*sicut dii*) rather than mental intemperance (*scientes bonum et malum*). Guyon, it is true, refuses to sit on the seat or pluck the apples; and he abuses Tantalus, who strives vainly to reach the fruit, as 'ensample . . . of mind intemperate' (vii. 60). But a somewhat different interpretation is made possible by a point which Kermode neglects concerning the two names of the sufferers, Tantalus and Pilate. In aspiring towards the divine condition, Tantalus made of his son Pelops a feast for 'high Iove' (II. vii. 59). Pilate delivered over God, the Son of Man, to human punishment. There is an additional twist in the point that both victims had an apotheosis. Cf. Kellogg and Steele, p. 315 n.

21 The evidence of the text of 1596 suggests that Spenser was not preoccupied with the symmetry involved in numerical centre-points of books when he came to put together in final form Bks IV, V, and VI; at least we find in them no significant central point except, possibly, for one noted by Fowler (p. 220): in Bk V, the stanza about the like race run in equal justice by Isis and Osiris (the sun and the moon) (V. vii. 4) is the 294th out of 588. But this

count includes the proem and the arguments. Whatever Spenser's inconsistencies may have been, and however attractive this citation may be, we do not here invite sceptics to attack variant ways of counting stanzas. We have counted only canto-stanzas.

# The unity of Spenser's *Amoretti*

ALEXANDER DUNLOP

The search for a unified principle of organization has dominated criticism of Spenser's *Amoretti*. John Erskine, in 1903, seeing in *Amoretti* 'the truest sequence of this decade', asserted that 'each sonnet has its inevitable place'. Erskine did not demonstrate this in detail, and subsequent studies have uncovered at best a rather general thematic coherence.[1]

Most critics have accepted the view that there is a general, if not too precise, progression of mood and story reflecting feelings and events in Spenser's courtship of Elizabeth Boyle. W. L. Renwick's 'simplest reading', which follows the events 'from late in 1592 to spring of 1594, or, allowing for a longer separation, 1591–4', is typical of this view. Other commentators have suggested an allegorical unity fusing autobiography, fiction, convention and myth in an ideal synthesis of spirit and flesh. Others, notably Louis L. Martz, have found a dramatic unity, which accounts for contradictory elements by the hypothesis that the lover assumes different roles in the course of the sequence.[2]

Even those who have seen in *Amoretti* a careless juxtaposition of earlier and later sonnets have admitted some element of unity. J. W. Lever, for example, sees 'an attempted blending of two collections of sonnets, differing in subject matter, characterization, and general conception'. After setting aside 18 sonnets, however, he finds that the remaining 71 form a unified whole – 'the solid core of the *Amoretti* sequence'.[3]

Despite Spenser's fascination with the calendar as a device of poetic organization it is only recently that the extent of his use of number and calendar symbolism has been recognized. A. Kent Hieatt's study of the *Epithalamion* and Alastair Fowler's study of

*The Faerie Queene* reveal that complex patterns of numerological and calendrical correspondences lie very close to the artistic heart of these works. William Nelson's objections notwithstanding, that 'the effect of [Hieatt's] thesis is to obscure what I take to be the obvious structure of the poem', the underlying symbolism uncovered by Hieatt and Fowler cannot be denied, and Hieatt's conclusion must be accepted as valid: 'The mode which Spenser follows requires before everything else a pursuit of an integral meaning, integrally expressed, below the surface of discourse.'⁴ Hieatt's and Fowler's studies have made it clear that intricate symbolic patterns were very much a part of Spenser's artistic consciousness and cannot be overlooked in the study of any of his works. They indicate that in the case of Spenser the 'simplest reading' is likely to be inadequate.

Previously unnoticed elements of calendar symbolism in *Amoretti* provide, I believe, the key to the unity of the sequence. Six sonnets are clearly associated with calendar events. Sonnets iv ('New yeare forth looking out of Ianus gate') and lxii ('The weary yeare his race now having run') mark the year's beginning; lxviii ('Most glorious Lord of lyfe, that on this day, / Didst make thy triumph over death and sin') is an Easter sonnet, and xxii ('This holy season fit to fast and pray') refers to Lent. Sonnets xix and lxx are specifically identified with spring.

While the familiar Julian tradition of beginning the year on 1 January was well known in Spenser's day, the liturgical year began on Lady Day, 25 March, the Feast of the Annunciation.⁵ Until 1752 it was much more common for Englishmen to reckon their years from Lady Day, even though the term 'New Year's Day' was reserved for 1 January. Spenser, for example, placed March at the head of the procession of months in the second of the Mutability Cantos. We thus have two dates for beginning the year. Sonnet iv, with its reference to the 'New yeare' and to 'Janus gate' in terms that echo phrases used by E. K. to describe 1 January in his preface to the *Shepheardes Calendar*, is unambiguous.⁶ Sonnet lxii, however, could refer as well to either date. The common assumption has been that it refers to a January New Year 12 months after that of Sonnet iv. The 25 March date, however, has much to recommend it. Assigning 25 March rather than a second 1 January to Sonnet lxii orders the sonnet logically in a progression from 1 January to Lent to 25 March to Easter, and thus has the effect of confining the *Amoretti* 'story' within a time period of a few months as against the generally accepted span of a few years.

If, beginning with 25 March at Sonnet lxii, we assign consecutive dates to the sonnets that precede and follow, we come at Sonnet lxviii to 31 March, and at Sonnet xxii to 13 February (assuming a non-leap-year). Consulting a church calendar, we find that these are precisely the dates on which the Church of England observed Ash Wednesday and Easter in 1594, the year preceding the publication of *Amoretti*.

Actually this pattern is applicable to any year in which Easter falls on 31 March, and there is one other year of Spenser's lifetime that fits, namely 1583. However, the inscription 'Written not long since' on the title page, and the references in Sonnets xxxiii and lxxx to *The Faerie Queene* impose the later date. Since the *Amoretti-Epithalamion* volume was entered in the Stationer's Register 19 November 1594, the inscription 'Written not long since' can be taken at face value.

The evidence thus seems conclusive that the 47 sonnets from xxii through lxviii correspond to the Lenten season of 1594, including Easter and the 6 Sundays before Easter. When we consider further that there are 21 sonnets preceding this central Lent-Easter group and 21 following, the sequence takes on a very symmetrical appearance, and it becomes clear that we cannot accept Lever's proposal to 'set apart' sonnets that are seemingly 'out of place'. Whether the sonnets were written in one or several periods of the author's life, their arrangement is intentional and unified, and was most likely conceived and executed in 1594.[7] In sum, the form imposed by the calendar symbolism of *Amoretti* is that of a cycle with symmetrical beginning and end sections of 21 sonnets each, and a central group of 47 sonnets in which each sonnet corresponds to a date in Lent of 1594.

A plan that assigns specific days and dates to specific sonnets invites speculation about a more detailed pattern of calendrical or numerological correspondences. A number of details suggest the existence of a pattern based on 7. The 2 groups of 21 sonnets before and after the central group, together with the Easter Sonnet and those of the 6 Sundays of the Lenten season, make 49 non-Lenten sonnets, 7 weeks if each sonnet is associated with a day. Further, Sonnet lxxxiii is an exact repetition of Sonnet xxxv; bracketing this group of sonnets, we find there are 49. Again, from the spring Sonnet xix to the last Lenten sonnet (lxvii, Easter Even being the last day of Lent) there are 49 sonnets; from the first Lenten sonnet (xxii) to the second spring sonnet (lxx) there are likewise 49. The number 7, notable as that of the planets, the days of the week and of creation, and the ages of man, was traditionally associated with body as opposed to mind and mutability as opposed to mortality. Both associations are relevant to the dominant theme of a sequence which depicts the process of the elevation of earthly desire to a higher form of love.

Spenser's symbolic use of events of the church calendar also suggests the possibility that the sequence is related to the themes of the liturgical readings for the various days. Sonnets xxii and lxviii are clearly liturgical. Some critics, recently Waldo F. McNeir, have interpreted xxii as a first Easter sonnet.[8] However, Easter is not a day of fasting, and the suggestions of burning and of the poet's preparing to sacrifice his heart at the altar seem appropriate both to Ash Wednesday and to the eucharistic symbolism that culminates in the Easter Sonnet lxviii.

xxii

This holy season fit to fast and pray,
  Men to devotion ought to be inclynd:
  therefore, I lykewise on so holy day,
  for my sweet Saynt some service fit will find.
Her temple fayre is built within my mind,
  in which her glorious ymage placed is,
  on which my thoughts doo day and night attend
  lyke sacred priests that never thinke amisse.
There I to her as th' author of my blisse,

will builde an altar to appease her yre:
  and on the same my hart will sacrifise,
  burning in flames of pure and chaste desyre:
The which vouchsafe O goddesse to accept,
  amongst thy deerest relicks to be kept.

The common medieval association of the number 22 with moderation or temperance may help explain the placement of the Ash Wednesday poem as Sonnet xxii.[9]

William Nelson's association of Sonnet lxviii with Christmas appears to be without foundation.[10] The joy of the day is contrasted throughout with the sorrows of the preceding crucifixion: 'having harrowd hell', 'thou diddest dye', and 'all lyke deare didst buy', we 'being with thy deare blood clene washt from sin'. The liturgical nature of Sonnet lxviii is underscored by the fact that its rhetorical form is derived from the Collects of the Book of Common Prayer.[11]

A number of sonnets, especially those surrounding Sonnet lxviii, reveal an artful ambiguity. The line between secular and religious becomes blurred in these sonnets, which have allusions that can refer equally to events of the Christian calendar and of the lover's courtship. For example, the 'weary chace', 'long pursuit', and 'vaine assay' described in Sonnet lxvii (Easter Even) as just past refer equally to the trials of the lover and the discipline associated with Lent. Sonnet lxvi (Good Friday) can refer equally to Christ's sacrifice and to the lady:

lxvi
To all those happy blessings which ye have,
  with plenteous hand by heaven upon you thrown,
  this one disparagement they to you gave,
  that ye your love lent to so meane a one.
Yee whose high worths surpassing paragon,
  could not on earth have found one fit for mate,
  ne but in heaven matchable to none,
  why did ye stoup unto so lowly state?
But ye thereby much greater glory gate,
  then had ye sorted with a princes pere:

for now your light doth more it selfe dilate,
and in my darknesse greater doth appeare.
Yet since your light hath once enlumind me,
with my reflex yours shall encreased be.

Other sonnets have isolated details that might be thought significant. Sonnet lxiv is an example; it begins 'Coming to kiss her
lyps, (such grace I found)'. Is it simply a curious coincidence that
the gospel reading for the corresponding day, Wednesday before
Easter, relates the incident of Judas kissing Christ (Luke xlvii–
xlviii)? It would seem so, for the remainder of the sonnet is a
frankly sensual enumeration of floral comparisons with the lady's
body.

Most of the sonnets have no explicit liturgical allusions.
However, there is good reason why this double allusiveness
becomes prominent with the sonnets preceding Easter. Easter in
the sequence is a point of transition. *Amoretti*, I have suggested,
depicts through Christian symbolism the progression of earthly
love towards a higher form of love. Easter, as the culmination of
earthly love, marks the transition from the earthly to the spiritual.
The thematic development of the sequence substantiates this interpretation.

The development of *Amoretti* parallels Spenser's description of
the workings of Love in 'An Hymne in Honour of Love'. First,
Love stirs desire in the lover (*HL*, 120–124). As his desire grows,
and to help it grow, Love hardens the Lady's heart (*HL*, 137–9),
so that the lover, continually thwarted, must suffer. These themes
of praise and suffering complaint dominate the first part of
*Amoretti*. The lover's desire and suffering increase until all his
other concerns are excluded: he sees only her (*HL*, 131–3, and
*Amoretti* xxxv). The long period of suffering which ensues is
described in the hymn (vv. 162–8) as a sort of trial; it corresponds
to the Lenten period in *Amoretti*. Verses 176–8 of the hymn
describe Love, the 'Lord of truth and loialtie', as 'lifting himselfe
out of the lowly dust / On golden plumes up to the purest skie'
in terms reminiscent of *Amoretti* lxviii, the Easter sonnet.

The lover's mind now becomes fixed (*HL*, 190–204) on a 'fairer

form that now doth dwell / In his high thought'; this corresponds
to the increasing fixation of the *Amoretti* lover, beginning with
Sonnet lxxvi, on the 'fairer form' of the lady. The fixation culminates in Sonnet lxxxiii, in which for a second time he sees only
her. The idea of intense fixation on the lady occurs at two places in
'An Hymne in Honour of Love,' at verses 131–3 and 204–7,
and in *Amoretti* at xxxv and lxxxiii. This parallel suggests that the
repetition of Sonnet xxxv as Sonnet lxxxiii is not a matter of
hurried or careless arrangement, as has been supposed. The idea
in the sonnet is exactly the same as that expressed in the hymn
and it is repeated at the same stages of the development.

Beginning at verse 250 of the hymn, envy, spite and 'that
monster Gelosie' begin to plague the 'fayning fansie' of the lover's
'troubled mind'. This development is enacted in *Amoretti* lxxxiv
through lxxxvi, which all show the poet-lover's emotional
agitation and his concern with asserted dangers to himself and the
lady.

These parallels indicate that the thematic development of
*Amoretti*, since it recurs in the hymn, proceeds according to a well-
defined plan, and that it is closely tied to the symbolic framework
of the sequence. They also corroborate the interpretation of the
framework as a progression from desire to a higher form of love.
The calendar symbolism, then, has not only a temporal correspondence but also a causal relationship to the central theme.
Clearly, Spenser saw the religious and the amatory elements not
as two levels of meaning, but as inseparable aspects of the same
story. Spenser's story of love is based on the proposition that
Christ is in man. Christ is Beauty, which causes and sustains
desire. And Christ is Love. Thus when Christ, who is Love, rises
from his human state to heaven, the love that is Christ in the
poet is also rising to a higher level. For Spenser this is not a pair of
separate, parallel, symbolic actions, but one occurrence. But the
lover in the story is also a historical person, Edmund Spenser,
identifiable by the details included from his life. Hence the
elevating act of love is represented in *Amoretti* at once on three
corresponding levels, and all three – the personal, the typical, and
the divine are subsumed in a single reality.

Within the calendrical, numerological, liturgical, and thematic bounds which Spenser has set for the sequence, the individual sonnets are arranged in precise and meaningful patterns. The group formed by the first 21 sonnets provides illustration of this. In the first sonnet the poet is characterized as captive and sorrowful; his heart is bleeding, his spirit is dying, and his soul lacks food. The heart, spirit (i.e., mind), and soul are the stages through which love passes in its elevation, and the levels at which the lover experiences love. The lady too is given threefold characterization. Although her might consists only of 'loves soft bands', she is a victor with 'dead doing might', the source of his sorrowful captivity and bleeding heart. Derived from Helicon, she is also the source of the poetic inspiration that can revitalize his dying spirit. Finally, as a blessed angel, she is his 'soules long lacked foode'. The source of his suffering on earth, she is also his 'heavens blis'. Thus the first sonnet is a digest of the entire sequence.

The first 4 sonnets are introductory. Sonnets ii through iv characterize the situation of the lover at the beginning of the sequence, ii and iii showing contrasting effects of the lady on him, and iv providing a specific temporal setting. Sonnet iv is associated with the secular New Year's Day, as opposed to that of the 'Year of Grace' observed by the Church. Instituted by the Julian calendar reform of 46 B.C., the January New Year was originally a pagan festival.[12] Spenser is careful to characterize this New Year with an eye to the pagan tradition. It is set in 'sad winters night', and although it promises 'hope of new delight', it is the delight of 'fresh love . . . with *wanton* wings and darts of *deadly* power' (italics mine). The spring it heralds is 'lusty spring', so that the earth must 'decke hir selfe'. Thus, as the sequence begins, the lover, in a pagan setting, is troubled on the one hand by the 'inward bale' of a baser desire that gives rise to 'unquiet thoughts' (Sonnet ii), and on the other by his recognition that the lady, as an embodiment of angelic qualities that kindle 'heavenly fire' in him, deserves worship rather than passion (Sonnet iii).

The development of the story begins with Sonnet v. The contrasting effects of the lady on the lover are the basis of two distinctly different kinds of sonnets. The first kind, like Sonnet ii, may be called the 'fayre proud' variety; it emphasizes the lady's pride, tyranny, cruelty, rebelliousness, obduracy. The second kind, like Sonnet iii, is the *donna angelicata* variety, which stresses the lady's beauty, goodness, divinity, or salutary powers.[13] In Sonnet v the poet praises the goodness and salutary effects of the lady's 'too portly pride'. It summarizes or unites, like Sonnet i, the dichotomous qualities. Here the 'moral' of the story is drawn. The poet recognizes that the lady's pride is a necessary corollary of her angelic qualities if the lover is to be lured on: 'Was never in this world ought worthy tride, / Without some spark of such self-pleasing pride.'

In Sonnet vi the poet-lover launches his campaign for the lady's favour; vi is a poem of self-encouragement in the face of the lady's 'rebellious pride': 'Be nought dismayd,' he tells himself. All the other sonnets of the first 21 are repetitions of these basic types.

Sonnets vii, viii and ix are *donna angelicata* sonnets. These 3 are followed by 3 'fayre proud' sonnets in which the lover's efforts come to nought and he is humbled. Sonnet xiii is, like v, a moralizing sonnet dealing with pride: 'Myld humblesse mixt with awfull maiesty.'

Sonnet xiii marks the end of the poet's first 'siege' to win the lady, but it also marks the beginning of a second 'siege' that proceeds according to exactly the same pattern as the first: a sonnet of encouragement, 3 *angelicata* sonnets, 3 'fayre proud' sonnets, and finally, another 'mixt' sonnet ('Myld humblesse mixt with awful maiesty') reiterating the moral. Not only is the arrangement parallel, but also each sonnet of the second 'siege' corresponds thematically to a sonnet of the first.

Sonnet xiv, a sonnet of self-encouragement like vi, notes the cyclic nature of the arrangement:

Retourne agayne my forces late dismayd
   Unto the siege by you abandon'd quite,
   great shame it is to leave like one afrayd,
   so fayre a peece for one repulse so light.

The military imagery and the force of the terminology in general indicate a considerable escalation in the second 'siege': 'Gaynst such strong castles needeth greater might, / . . . Bring therefore all the forces that ye may.' Thematically there is little change in the second set of sonnets; the only progression seems to be in intensity.

Sonnet xv is, like viii, a celebration of the lady's beauty. The emphasis is on the beauty of 'her mind adorned with vertues manifold', as in viii it was on the effects of her virtue.

Sonnet xvi is a little anecdote based, like vii, on her power of life and death. Both sonnets, despite the overtones of her power over his life, stress the angelic nature of her 'immortal light'.

Sonnets xvii and ix proclaim the lady's divine origin. Her eyes have a central place in both sonnets. The tone has now mounted from admiration to adoration; the lover, with increasing insistence but little apparent effect, has plied his battery of compliments and is ready to turn to other means. In all of these sonnets the lady remains unyielding; what changes is the lover's strategy in his effort to change her.

As the lover in xi sought to change the lady with 'reason' and 'rewth', so in xviii he tries 'long intreaty' and 'dropping tear'.

In Sonnet x the lover called upon the 'unrighteous Lord of love' to humble the lady; in xix he asks Love's help again, this time for a stronger redress: 'Therefore O love, unlesse she turne to thee / Ere Cuckow end, let her a rebell be.' Sonnet xix also reinforces the secular temporal setting established by Sonnet iv. Spring in this sonnet is seductive and earthly rather than elevating, for it is heralded by 'the merry Cuckow', whose note is derided in Sonnet lxxxv as 'witlesse'; love's influence is described as an 'idle message'.

In Sonnet xx the lover complains that the lady takes unfair advantage of him: '[I] doe myne humbled hart before her poure / The whiles her foot she in my necke doth place.' This echoes the situation of Sonnet xii, in which the lady sets 'a wicked ambush' for him, while he, disarmed, 'sought with her hart-thrilling eies to make a truce'. The tone of the 'fayre proud' sonnets has intensified from plaint to abject humiliation. Thus the increasingly positive effort depicted in the *donna angelicata* sonnets is followed by an increasingly negative reaction in the 'fayre proud' sonnets.

Finally, xxi, parallel to v and xiii, summarizes the activity of the two 'sieges' ('her smile me drawes, her frowne me drives away') and draws the moral: 'Thus doth she traine and teach me with her lookes.'

The lover and the poet are of course the same person. However, at different times one or the other of these roles takes precedence. In the sonnets that comment on his situation he is the narrator, the poet. Sonnets i through iv, and v, xiii and xxi are like asides by the poet-lover to the audience, explaining and interpreting what is going on. In sonnets that show actions, such as plaints or pleadings, he abandons his stance of narrator and plays the part of the lover, demonstrating rather than narrating. Sonnets vi through xii and xiv through xx are poetic enactments of interludes of courtship.

The arrangement of Sonnets i–xxi invites diagrammatic representation:

<pre>
                                      ⎧i
                          intro-      ⎪ii
                          ductory     ⎨iii
                                      ⎩iv


'mixt'                      v ——moral valuation ——xiii

self-encouragement          vi ——self-encouragement ——xiv

donna    ⎫                       ⎧vii ——beauty              ⟍  ⟋ xv
ange-    ⎬        praises        ⎨viii ——life/death power    ⟋⟍ xvi
licata   ⎭        her            ⎩ix ——divine origin              ——xvii

'fayre   ⎫       seeks           ⎧x   ⟍  ⟋ entreaty              ——xviii
proud'   ⎬       to move         ⎨xi  ⟋⟍ Love's redress         ——xix
         ⎭       her by          ⎩xii ——self-abasement          ——xx

'mixt'                      xiii ——moral valuation ——xxi
</pre>

The lover is active in assuming the stances of conventional courtship, although his actions are ineffectual; the lady is static. Although she is described in many of the sonnets, it is the lover who is characterized by his own descriptions. It is only in the changes of his attitudes that the story of *Amoretti* can be followed.

In sum, this alternation of dramatic and narrative sonnets and of positive and negative attitudes determines the arrangement of the individual sonnets in meaningful patterns that function as units of development.

The groups formed by Sonnets xxii through lxviii and Sonnets lxix through lxxxix develop in similar patterns according to the thematic progression outlined in 'An Hymne in Honour of Love'. With Sonnet xxii the focus moves within the poet's mind. The sanctification of the lady links the development of the courtship to a spiritual development of which the lover's suffering forms an integral part. His heart, the locus of his love in the first group, he now sacrifices, 'burning in flames of pure and chaste desyre', to his 'sweet Saynt'.

Sonnets xxii to lxviii show a uniformity in tone and theme corresponding to the Lenten season. Characteristic of this tone is the almost complete disappearance of the *donna angelicata* sonnets, which do not become prominent again until Sonnets lix through lxviii. With the exception of xxii, xxxix and xl, virtually all the other sonnets – xxiii through xxxviii and xli through lviii – stress the cruelty of the lady, the suffering of the lover, or both of these.

In Sonnets lix through lxviii the poet's love moves toward fulfillment. Sonnets v and lix mark the beginning and end of his period of suffering, and have the same themes: praise of the lady's pride. While he has been lost in the storms of baser passion, she has remained strong, just as 'a steddy ship doth strongly part / the raging waves and keepes her course aright: / ne ought for tempest doth from it depart'.

Sonnet lxii begins a new year, this time the liturgical 'Year of Grace', bringing with it a 'change of weather'. The lover repudiates the sins of the past year: 'the old yeares sinnes forepast let us eschew'. Everything has changed: 'Chaunge eeke our mynds and former lives amend'. The 1 January New Year at Sonnet iv was said to be calling forth 'out of sad Winters night', as love 'about him dight / his wanton wings and darts of deadly power'. Here, on 25 March, 'with shew of morning mylde he hath begun, / . . . and all these stormes which now his beauty blend, / shall

turne to caulmes and tymely cleare away'. In lxiii, he declares 'I
doe at length descry the happy shore.' Finally the culmination of
the love of the poet and his lady, which is the culmination for
Spenser of earthly love, is celebrated in the resurrection paean
at Sonnet lxviii.

For a brief period the lover enjoys the presence of his lady,
although his mind is troubled by 'burden of mortality' (Sonnet
lxxii). The theme and images of Sonnets lxix to lxxv are notably
material and worldly. In lxxv, however, the lady's name is
washed away in the sand, and in lxxvi to lxxxiii the emphasis
shifts to the incorporeal – from the lady to her 'gentle spright',
her 'aspect', her 'ymage'.

This shift is accompanied by renewed poetic inspiration. In
Sonnet xxxiii the poet complained he could not continue *The
Faerie Queene* because his wit was 'tost with troublous fit of a
proud love, that doth my spirite spoil'. In lxxx the reverse is true:
'the contemplation of [her] heavenly hew, / my spirit to an higher
pitch will rayse'. Likewise in Sonnet iii he was silenced by the
beauty of the lady: 'So when my toung would speak her praises
dew, / it stopped is with *thoughts* astonishment.' In lxxxi, considering her mind, he is differently affected: 'The rest be works of
natures wonderment, / but this the worke of *harts* astonishment'
(italics mine). Likewise, Sonnet xxxv, repeated as Sonnet lxxxiii,
gains a different meaning from its new context: 'Yet are myne
eyes so filled with the store / of that fayre sight, that nothing else
they brooke: / but loath the things which they did like before.'
As xxxv the sonnet distinguishes between different objects of
beauty; as lxxxiii, between different kinds of beauty.[14]

In the last 6 sonnets the lover is plunged back into suffering.
He has seen love, the true light; 'some glance' of 'that heavenly
ray' has remained in his eye to fortify his soul. But in this life he
must sustain himself with that glance only. The dominant mood
of the last 3 sonnets is one of expectation and waiting: 'Thus I the
time with expectation spend'. The world has sunk into darkness
corresponding to the 'sad winters night' with which the sequence
began. The light of the 'Idaea playne', which transcends the realm
of heart and mind, has become the only light for the lover:

with light thereof I doe my selfe sustayne,
and thereon feed my love–affamisht hart.
But with such brightnesse whylest I fill my mind,
I starve my body and mine eyes doe blynd.

The lover is left mourning like the culver, awaiting reunion with love.[15]

This reunion is that celebrated in *Epithalamion* – the reunion of the lover with the lady in marriage. But it is also much more. Here, as elsewhere in Spenser, the full significance can be perceived only in terms of 'an integral meaning, integrally expressed, below the surface of discourse', as Professor Hieatt has asserted. The key to this integral meaning in *Amoretti* is the identification of love with Christ, revealed in the calendar symbolism of the sequence and in the arrangement of the dominant themes. It is above all the *oneness* of love that is expressed in *Amoretti* – the love of the poet for his lady *is* the love of the Christian for his God. The pattern of religious symbol and image in *Amoretti*, then, is not an exercise in poetic virtuosity, but an integral expression of the central theme, 'for Love', as Spenser observes in 'An Hymne in Honour of Beauty', 'is a celestiall harmonie'.

# NOTES

1 John Erskine, *The Elizabethan Lyric* (New York, 1903), p. 153, cited by William Nelson in *The Poetry of Edmund Spenser: A study* (New York, 1963), p. 88. Nelson feels that the statement 'is surely an overstatement of the case'. Erskine found the sequence divided at Sonnet lxii into two parts, describing courtship and betrothal respectively.

2 'Simplest reading': W. L. Renwick (ed.), *Daphnaïda and Other Poems by Edmund Spenser* (1929), pp. 192–3. Allegorical interpretation: see e.g. Diethild Bludau, 'Humanismus und Allegorie in Spensers Sonetten', *Anglia*, lxxiv (1956), and Robert Kellogg, 'Thought's Astonishment and the Dark Conceit of Spenser's *Amoretti*', *Renaissance Papers 1965 of the Southeastern Renaissance Conference* (1966). Dramatic interpretation: see Louis L. Martz, 'The *Amoretti*: "Most Goodly Temperature",' *Form and Convention in the Poetry of Edmund Spenser*, ed. William Nelson (New York, 1961), and Waldo F. McNeir, 'An Apology for Spenser's *Amoretti*', *Die Neueren Sprachen*, xiv (1965).

3 *The Elizabethan Love Sonnet* (1965), pp. 99–103.

4 Alastair Fowler, *Spenser and the Numbers of Time* (1964); Fowler's suggestions for revision much improved an earlier form of the present article, published in *N & Q*, cciv (1969), 24–26. A. Kent Hieatt, *Short Time's Endless Monument* (New York, 1960), pp. 80–2. Cf. William Nelson, *The Poetry of Edmund Spenser*, p. 321, n. 9, also pp. 95–6. The difference between Nelson's and Hieatt's views would seem to be one of emphasis: Nelson stresses theme and image, denying the primacy but not the existence of underlying numerical relationships; Hieatt stresses number symbolism as the primary structural determinant in the *Epithalamion*. Important clarifications of some aspects of Hieatt's analysis of the structure of the *Epithalamion* are made by Max A. Wickert, 'Structure and Ceremony in Spenser's *Epithalamion*', *ELH*, xxxv (1968), 135–57.

5 'The yeere of our Lorde beginneth the .xxv. day of March, the same day supposed to be the first day upon which the worlde was created, and the day when Christ was conceived in the wombe of the virgin Marie.' *New Calendar of 1561* (1578), *Liturgical Services*

*of the Reign of Queen Elizabeth*, ed. William Keeling Clay (Cambridge, 1847), p. 441. Other traditions began the year at 25 December, 1 March, or 1 September. A summary of the various traditions is given by Reginald L. Poole, 'The Beginnings of the Year in the Middle Ages', *Proceedings of the British Academy*, x (1921), 113–37. Samuel Seabury, *The Theory and Use of the Church Calendar in the Measurement and Distribution of Time* (New York, 1872) gives a valuable description of the functioning of the church calendar. See also C. R. Cheney, *Handbook of Dates* (1945).

6 See E. K.'s 'Generall Argument' in *Spenser: Poetical Works*, ed. J. C. Smith and E. de Selincourt (1912), pp. 419f.: 'That wise king minded upon good reason to begin the yeare at Januarie, of him therefore so called *tanquam Ianua anni* the gate and entraunce of the yere, or of the name of the god Ianus.' A. Kent Hieatt, p. 71, has linked *Amoretti* iv, *Amoretti* lxii, and *Epithalamion*, vv. 30–6, with the beginning of the year at 25 March.

7 If that line of reasoning is correct by which the year of Spenser's birth is set at 1552 on the basis of Sonnet lx, association of *Amoretti* with 1594 necessitates revision to 1554. According to the same logic the date could be specified as 23 March, the date corresponding to Sonnet lx.

8 Waldo F. McNeir, p. 3.

9 See Jerry Leath Mills, 'Spenser's Castle of Alma and the Number 22: A Note on Symbolic Stanza Placement,' *N & Q*, ccxii (1967), 456–7.

10 William Nelson, *Poetry of Edmund Spenser*, p. 88.

11 The similarity to the Collects has been pointed out by O. B. Hardison, Jr, '*Amoretti* and the Dolce Stil Nuovo', unpublished paper presented at the annual meeting of the MLA in New York, 27 December 1968.

12 See Sherman Hawkins, 'Mutabilitie and the Cycle of the Months', *Form and Convention in the Poetry of Edmund Spenser*, p. 90.

13 I am indebted to O. B. Hardison, Jr, Director of the Folger Shakespeare Library, for the important distinction between these two types of sonnets; the terms are also his. Nelson, Bludau and others have noted in a more general way the pattern of thematic oppositions in *Amoretti*.

14 *Amoretti*, as Robert Ellrodt has pointed out, *Neoplatonism in the Poetry of Spenser*, Travaux d'Humanisme et Renaissance, xxxv (Geneva, 1960), is not primarily Neo-platonic in inspiration. How-

ever, Ellrodt is wrong, I believe, in denying a progression in *Amoretti* to a higher form of love. The divinity of the lady is more than a question of 'outdoing the hyperboles of his predecessors' (p. 40). The development of *Amoretti* corresponds in fact to the first three stages (Grade II) of the Neoplatonic process as noted by Ellrodt. Spenser does not continue in the ascent. He follows the working of love in its progress through the levels of the heart and the mind to the frontier of the soul, but he can go no further. Spenser is no mystic. This is for him the limit of human experience; beyond this he can only wait.

15 Typically, Spenser suggests the inner intangible by the tangible exterior. Birds reflecting the lover's state in *Amoretti* progress from the cuckow to the mavis (thrush) to the culver (dove).

# 'To Shepherd's ear':
# the form of Milton's *Lycidas*

ALASTAIR FOWLER

I

Few English poems have been more minutely examined by prosodists than Milton's *Lycidas*. Yet its external form continues to present many problems – so many that one doubts whether prosodic solutions can really be in the offing. The main difficulty is the irregularity of the stanzas or paragraphs. In 'A Poem Nearly Anonymous' John Crowe Ransom even advanced the amusing theory (which everyone including Ransom seems to have taken seriously) that an 'insubordinate' Milton disturbed the anonymity of the *canzone*, varied the stanza pattern and introduced unrhymed lines, all 'as a gesture of his rebellion against the formalism of his art'.[1] Others have tried to explain the form of *Lycidas* more rationally by referring it to Italian models. Professor F. T. Prince cogently demonstrates resemblances to the *stanze divise* of the *canzone* with their short dividing lines, but finds the variation in stanza length and short line disposition so wide that he also has to invoke the precedent of choruses in pastoral dramas such as *Aminta*.[2] M. C. Battestin in effect follows suit.[3] Gretchen Finney compares Striggio's musical drama,[4] Ants Oras the Italian madrigal.[5] We may distinguish between these attempts and find more justice in the comparison with non-dramatic lyric; but it must be said of all of them that they leave the impression of differences from Italian precedents as well as resemblances. Prince remarks: 'The wide deviations from the strict form of the *canzone* are . . . the first thing to be noticed' (p. 72). We may readily agree with him that Milton 'has made his own rules for this poem, but made them out of his knowledge and enjoyment of the strictest Italian practice' (p. 87). At the same time, we naturally wonder which principles governed Milton's rules, which ideas he expressed through the form of what is arguably the most serious English poem about death. These questions are not quite the province of prosody, however. *The Italian Element of Milton's Verse* contains a brilliant account of texture and of such rhythmic effects as the counterpointing of syntactic pauses with pauses enforced by rhyme. But the symbolism of the external structure is outside its brief. That is a matter for numerological enquiry.

When it first appeared in 1638, *Lycidas* was accompanied by 35 other elegies for King, some of them obviously organized on a numerical basis.[6] By comparison, its own numerology is both subtle and complex, as indeed we might expect from a young poet of Milton's intellect and artistry. Yet some of its structural features would once have seemed patent enough. A division into 11 paragraphs or stanzas, for example, seems to have been considered appropriate for funeral odes: another famous instance is Henry King's 'The Exequy'. The basis of this convention lay in the ancient association of 11 with mourning and specifically with its termination. Tombs were honoured in February, according to Ovid, so long as the shades wandered; but this stopped on the day of the Feralia, when 11 days of the month remained – 'as many days of the month as there are feet in my verses' (*Fasti* ii. 561–70). Pietro Bongo, citing this passage in his discussion of the symbolism of the number, further observes that the Spartan legislator Lycurgus limited ritual mourning at funerals to the space of 11 days.[7]

Turning to the arrangement of finer external structure, the fit reader will see that on the *canzone* analogy *Lycidas* consists of 10 stanzas, varying in length between 12 and 33 lines, together with a final 8-line *commiato*. But he will also notice a gross prosodic irregularity. Whereas all the other stanzas resemble *stanze divise* broken by the interposition of short 6-syllable lines, Stanza x, like the *commiato* that follows it, remains unbroken: a variation for which it would not be easy to find Italian authority. Numerologically considered, on the other hand, the unbroken form of the tenth stanza is highly appropriate. For it coincides with a decisive transition to the Christian consolation that is to end mourning:

'Weep no more, woful Shepherds weep no more, / For *Lycidas*
your sorrow is not dead.' The decorum rests on two poetic ideas,
one simple and the other philosophical. By a simple self-referring
ambiguity, of a sort typical of mannerist poetry, the broken
stanzas are broken with grief. (Comparably, the divided eighth
song in Astrophil and Stella refers to its own form in 'my song
is broken'.[8] It is also significant, however, that the only stanza
without an incomplete line, the only unbroken stanza, should be
the tenth. For, in the Pythagorean system, the decad symbolizes a
return to unity. It is a form of the *tetraktus*, the creative principle,
which unfolds the divine One into his creation, then restores it
again to unity and to God. It is fitting, therefore, that the mourners, broken in their grief at the disememberment of King in re-
enactment of the archetypal dismemberment of Orpheus, should
be made whole – and with them the form of the ode itself – in a
stanza bearing the number that denotes the summed form of the
*tetraktus*.[9] Commonly the *tetraktus* also symbolizes the integrative
virtuous soul; and in the end Lycidas is seen to have become,
through his virtue, 'the Genius of the shore' and the informing
spirit of the shepherds who survive. Thus the short lines, besides
signalizing shifts in tone, mime by their spatial disposition the
processes of integration and of *remeatio* to the divine.

A closely analogous external feature is the 10 unrhymed lines
(1, 13, 15, 22, 39, 51, 82, 91, 92, 161: the total remains invariable
through manuscript revisions, as Battestin points out in rebuttal of
Ransom's notion of impatience with rhyme). Just as the short lines
are incomplete and break the stanzas, so the unrhymed lines break
the bond of rhyme and the unison of line-endings.[10] The 10 unrhymed lines are arranged like this:

| stanza | i | ii | iii | iv | v | vi | vii | viii | ix | x | xi |
|---|---|---|---|---|---|---|---|---|---|---|---|
| *unrhymed lines* | 2 | 2 | 0 | 1 | 1 | 1 | 2 | 0 | 1 | 0 | 0 |

That the tenth stanza and the *commiato* should attain the uninter-
rupted harmony of continuously rhyme-linked endings is what
we should expect, on the analogy of the pattern of stanzas broken
by short lines. But it is less obvious why Stanzas iii and viii should

be completely rhymed. Until, that is, we see a touching decorum of form. For the third stanza looks back nostalgically to the harmony, now lost, of the time before Lycidas' death, when 'Rural ditties were not mute, / Temper'd to th'Oaten Flute'; and the eighth, while it contrasts the 'scrannel Pipes of wretched straw' of bad shepherds surviving him, also introduces the virtue of Camus[11] and St Peter's massy keys to the bliss that Lycidas is imagined enjoying in heaven as he listens to 'the unexpressive nuptiall Song' among saints 'that sing, and singing in their glory move' in the tenth (again completely rhymed) stanza.

The poem's decasyllabic couplets have a significance opposite to that of the 'incomplete' and the unrhymed lines. By enforcing the closest possible bond of rhyme the couplets serve the poet's sympathetic magic. Consequently, while the incidence of short and unrhymed lines diminishes towards the end, decasyllabic couplets become, on the contrary, more frequent, until in Stanzas ix and x they even occur doubled (ll. 135–9, 182–5). Their distribution among stanzas runs 1, 2, 2, 0, 1, 3, 1, 4, 4, 5, 1. The idea that Milton designed the harmony of close rhyme to soothe the dissonance of unrhymed and incomplete lines would remain speculative, however, were we not in the fortunate position of being able to support it numerologically. For the couplets, which number just 24, exactly compensate for the 10 unrhymed and 14 short lines:[12] $10 + 14 = 24$. Perhaps we glimpse the magical process actually at work in the pivotal stanza vi, where couplets immediately enclose the unrhymed line 82.

As Prince has noticed (p. 87), the short lines of *Lycidas* 'always rhyme with a previous longer line' – another instance of rhyme's compensating for the incomplete line's dissonance. But one has to give a more exact description, to appreciate Milton's full intention. As a rule, we find, each short line rhymes with the long line *immediately* preceding. Of the exceptions to this rule, two infringe it minimally and rhyme with preceding long lines at one remove only. These 'second distance' rhymes (to use Puttenham's term) mark the entry of the first and last mourners in the central exequy or funeral procession: 'But now my Oate proceeds, / And listens to the Herald of the Sea' (88f.); 'Last came, and last did go' (108).

The remaining exceptions (41, 48) are more egregious, since they rhyme with long lines at two removes. Moreover, these third distance rhymes occur both in the same stanza. And this same Stanza iv is also the only one in the ode without a decasyllabic couplet. The conclusion seems ineluctable, that all three irregularities have a formal decorum befitting the content of stanza iv, an account of the 'heavy change' brought by Lycidas' death. The concluding line of the stanza, which itself avoids close rhyme, is thus self-referring: 'Such, *Lycidas*, thy loss to Shepherds ear' (49).

2

Since so many lines of *Lycidas* have a formal self-reference or accompanying formal decorum, since the poet is so careful to give a conscious sense of his *maniera*, we turn with special interest to the *commiato*, where he introduces himself in the act of making the preceding stanzas' music and so sets the ode itself at an artistic distance, within a frame that forms part of the picture, as in a mannerist *trompe l'oeil* painting.[13] The swain is also deeply involved in his ode as a participant: he mourns like the other shepherds. But, again like them, he survives, and therefore must purge and assuage his grief, twitch[14] his mantle to remind himself of his duty and go on to other concerns with a new resolve. His 'mantle blue' is related not merely to the academic mantle of Camus (104), but through that to the emblematic *camus* or collar of rational integration and discipline.[15] It is the robe of a rededicated student body, the bands of a *Musarum sacerdos*, even a prophetic mantle fallen from the ascended King to Elisha-Milton below, in whose cerulean colour we are no doubt to recognize the poet's hope of ascent from his own destined urn to heaven.[16]

The most complex participation of the swain is in an Orphic role. 'Uncouth' (186) partly in the sense strange or foreign,[17] he communicates to England an ancient and Italian art, just as the head of Orpheus was believed to have transmitted a poetic tradition to the island of Lesbos. Thus the swain sings 'to th' Okes', English trees, what he invoked the exotic and academic myrtles to provide.[18] Orpheus, too, sang to trees: central to his myth was a magical influence over nature, whereby he moved vegetation and even rocks with the music of his lyre. His final magic was to move the spheres with his stellified lyre:

> once Woods and Stones, now Stars it draws
> And leads about the revoluble Spheres.[19]

Similarly the Orphic Milton exerts magical influence over his poetic cosmos. The succession of times of day in the *commiato* –

> Thus sang the uncouth Swain to th'Okes and rills,
> While the still morn went out with Sandals gray,
>
> .    .    .    .    .
>
> And now the Sun had stretch'd out all the hills,
> And now was dropt into the Western bay;
> (186f., 190f.)

– implies a close association between swain and sun, which recalls Lycidas' comparison with the sinking and rising daystar.[20] This association is from one point of view magical harmony and influence: the swain no sooner 'touch'd the tender stops' than 'the sun had stretch'd out all the hills' with a promptness it takes the pluperfect to express. But in a deeper sense the poem's day signifies the day of human life:[21] a symbolism common in funeral odes.[22] If the life is considered as King's, the sun's course ends in death, though with hope of a rising 'in the forehead of the morning sky' (171). If the life is Milton's, however, the sun may either measure his purgative day's work composing sad thoughts into the harmony of a true poem, or proleptically accomplish his whole life's day – in which case 'At last he rose . . . Pastures new' expresses faith in a day beyond that of the visible sun. The 8-line total of the *commiato* suits both sides of the ambiguity, since it may symbolize either the octave of harmony or the eternal life beyond mortality's 7s.[23]

Some will object that the swain plays a pipe, not a lyre. But I am far from sure that Orpheus' lyre is not alluded to verbally.

Certainly Milton invokes the Muses with respect to a stringed instrument: 'somewhat loudly sweep the string' (17). And even the shepherd's pipe may be pastoral disguise. The beautifully ambiguous phrase 'tender stops of various Quills' only primarily refers to the finger-holes of reed pipes: the *quill* might also be a plectrum, the *stop* a part of the string pressed to raise the pitch (by half a tone in the case of the lute). Even *twitched* carries on the word play, since it was used for the action of plucking a stringed instrument.[24]

The Orphic magic whereby Milton leads round the revolving heavens works in part through numbers. (Numbers were often thought of as a means of power; not unreasonably, as it has turned out, considering science's dependence on mathematics.)[25] Thus the swain's quills are 'various' not merely to boast rhetorical *varietas* but also to draw attention to the significance of number. Traditionally, Orpheus' lyre had been interpreted numerologically and its strings related to the cosmic spheres or (after Timotheus of Miletus) to the zodiacal signs.[26] And the stringed instrument of Apollo, like that of David, was in much the same way associated with the decad and hence with the 10 spheres (7 planetary, firmament, crystalline, *primum mobile*).[27] In this context it is not hard to see that Milton sympathizes with the heavens' rotation, and consequently with the sinking and rising of the poet-sun, by dividing his ode into 10 stanzas that match the cosmic spheres. But the swain's various quills express the measure of the spheres' rotation in other ways too. Most obviously, the 24 couplets correspond to the hours of a complete day: least obviously, the 14 short lines correspond to the artificial hours of day on the fatal 10 August 1637 (sunrise to sunset was about 14 hours 20 minutes): and most conclusively from an apologetic stand-point – the numbers involved being larger – the total of long lines corresponds to the degrees of the sun's diurnal half-orbit. For, though the apparent daily orbit of the sun is 360°, the retardation of about 1° per day that causes his seasonal course round the ecliptic means that his true diurnal orbit is about 359° and the half-orbit, during which the shepherd sings his pastoral elegy, 179½°. And *Lycidas* has 179 long lines.

3

Besides keeping to temporal measures in obedience to the Unity of Time, *Lycidas* exhibits the equal divisions and centralized symmetries that were once a regular feature of formal style.[28] This aspect of its numerology has a bearing on current vacillations of criticism between two- and three-part structural interpretations.

If we regard the short lines as dividers, the centre by line-count is the central, ninetieth long line, 102. On the analogy of many poems of its time, and in view of the long-standing iconographical tradition of central accent, *Lycidas* might be expected to have a sovereign or triumphal image at this point. And in fact the central long line refers to Lycidas' 'sacred head'. But instead of mounting to its zenith, the orb-like part[29] is here brought to its nadir by death working through the mortal bark –

Built in th' eclipse, and rigg'd with curses dark,
That sunk so low that sacred head of thine.   102

To compensate for this sinking of the sun-poet into darkness at one structural centre, a far more prominent solar image mounts high at another. For the central paragraph, Stanza vi, enthrones Phoebus the sun-king himself, midmost of the planetary deities.

Some have thought Phoebus merely a pagan deity, and Daiches even detects irony in what he considers the 'deliberately false climax' of the reply of the god to the poet's nihilism.[30] But the Phoebus who plucks Milton's ear in warning, who touches the trembling lyre of his inspiration with a strain of 'higher mood' (77, 87) and who occupies the central position of sovereignty in the ode can only be a persona of the true God – the Christian *Sol iustitiae* rising to heal the believer (Mal. iv. 1). Phoebus' intervention to raise the poet's thought to a spiritual level is decisive enough to be given structural expression in another pattern, the symmetrical array of short-line distribution, which suggests a just division at this very point in the ode:

| Stanza | iii | iv | v | vi | vii | viii |
|---|---|---|---|---|---|---|
| Total of short lines | 1 | 3 | 1 | 1 | 3 | 1 |

Moreover, the stanza proportions reaffirm this effect, since the only repeated line-totals are those of i, v, vi and x:

| Stanza | i . . . v | | vi . . . x | |
|---|---|---|---|---|
| Line total | 14 | 14 | 21 | 21 |

Omitting the *commiato*, the ode again divides at the point of Phoebus' speech. Primarily, of course, this division expresses the justice of 'all judging *Jove*' the divider. But it is also of interest that line-totals forming the last symmetry are multiples of 7 that add to 70 (i.e. $14 + 14 + 21 + 21 = 10 \times 7$). For Valeriano interpreted the lyre as a symbol of human life, on the ground that its 70 notes correspond to the 10 hebdomads of the life-span.[31] Thus the proportions of *Lycidas* express God's equal judgement of human life, even where he appears to cut it off prematurely.

Phoebus' intervention is all the more salient since it comes as an unexpected irruption into a series of invocations. The latter belong themselves to an independent symmetrical array of substantive units. An initial series of 7 invocations – of *laurels*, *myrtles*, *Muses*, *Lycidas*, *nymphs*, *Arethuse*, *Mincius* – gives way to an exequy of the 4 mourners *Triton*, *Aeolus*, *Camus* and *St Peter*, succeeded in turn by 7 further invocations – of *Alpheus*, *Sicilian Muse*, *valleys*, *Lycidas*, *angel*, *dolphins* and *shepherds*.[32] Milton signalizes the tripartite division explicitly: 'now my Oate proceeds' (88); 'Return *Alpheus*, the dread voice is past' (132). But the dramatic sequence hardly needs such signposts: it is nothing if not an alternation between the poet's voice (addressing silent, mostly unseen, beings) and the voices of mourners at the funeral. Thus the primary large-scale movement resembles the *choresis* of a Neoplatonic triad. Looking at the arrangement of speeches in more detail, we see a number symbolism in the central placing of 4 speeches between groups of 7 invocations: 7s of mutability ordered and transformed by the virtuous *tetraktus*, the form-giving *vinculum* or spirit linking earth and heaven. On an even finer scale, the groups of 7 invocations contain further central accents, since the invocations of Lycidas himself come fourth in each case: 3 | *Lycidas* | 3 || *Exequy* || 3 | *Lycidas* | 3.

Any reader who notices this scheme will also notice two anomalies in it. The first, already mentioned, is Phoebus' interruption, breaking into the sequence of invocations from outside and above its order. The other is the fact that only 5 of the 7 invocations following the exequy can be called new invocations. (Invocations of Lycidas himself and of the Muses also figured in the first 7.) Thus, disregarding repetitions, we are free to regard the swain's fresh invocations as 12 in all, a number corresponding to the hours of his poem's day; forming, together with the speeches of others, the following symmetrical pattern: 5 | *Phoebus* | 2 | *Mourners at exequy* | 5. This more complex pattern draws attention to the structural relation between the first climax, Phoebus' speech, and the second, St Peter's. The apocalyptic *Sol iustitiae* at the zenith, in the central position of judgment,[33] logically brings on denunciation of the false church, the two-handed engine and the gate of heaven: the ode accomplishes time, looking forward with a sense of ending to the dread day when God 'pronounces lastly'. By reminding that death is not the end of human effort, Phoebus moves the ode from regret and nihilism to a higher plane of values. Camus and St Peter represent human and Christian responses to this challenge, their descriptions implying in symbolic terms the idea that death is a door for the reformed and the dedicated. Subsequently the Christian poet can look with hope even on the horror of bodily dismemberment.

Some will see the multiplicity of the patterns described above as an obstacle to belief that Milton intended them. But familiarity with the structural ambiguities of mannerist art – especially in garden design and in the articulation of architectural façades – accustoms us to accept such intricacies as a matter of course. Complex ambiguous patterns with multiple centres of interest were in keeping with the artistic ideals of Milton's time. In any case, Arthur Barker and other critics of *Lycidas* have shown that several structural interpretations are tenable; and such a sophisticated notion as that of a triple suite of climaxes in the content is quite in keeping with the complex formal patterns described above.[34]

Far from the 'accumulation of magnificent fragments' described by Wilson Knight,[35] we have in *Lycidas* one of the best-built poems in our literature; though its architectural style is now an unfamiliar one. On the other hand, it would be wrong to infer that Milton was mainly interested in formal finesse. On the contrary, his conception of the poet's role is religious and cosmic in its range. He means his Orphic lyre to link heaven with earth, his poem's numbers to form in the reader the resolution its content describes.

# NOTES

1 *AR*, i (1933), 179–203.

2 *The Italian Element in Milton's Verse* (Oxford, 1954), pp. 71–88.

3 *College English*, xvii (1956), 223–8.

4 *HLQ*, xv (1951–2), 325–50.

5 *MP*, lii (1954), 12–22.

6 In the following analysis I deal exclusively with the more carefully printed 1645 edn, since the 1638 paragraphing is inaccurate. Yet the whole volume of *Justa* and vernacular *Obsequies* was probably designed as a numerological construction. It contains 23 + 13 poems (= 36, the Great Quaternion), so that, if these are regarded as forming a circle, *Lycidas* (the last poem in the volume) would complete the 24-poem-hour sequence of the former group. As 24 + 12, the array would then be in the harmonious 1:2 proportion of the octave. Numerological considerations thus support M. Lloyd's suggestion, *N & Q*, cciii (1958), 432–4, that *Justa Eduardo King* was meant as a unified work. See further n. 22 below.

7 *Numerorum mysteria* (Bergamo, 1591), p. 383. Cf. p. 94 above and pp. 251f. below.

8 See my *Triumphal Forms* (Cambridge, 1970), ch. ix.

9 In this connection it is interesting that, as the thirty-sixth poem in *Justa Eduardo King*, Milton's completes yet another form of the *tetraktus* (see n. 6; the Great Quaternion 36 sums the first 4 odd and the first 4 even numbers). If this pattern is intentional, *Lycidas* serves as a coda to the volume, terminating the whole mourning rite.

10 For the conception of rhyme as a bond like that used in masonry, see Puttenham, *The Arte of English Poesie*, ed. G. D. Willcock and A. Walker (Cambridge, 1936), p. 89.

11 See below p. 174 and n. 15.

12 Other counts have been given, but there are in fact 14 short lines: 4, 19, 21, 33, 41, 43, 48, 56, 79, 88, 90, 95, 108, 145.

13 Such as Jan Porcellis' *Stormy Sea* (1629) at Munich, Bayerische Staatsgemäldesammlungen, no. 5742; illus. Wolfgang Stechow, *Dutch Landscape Painting of the Seventeenth Century* (1968), Fig. 219.

14 For *twitch* = pluck by the clothing, often as a cautionary gesture, see

*OED* s.v. *Twitch* v.[1] 1; e.g. Philippe de Mornay, *Trewnesse of the christian religion*, tr. Arthur Golding (1592), p. 341: 'Notwithstanding that our Lawe in every line ... doe reprove us for it, and after a sort twich us every hour by the Cote, to pull us from it.'

15 The *camus* (Lat. = collar, muzzle) was regularly an emblem of temperance and virtue; see, e.g., Valeriano, *Hieroglyphica* (Frankfort, 1613), p. 606, citing Vulg. Ps. xxxi. 9 *In camo et freno maxillas eorum constringe* ('Be ye not as the horse, or as the mule, which have no understanding: whose mouth must be held in with bit and bridle'). The fact that Camus' mantle is *hairy* strengthens this implication of discipline.

16 R. C. Fox, *Explicator* ix (1951), 54, interprets blue as a symbol of hope, and John Carey, *The Poems of John Milton*, ed. Carey and Fowler (1968), p. 254, compares *Faerie Queene*, I. x. 14, where Speranza wears blue. But see also Ben Jonson, *Part of the Kings entertainment* (1616), ed. Herford, Simpson and Simpson, vii. 89: 'Unanimity in blew, her roabe blew, and buskins. A chaplet of blew lillies, shewing one trueth and intirenesse of minde.' It is a coincidence Milton perhaps welcomed, that blue is associated with the isles of Elisha in Ezek. xxvii. 7: 'Blue ... from the isles of Elisha was that which covered thee.' On the *Musarum sacerdos* see Raymond Klibansky and others, *Saturn and Melancholy* (1964), p. 245. Cf. William Belsham, *Essays* (1789–91) I. xii. 229; 'the sacred mantle which descended from Shakespeare to Milton'.

17 The commoner meaning at the time (Carey 253); though the modest sense 'clumsy' is also functional.

18 Carey, who discusses the opening invocations at some length (239f.), notes that a crown of laurel, myrtle and ivy occurs in Ripa's image of *Accademia*. For a fuller account of these emblematic literary trees see Robert J. Clements, *Picta poesis*, Temi e Testi, vi (Rome, 1960), pp. 229 *et passim*, and Joseph B. Trapp in *JWI*, xxi (1958), 227–55.

19 Manilius, *The Sphere*, tr. Edward Sherburne (1675), p. 26. On the theological significance of Orpheus in Renaissance thought, see D. P. Walker, 'Orpheus the Theologian and Renaissance Platonists', *JWI*, xvi (1953), 100–20.

20 Ll. 168ff. Throughout, imagery suggests the rotation of the heavens; see, e.g., 30f.: 'Oft till the Star that rose, at Ev'ning, bright, / Toward Heav'n's descent had slop'd his westering wheel.' Northrop Frye discusses natural cycles referred to in the ode (C. A.

Patrides [ed.], *Milton's 'Lycidas': The Tradition and the Poem* [New York, 1961], pp. 200–11); but draws conclusions relating to mythic archetypes I can find no sign of in the poem.

21 Ending perhaps in the Orphic night, which is oneness with God in the abyss of original unity; see Edgar Wind, *Pagan Mysteries in the Renaissance* (rev. edn 1967), pp. 65 n., 276ff.

22 Again cf. Henry King's 'The Exequy'. Several of the *Obsequies* for Edward King express the same idea numerologically by the use of temporal measures. Beaumont's and Henry King's Obsequies – like 'The Exequy' – are in 60 couplets (the latter with an indented concluding couplet epitaph); though here a Biblical number symbolism, whereby the line-total 120 stands for the ideal duration of the good life (Bongo, p. 588), complicates the issue. Another of the *Obsequies*, C. B.'s, is in 24 lines. In a wider context, cf. Michelangelo's Medici Chapel, with its Times of Day expressing the destructive power of the temporal process.

23 St Augustine, *Epist.* LV. ix. 17. See also Otto von Simson, *The Gothic Cathedral* (New York, 1956), p. 40; and above, pp. 43, 50, 98ff.

24 *OED* s.v. *Quill* sb.¹ 3 c; *Stop* sb.² 15 b (e.g. Bacon, *Sylva*: 'to raise or fall his Voice, still by Halfe-Notes, like the Stops of a Lute' – perhaps the *commiato* is to count as a half-tone compared with the whole tones of the stanzas); and *Twitch* v.¹ 3. In Renaissance visual art Orpheus was commonly portrayed holding a lute or viol.

25 The magical power of numbers is a principal theme of H. C. Agrippa's *De occulta philosophia* (Antwerp and Paris, 1531).

26 J. E. Cirlot, *A Dictionary of Symbols*, tr. J. Sage (1962), p. 186; Natale Conti, *Mythologiae* VII. xiii (Lyons, 1653), p. 761. According to Ptolemy's setting, as it happened, the constellation Lyra comprised 10 stars; according to Kepler's, 11. The pipes of Pan were similarly interpreted in a cosmic sense; see Conti V. vi; p. 454.

27 Bongo, pp. 359, 371; see above, pp. 46f., 49.

28 The phenomenon of central accent, first explicitly discussed with reference to English Literature by Gunnar Qvarnström, *Dikten och den nya vetenskapen*. Acta Reg. Soc. Humaniorum Litterarum Lundensis lx (Lund, 1961), but earlier noticed by critics of the Elizabethan lyric (e.g., on *Epithalamion*, Janet Spens, Variorum Spenser *Minor Poems* ii 647 and T. M. Greene, *Comp. Lit.* ix [1957] 225 n.), has since been extensively analysed. See above, pp. 56ff., 149; Maren-Sofie Røstvig, 'The Hidden Sense' in *The Hidden Sense and*

*other Essays*, Norwegian Studies in English, ix (Oslo, 1963); and my own *Spenser and the Numbers of Time* (1964), Index, s.v. *Central position of sovereignty*; and *Triumphal Forms*, chs ii–v.

29 The connection of Orpheus' and Lycidas' heads with the sun would be an obvious one, when the circular part of the body was often compared by symbologists with the heavenly orbs. See *Spenser and the Numbers of Time*, pp. 262f., citing Lactantius and Francesco Giorgio.

30 David Daiches, *Milton* (1957), p. 84.

31 *Hieroglyphica*, p. 593; cf. p. 591, where Orpheus' lyre symbolizes *Bona disciplina*. The second half of the ode is framed by references to mantles (104, 192) in such a way as to imply a connection between the image and formal bisection; thus recalling Elisha's division of his clothes into 2 parts as an act of mourning, before he took up the mantle of Elijah, in II Kings ii. 12 – a text that provided the basis for several numerological programmes during the seventeenth century (see *Triumphal Forms*, ch. iv).

32 Ivy (l. 2), though grouped 'with' the laurels and myrtles, is not addressed in the second person as they are.

33 On the astronomical development of the *Sol iustitiae* type with the sun in mid-heaven, see Erwin Panofsky, *Meaning in the Visual Arts* (Garden City, N.Y., 1955), pp. 262f.

34 'The Pattern of Milton's "Nativity Ode" ', *UTQ*, x (1941); M. Y. Hughes (ed.), *John Milton: Complete Poems and Major Prose* (New York, 1957), p. 118; and J. S. Lawry, 'Eager Thought: Dialectic in *Lycidas*', *PMLA*, lxxvii (1962). On the relation of Milton's poetry to the art styles of his time much has been written. Little or none of it, however, deals with formal structure, with respect to which comparisons between the sister arts are appropriate and relatively exact. See Roy Daniells, *Milton, Mannerism and Baroque* (Toronto, 1963); Rosemond Tuve, 'Baroque and Mannerist Milton?', *JEGP*, lx (1961).

35 *The Burning Oracle* (1939), 70.

# The structure of Dryden's
## *Song for St Cecilia's Day, 1687*

ALASTAIR FOWLER

DOUGLAS BROOKS

*A Song for* ST CECILIA's *Day, 1687*

From Harmony, from heav'nly Harmony
  This universal Frame began.
    When Nature underneath a heap
      Of jarring Atomes lay,
        And cou'd not heave her Head,
The tuneful Voice was heard from high,
      Arise ye more than dead.
Then cold, and hot, and moist, and dry,
    In order to their stations leap,
      And MUSICK's pow'r obey.
From Harmony, from heav'nly Harmony
  This universal Frame began:
From Harmony to Harmony
  Through all the compass of the Notes it ran,
  The Diapason closing full in Man.

  ii

What Passion cannot MUSICK raise and quell!
When *Jubal* struck the corded Shell.
  His list'ning Brethren stood around
And wond'ring, on their Faces fell
  To worship that Celestial Sound.
Less than a God they thought there cou'd not dwell
Within the hollow of that Shell
That spoke so sweetly and so well.
What Passion cannot MUSICK raise and quell!

iii

The TRUMPETS loud Clangor
  Excites us to Arms
With shrill Notes of Anger
  And mortal Alarms.
The double double double beat
  Of the thundring DRUM
  Cryes, heark the Foes come;
Charge, Charge, 'tis too late to retreat.

iv

The soft complaining FLUTE
  In dying Notes discovers
  The Woes of hopeless Lovers,
Whose Dirge is whisper'd by the warbling LUTE.

v

Sharp VIOLINS proclaim
  Their jealous Pangs, and Desperation,
  Fury, frantick Indignation,
  Depth of Pains, and height of Passion,
For the fair, disdainful Dame.

vi

But oh! what Art can teach
What human Voice can reach
  The sacred ORGANS praise?
  Notes inspiring holy Love,
  Notes that wing their heav'nly ways
    To mend the Choires above.

vii

*Orpheus* cou'd lead the savage race;
And Trees unrooted left their place;
  Sequacious of the Lyre:
  But bright *CECILIA* rais'd the wonder high'r;

When to her ORGAN, vocal Breath was giv'n
  An Angel heard, and straight appear'd
Mistaking Earth for Heaven.

(GRAND CHORUS)

*As from the pow'r of sacred Lays*
  *The Spheres began to move,*
*And sung the great Creator's praise*
  *To all the bless'd above;*
*So when the last and dreadful hour*
  *This crumbling Pageant shall devour,*
*The* TRUMPET *shall be heard on high,*
*The Dead shall live, the Living die,*
*And* MUSICK *shall untune the Sky.*

[Text from first edn, 1687]

Two recent articles have suggested that Dryden's *A Song for St Cecilia's Day, 1687* may be altogether a more complex poem than it at first appears to be.[1] The aim of the present paper is to demonstrate that this is in fact the case; and that a way into the complexity lies through the *Song*'s structural pattern, which is built according to a coherent system of number symbolism.

Before discussing the poem's numerical structure it will be useful to recall what, in a simple sense, it is about. Dryden is celebrating creation; from the creation of the universe, through the creation of man, to the ultimate destruction of both on the Day of Judgment. Throughout, creation is considered as a form of music. This is the direct subject of the first and last stanzas. The inner stanzas, however, deal with what seems at first a different and much more specific subject, the effect of music on man: 'What Passion cannot MUSICK raise and quell!'[2] But in fact the ordering of the passions of man is presented as a microcosm of the larger operation of cosmic harmony. In particular, stanzas iii–vi describe forms of music conducive to the 4 temperaments, the choleric, melancholic, phlegmatic, and sanguine: equivalents in man of the 4 concordant elements that separate from chaos to form the macrocosm.[3]

**187**

Since this last point already brings us to a structural scheme not previously noticed, it is worth demonstrating at some length.

The martial preoccupations of Stanza iii are sufficient to indicate that it deals with music producing the choleric temperament. This is confirmed by the explicit mention of 'Anger' at line 27. But it would once have been no less clearly confirmed by the introduction of trumpet and drum; for from an iconographical standpoint both instruments were traditional attributes of the choleric temperament. Thus in Athanasius Kircher's *Musurgia* (Rome, 1650) we read that 'On account of the strength of their raging bile, cholerics long for similar motions in music. Hence warlike men, accustomed to trumpets and drums, seem to dislike all music of a softer kind.'[4]

Marin Mersenne's *Harmonie Universelle* (Paris, 1636) mentions the same instruments when discussing how to represent the various passions in music by accentuation. Accentuation, he says,

> donnera une telle grace et un tel air aux chants, et aux recits, que tous ceux qui les oyront, avoueront qu'ils sont animez, et pleins de vigeur et d'esprit, dont ils sont destituez sans ces accents, esquels les Compositeurs se peuvent instruire en considerant les batemens des chamades, et des charges sur le tambour, et celles des trompettes, dont les derniers sons de chaque mesure representent la cholere par la promptitude, et la force du coup be baston ou de langue.[5]

It is important to note this association of *promptitude* with the choleric temperament; it accounts for the *Song's* change, in this stanza only, to a partially anapaestic metre. Swiftness, continues Mersenne, can be conveyed by quavers, semi-quavers, and the like: '*Quant à la promptitude, l'on a des notes crochues, ou doubles, et triples crochues, qui vont assez viste pour marquer la vitesse de tous les degrez des passions les plus rapides. . . .'[6]*

Dryden's change of metre produces an exactly analogous effect, in prosodic terms.

Stanza iv is just as obviously concerned with the effect of music on the melancholic temperament. The overt portrayal is of a lover's melancholy: a 'Dirge' disclosing lovers' 'Woes' is described in terms applicable to the lovers themselves: 'complaining', 'dying'. More obliquely, the instruments referred to are those symbolically appropriate to the melancholic temperament in general. Thus Mersenne, writing of the organ and its various stops (quoting Giovanni Doni's *Trattato dei Generi e Modi*), says that '*les tuyaux qui font la flute d'Allemand [sont bons] pour [exprimer] le Lidien*'. And the Lydian mode is, of course, the mode assigned to melancholy, as Mersenne reminds us only a few lines earlier: '*la [Musique] Systaltique remplie de tristesse [est propre] pour le Lidien*'.[7] The passage also associates the lute with the Lydian mode: an association that was ancient and general.

In the same way, the phlegmatic temperament is treated in Stanza v. Here the clue lies in the opening reference to 'Sharp VIOLINS'; for the phlegmatic's affinity to sharp sounds was well known. Kircher remarks: 'Phlegmatics are influenced by the harmony of soprano female voices; since a sharp sound affects the phlegmatic humour favourably'.[8] Even the specification of violins as the instrument producing sharp sound was traditional. Mersenne writes that '*les airs . . . des Violons excitent davantage à raison de leur gayeté qui vient . . . de leurs sons aigus*'.[9]

Finally, Stanza vi completes the scheme by dealing with the music of the sanguine temperament. The final position has a climactic force, because the sanguine man enjoys the best-tempered constitution. His is the *complexio temperata*, the complexion 'almost always considered the best or noblest'.[10] Medieval tradition even had it that the *homo sanguineus* most nearly resembled the sinless Adam. Before the Fall, the natural temperament of man had been sanguine.[11] It is easy to see, therefore, why the sanguine temperament should have as its attribute the 'sacred ORGAN'. For, just as the sanguine is the Christian, and the only tempered, disposition, so is the organ the supreme instrument. Within itself it contains, because of the variety of its stops, all the modes. As Mersenne puts it, quoting Doni again: '*l'Orgue peut servir à exprimer chaque mode, à raison du grand nombre de ses jeux*'.[12] The organ is also the instrument of St Cecilia, the exemplary Christian of the poem.

Thus, the middle stanzas of the *Song* enact the raising of passions characteristic of the 4 elementally-based human temperaments. The harmonizing of these, and the framing of a divinely-inspired nature including and surpassing them, is a musical image of the creation of the microcosmic man, and of his sanctification.


2

This in itself leads one to suspect some numerical expression of the *Song*'s ideas. For in Dryden's time such musical or poetical analogies of creation were invariably based on the notion of numerical proportion. It was commonplace to compare creation to a poem; and it was commonplace to substantiate the comparison by referring to the common basis of number. The idea had a long history; Cowley pillaged St Augustine to write:

> Such was *Gods Poem*, this *Worlds* new *Essay*;
> So wild and rude in its first draught it lay;
> Th'ungovern'd parts no *Correspondence* knew,
> An artless *war* from thwarting *Motions* grew;
> Till they to *Number* and fixt Rules were brought
> By the *eternal Minds Poetique Thought*.[13]

and annotated the passage as follows:

> the *Scripture* witnesses, that the World was made in *Number*, *Weight*, and *Measure*; which are all qualities of a good *Poem*. This order and proportion of things is the true *Musick* of the world. . . .[14]

The most striking formal feature of the first stanza of the *Song* is the repetition of the opening 2 lines –

> From Harmony, from heav'nly Harmony
> This universal Frame began –

as lines 11–12. It is natural to ask what may be the *function* of this repetition. The poem's formal reply to this question is clear. The repeated lines are, on the occasion of their first use, opening lines. It is reasonable, therefore, to regard their function as in some sense inceptive on the second occasion also. In other words, to think of the stanza as consisting of 2 parts, each beginning with the same pair of lines. The first part thus contains 10 lines; the second, 5. Or, expressing the structure as a proportion, we can say that the stanza is divided in the ratio 10 : 5 or 2 : 1. Now this is the octave proportion, i.e., the numerical expression of the relationship between a musical note and the note one octave above or below it. Thus the stanza can be seen as conveying, in formal terms, the 'Diapason' mentioned in its final line, 'The Diapason closing full in Man'. And even the notion of a 'Diapason . . . in Man', of little significance to most modern readers, can be unpacked in some detail. In Macrobius, the medieval authority on the symbolism of musical intervals, we read that 'the Soul had to be a combination of those numbers that alone possess mutual attraction since the Soul itself was to instill harmonious agreement in the whole world. Now two is double one and . . . the octave arises from the double.'[15]

And since the time of Pico della Mirandola it had been quite fashionable to treat the adjustment of the three Platonic faculties as a 'composition' of the intervals fifth and fourth into an integrated octave.

It will have occurred to some of our readers, however, that it is possible to consider the repeated lines of the first stanza in a different way. With J. A. Levine,[16] we may see them as *framing* the 8 lines on the composition of chaos into a 'universal Frame': *repeated lines | 8 lines | repeated lines.*

The repetition would then enact, as it were, creation's cyclic return to unison and to the One from which it took its origin: 'This monad, the beginning and ending of all things, yet itself not knowing a beginning or ending, refers to the Supreme God. . . .'[17] But what now becomes of the division of the stanza into the octave proportion? In a curious way that felicity is not only preserved, but even enhanced. For now lines 1–12 constitute a completed framed universe, leaving 3 lines outstanding. Hence the stanza is divided into the ratio 12 : 3 or 4 : 1, the proportion of the disdiapason or double octave.[18]

The stanza is also able to mime the double octave in quite a different, and most ingenious manner. Line 14 – 'Through all the compass of the Notes it ran' – can hardly, in this context, be anything but an invitation to look for a formal correlative to the separate notes of the diapason. The most obvious possibility is that lines correspond to notes, just as the stanza (set of lines) corresponds to the octave (set of notes). Now the lines of the stanza total 15, and 15 is, in fact, the number of notes in a double octave.[19] For in running through all the notes of 2 octaves of the diatonic scale, the tonic is sounded only 3, not 4, times; so that there are 15, not 16, notes.

## 3

The first stanza's formal insistence on the octave is repeated on a larger scale in the overall structure of the *Song*. For it consists of just 8 stanzas: a macrocosm, as it were, of which the first stanza is the microcosm.

J. A. Levine has drawn attention to the circularity of the diapason's compass. Every octave returns to its first note, repeating the octave below it in a progression that can be continued (in the imagination at least) to infinity.[20] This circularity finds its reflection in many ways in the poem's substantive structure. Thus it has already been noted that line 61, '*The* TRUMPET *shall be heard on high*', is in unison with line 6, 'The tuneful Voice was heard from high'; just as Stanza ii, dealing with Jubal, Biblical founder of music, matches Stanza vii, dealing with Orpheus and Cecilia. The latter pairing is made obvious by the exact response of Jubal's 'corded Shell' (i.e. lyre) to Orpheus' powerful instrument of civilization.[21] To these substantive circularities may be added formal ones, such as the echo of 'The tuneful Voice' of Stanza i in the mention of 'untuning' in Stanza viii, and the poem's ending with the same rhyme with which it begins.

Further patterns of return to unison can be traced in individual stanzas of the *Song*. Thus in Stanza ii, the first line ('What Passion cannot MUSICK raise and quell!') is repeated verbatim as the last (line 24). Similarly, in Stanza iv the external rhyme-words 'FLUTE' and 'LUTE' make a return to unison, the 2 outer lines encircling the 2 inner – which are themselves in unison by virtue of rhyme, length, and feminine ending. And in Stanza v, 2 outer lines unified by rhyme encircle 3 inner. The point of this circularity – this persistent return to unison not only in the large structure of the poem (Stanza i answered by Stanza viii) but also in the organization of individual stanzas – lies in the conception of the monad as a symbol of 'the Supreme God'. The monad gives rise to all numbers and all being, and having done so returns to itself.

Hence, in Pythagorean thought, the decad was a number of perfection because it marked a circular return to the One from the multiplicity of the preceding digits. It was identified with the monad on the ground that succeeding decads (10, 20, 30 . . . 100) merely repeat the progression of the initial decad (1, 2, 3 . . . 10), just as one octave repeats another.[22] The link between numerical and musical circularities is beautifully effected by Dryden when he makes the number of instruments mentioned in the *Song* number 10: 'corded Shell', 'TRUMPET' (twice), 'DRUM', 'FLUTE', 'LUTE', 'VIOLIN', 'ORGAN' (twice), and 'Lyre'. For 10 was a form of the *tetraktus* $(1 + 2 + 3 + 4 = 10)$; and the *tetraktus* was believed to contain the intervals on which the harmony of the universe was based. From it were generated the ratios $2:1$ (diapason), $3:2$ (diapente), $4:3$ (diatessaron), $3:1$ (diapason kai diapente), $4:1$ (disdiapason), and $9:8$ (superoctave).[23]

## 4

We have now to consider the symbolism of the line totals of certain other stanzas of the *Song*. It is obvious that the fact that Stanza iv has 4 lines, Stanza v 5 lines, Stanza vi 6 lines, and Stanza vii 7 lines, alludes to the series of whole integers, and in this context, consequently, to the Pythagorean decad. The remaining stanzas, however, present at first more difficulty.

The notion underlying their numerology is one that is encountered in many literary works of the sixteenth and seventeenth centuries: namely, an antithesis of 7 and 9. In this antithesis the former is always corporeal, the latter spiritual. 7 is the number of the body, and of this world considered as a physical and mutable entity;[24] 9 is the number of the mind, of the spheres, of the angelic hierarchies, and of heaven itself.

A good example of the substantive application of this symbolism is Spenser's mathematical description of human nature in *The Faerie Queene*, II. ix. 22. The stanza opens with the pun on *frame* (temperament, building) that we have already eneountered in Dryden's opening lines: a pun that implies the notion that man is a microcosm by virtue of the moral ordering, as well as the structure, of his nature:

> The frame thereof seemd partly circulare,
>     And part triangulare, O worke divine;
>     Those two the first and last proportions are,
>     The one imperfect, mortall, foeminine:
>     Th'other immortall, perfect, masculine,
>     And twixt them both a quadrate was the base,
>     Proportioned equally by seven and nine;
>     Nine was the circle set in heavens place,
> All which compacted made a goodly diapase.

Spenser's just proportioning of human nature by 7 and 9 refers to the harmonious adjustment of corporeal and spiritual parts. The meaning of 'quadrate' is more controversial; but from our present point of view it is perhaps enough to cite Sir Kenelm Digby's interpretation. Writing in 1644 he identified it with the 4 humours,

> viz. *Choler, Blood, Phleme,* and *Melancholy*: which if they be distempered and unfitly mingled, dissolution of the whole doth immediately ensue: like to a building which falls to ruine, if the foundation and Base of it be unsound or disordered. And in some of these, the vitall spirits are contained and preserved, which the other keep in convenient temper; and as long as they do so, the soul and bodie dwell together like good friends, so that these foure are the Base of the conjunction of the other two, both which he saith, are

Proportion'd equally by seven and nine.[25]

The compacting of 7 and 9 into a diapason is a more complex idea. Arithmetically, Spenser implies that the mean between 7 and 9 is 8. Or, $7+9=2\times 8$. But he probably also means to invoke an arithmological tradition, going back to the *In somnium Scipionis*, according to which

> the soul was . . . derived from musical concords. Among these an important one is the diapason, which consists of two others, the fourth and the fifth. The interval of the fifth is based on the ratio of three to two and the interval of the fourth on the ratio of four to three; in one the first term is three and in the other four. . . .[26]

(It is worth noting that Macrobius carefully points out that 'in one the first term is three and in the other four'. The passage occurs in the course of his explanation of the meaning of the heptad.) Pico, in his Pythagorean *Conclusiones*, gave the symbolism a more psychological though also a more arbitrary flavour, when he identified the fifth as the proportion between the irascible and concupiscible faculties, and the fourth as the proportion between the reasonable soul and the irascible faculty. Compacted, these intervals give the diapason, the correct proportion between the rational soul and the concupiscible faculty.[27] This notion attained a certain vogue, and seventeenth-century mystics sometimes developed it with grotesque particularity. In that school we may mention Fr. Athanasius Kircher, who constructed a complete *Pentedecachordon animae* (Fig., p. 196):

Returning to Dryden's *Song* with these ideas in mind, we see at once that there is a relation of line-count numerology between two stanzas already shown to be paired in another way. Stanzas ii and vii (which are connected by the correspondence of Jubal's and Orpheus' lyres) have 9 and 7 lines respectively. Together, they compose a double diapason of harmony, which 'frames' or tempers the same 4 central stanzas (the passions) that it – in another sense – 'frames' spatially. The pattern is completed by the creation of another double diapason, for the 7 lines of Stanza vii

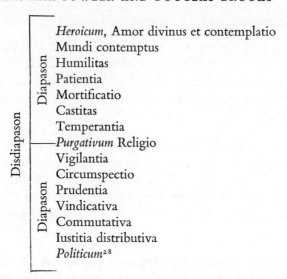

*Heroicum*, Amor divinus et contemplatio
Mundi contemptus
Humilitas
Patientia
Mortificatio
Castitas
Temperantia
*Purgativum* Religio
Vigilantia
Circumspectio
Prudentia
Vindicativa
Commutativa
Iustitia distributiva
*Politicum*[28]

are succeeded by the 9 lines of Stanza viii. We are no doubt intended to hear this last double diapason as a response to the initial one announced in Stanza i. The octave symbolism, it seems, is meant to convey much more than a diffuse sense of harmoniousness.

The full harmony between Stanza ii and Stanza vii is not heard, however, until the detailed structure of Stanza ii is recalled. As we have shown, it possesses a circular, framed structure of its own (the repetition of its first line as its last). Thus, its 9 lines can be analysed as a seven-line narrative of the effects of Jubal's 'corded Shell' on his listeners, framed by 2 single lines in unison. Not only is this pattern a microcosm of the larger framing of the 4 temperaments by Stanzas ii and vii: it also underlines the relationship with Stanza vii and its 7 lines. We are to think, it seems, of a *7 contained in a 9*. The same point is made in the substantive connection between Stanzas ii and vii, the recurrence of the lyre: in the classical period it was customary for the lyre to have 7 strings,[29] and these were regularly interpreted as corresponding to the 7 planets.[30]

These same 2 numbers control, in another way, the structure of the whole *Song*. Because 7 was the corporeal and 9 the spiritual number, 7 and 9 were thought to have the power to determine the critical stages of human life. According to the widely-known theory of the 'grades' of human life,[31] there were certain climacterics, of which the first and last were 49 years and 81 years ($7^2$ and $9^2$). But the most important climacteric, since it pertained to both the corporeal and spiritual qualities of human nature, was the median one derived from the multiplication of 9 by 7. It is surely in allusion to this theory that Dryden has given his poem an overall line total of 63.

## 5

Finally, we note that the *Song* is divided into 7 numbered stanzas, together with a 'Grand Chorus' which stands apart by being unnumbered and also through italicization. In view of the overall subject of the poem – the creation leading to the Day of Judgment when '*The Dead shall live, the Living die*' – this adding of a further stanza to a 7-stanza unit to bring the total to 8 again seems to possess symbolic significance. 7 is, as we have seen, the corporeal number, mutable and earthly. It is therefore appropriate that the first 7 stanzas should recount the creation and the effects of music on man, and end by explicitly mentioning 'Earth'. But 8, because it succeeds the mutable 7, was understood by arithmologists to be the number of eternity and regeneration. A specifically Christian significance accrued to it since the resurrection occurred on the eighth day after the beginning of Holy Week. Hence baptismal fonts were often given octagonal form.[32] It is for this reason that in Stanza viii, and only there, Dryden announces the ultimate resurrection.

The *locus classicus* for the symbolism is the Epistles of St Augustine, but Spenser's *Faerie Queene* also provides a good, and readily available, source. Canto vii of the incomplete Book VII is devoted, appropriately enough if we recall the significance of 7, to Dame Mutabilitie's assertion of her sovereignty in the universe. This is immediately followed by Spenser's vision of eternity, situated in the 'unperfite' Canto viii:

> For, all that moveth, doth in *Change* delight:
> But thence-forth all shall rest eternally
> With Him that is the God of Sabbaoth hight:
> O! that great Sabbaoth God, graunt me that Sabaoths sight.

Just as Spenser expressed the end of earthly flux in 'eternal rest' through the symbolism of 7 and 8, so, it appears, does Dryden in his *Song*. It is worth recalling that, against Book VII. vii. 12 in his 1679 copy of *The Faerie Queene*, Dryden wrote the words 'groundwork for a song on St Cecilia's day'.[33]

The *Song* contains other numerical subtleties – the mention of the virgin Cecilia in Stanza vii alone probably alludes to the traditional association of 7 with virginity, for example;[34] while the fact that Stanza vi deals with the harmonious organ and the sanguine, tempered, complexion alludes to the connection of the number 6 with harmony.[35] But clearly these are peripheral considerations beside the much more detailed and profound number schemes outlined above. When Dryden composed his *Song* in honour of God's creation of the world and of man, he organized it in such a way that it generated, through its form, the very harmonies it was celebrating. To those with ears to hear it expressed what Cowley, in his *Davideis*, called 'the true *Musick* of the world'.

# NOTES

1 E. R. Wasserman, 'Pope's "Ode for Musick"', *ELH*, xxviii (1961), 163–86; J. A. Levine, 'Dryden's "Song for St Cecilia's Day, 1687"', *PQ*, xliv (1965), 38–50.

2 Quotations are from the first edn as reprinted in Vol. ii of *The Poems of John Dryden*, ed. James Kinsley, 4 vols. (Oxford, 1958).

3 The connection between the temperaments and elements is discussed at length in R. Klibansky, E. Panofsky and F. Saxl, *Saturn and Melancholy* (1964), Pt I, Ch. i.

4 (Rome, 1650), i, 544: 'Cholerici ob bilis effervescentis vehementiam similes harmonicos motus appetunt. Hinc martiales viri ad tubas, et tympana assuefacti, omnem delicatiorem musicam respuere videntur.'

5 '*Harmonie Universelle contenant la Théorie et la Pratique de la Musique* (Paris, 1636); facs. ed. François Lesure (Paris, 1963), *Traitez des Consonances, des Dissonances*, Bk VI, Pt iii, Proposition 15.

6 *Ibid.*

7 *Ibid.*, *Traité des Instrumens à chordes*, Bk VII, Proposition 30.

8 'Phlegmatici acutarum muliebrium vocum symphoniis afficiuntur, siquidem acutus sonus humorem phlegmaticum benigne afficit.' (*Musurgia*, i, 544.)

9 *Harmonie Universelle, Traitez de la Voix, et des Chants*, Bk II, Proposition 26.

10 Klibansky *et al.*, *Saturn and Melancholy*, p. 59. See also pp. 13, 62, 64.

11 *Ibid.*, pp. 103, 105.

12 *Harmonie Universelle, Traité des Instrumens à chordes*, Bk VII, Proposition 30.

13 *Davideis*, i, in *Works* (1668), p. 13.

14 *Ibid.*, p. 36.

15 *Commentary on the Dream of Scipio*, II. ii. 18; tr. W. H. Stahl (New York, 1952), p. 192.

16 'Dryden's "Song"', pp. 38–40.

17 Macrobius, *Commentary*, I. vi. 8 (pp. 100–1).

18 *Ibid.*, II. i. 19 (p. 188).

19 It was also the traditional number of keys.

20 'Dryden's "Song"', pp. 41–2.

21 *Ibid.*, pp. 40, 45–8.
22 The association of the decad with the circle, and its identification with the monad, is made, for example, by Pietro Bongo, *Numerorum mysteria* (Bergamo, 1599), p. 358.
23 See Bongo, pp. 197–8 and 356–7 on the decad's containing the *tetraktus*, and p. 223 for his working out of the ratios yielded by the *tetraktus*. Macrobius, *Commentary*, II. i. 15–20 (p. 188) also gives an account of these ratios.
24 See *Macrobius*, I. vi. 48–81 (pp. 109–17).
25 *Observations on the 22.Stanza in the 9th Canto of the 2nd.Book of Spencers Faery Queen* in *Variorum Spenser*, ed. E. Greenlaw *et al.*, 10 vols. (Baltimore, 1932–57), ii, 475–6.
26 I. vi. 43 (p. 108).
27 Pico della Mirandola, *Conclusiones secundum mathematicam Pythagorae*, Nos 8–10 (*Opera omnia* [Basel, 1601], i, 53).
28 *Musurgia*, ii, 431.
29 See *Encyclopaedia Britannica* (1964 edn), s.v. *Lyre*.
30 The association is made, for example, by Kircher, *Musurgia*, i, 537.
31 Vincent F. Hopper, 'Spenser's "House of Temperance" ', *PMLA*, lv (1940), 962.
32 V. F. Hopper, *Medieval Number Symbolism* (New York, 1938), pp. 77, 85, 90, 101, 114, and 178.
33 C. E. Ward, *The Life of John Dryden* (Chapel Hill, N.C. and London, 1961), pp. 234–5, 360, n. 16.
34 See Macrobius, *Commentary*, I. vi. 11 (p. 102): 'The reputation of virginity has so grown about the number seven that it is called Pallas.'
35 The symbolism was based partly on the fact that there are 6 tones in the octave. See Martianus Capella, *De nuptiis Philologiae et Mercurii*, ed. A. Dick (Leipzig, 1925), sect. 737, p. 372. Bongo, *Numerorum mysteria*, pp. 267–8 refers to the harmonious quality of 6 and Martianus Capella's attribution of it to Venus, 'mother of harmony'.

Supporting considerations for the suggestion that Dryden is using 6 in this sense here are the mention of 'Harmony' 6 times in Stanza i; the appearance of 'The tuneful Voice' in line 6; and the fact that there are 6 stanzas (ii–vii) devoted to earthly music, from Jubal to Cecilia. (It is also worth bearing in mind that there were traditionally 6 ages to the world; so that the creation (St. i) and Last Judgment (St. viii) frame the correct number of stanza-ages.)

# The structure of Shadwell's
## *A Song for St Cecilia's Day, 1690*

H. NEVILLE DAVIES

I

During the 1680s and 90s it became the custom in London for the so-called Musical Society to celebrate St Cecilia's Day with the performance of a specially commissioned ode and with a feast.[1] The two most distinguished of these odes are Dryden's *A Song for St Cecilia's Day, 1687* ('From Harmony, from heav'nly Harmony') and his 'Alexander's Feast' of ten years later. Three recent articles about the first of Dryden's Cecilian odes have examined its structure, and though some of this analysis may seem over-ingenious, the broad outlines of the poem's numerological structure are now firmly established.[2] The precise point at which objective description of a text becomes creative invention prompted by that text is an issue on which opinion may differ. Universal approbation may not be given to the contention that 'the link between numerical and musical circularities is beautifully effected by Dryden when he makes the number of instruments mentioned in the Song number 10,[3] but few will doubt that Dryden's choice of 8 stanzas for his poem relates to the musical octave.

During the two years following 1687 the Musical Society seems not to have celebrated its patronal festival, no doubt because of the political situation in November 1688 (William landed less than three weeks before St Cecilia's Day) and possibly for the same reason in 1689. In 1690 the celebrations were resumed, and Thomas Shadwell, who the previous year had replaced Dryden as Poet Laureate and Historiographer Royal, was the author of the commissioned ode; though whether, as is just possible, he had written it for one of the two intervening years in which there had been no celebrations is not known. Whatever the circumstances, Shadwell must have found his great rival's fine poem a daunting example: comparisons were bound to be made and it was known

that Shadwell prided himself on competence in musical matters.[4]
We would expect Shadwell to have studied Dryden's ode closely,
and are not surprised to find verbal echoes of it in his own poem
(e.g. 'jarring atoms' / 'warring Atoms', 'the universal frame' /
'The Universe you fram'd', etc.), as well as Renaissance ideas
about cosmological music, which Dryden had handled so well
but which are much less important in the earlier and rather trivial
St Cecilia odes of Fishburn (1683), an anonymous versifier of
1683, Oldham (1684) and Tate (1685); though there are hints of
more serious notions in Fletcher's (1686, possibly for celebrations
at Oxford, not published until 1693).

Shadwell responded intelligently to the commission of the
stewards of the society, and though his poem is a pale affair beside
its predecessor, it is a good deal better than any of the earlier
poems, except Dryden's, and than many of the later ones. It
rises to, even if it does not transcend, its occasion. If Shadwell
has perhaps only laboured to be dull, at any rate his ode is not
nonsensical:

i

O Sacred Harmony, prepare our Lays,
While on *Cecilia*'s Day, we sing your Praise,
From Earth to Heav'n our warbling Voices raise!

ii

Join all ye glorious Instruments around,
The yielding Air with your Vibrations wound,
And fill Heav'n's Concave with the mighty Sound.

iii

You did at first the warring Atoms join,
Made Qualities most opposite combine,
While Discords did with pleasing Concords twine.

iv

The Universe you fram'd, you still sustain;
Without you what in Tune does now remain
Wou'd jangle into *Chaos* once again.

V

It does your most transcendent Glory prove,
That, to compleat immortal Joys above,
There must be Harmony to crown their Love.

vi

Dirges with Sorrow still inspire
The doleful and lamenting Quire,
With swelling Hearts and flowing Eyes,
They solemnize their Obsequies;
For Grief they frequent Discords chuse,
Long Bindings and Chromaticks use.
Organs and Viols sadly Groan
To the Voice's dismal Tone.

vii

If Love's gentle Passions we
Express, there must be Harmony;
We touch the soft and tender Flute,
The sprinkling and melodious Lute,
When we describe the tickling Smart
Which does invade a Love-sick Heart:
Sweet Nymphs in pretty Murmurs plain,
All chill and panting with the pleasing Pain,
Which can be eas'd by nothing but the Swain.

viii

If Poets, in a lofty Epic Strain,
    Some ancient-noble History recite,
    How Heroes love, and puissant Conquerors fight,
Or how on cruel Fortune they complain:
        Or if a Muse the Fate of Empires sings,
        The Change of Crowns, the Rise and Fall of Kings:

CHORUS

*'Tis sacred Musick does impart*
*Life and Vigour to the Art;*
*It makes the dumb-Poetic Pictures breath,*
*Victor's and Poet's Name it saves from Death.*

ix

How does the thund'ring Martial Song
Provoke the Military Throng!
  The Haut-Boys and the Warlike Fife,
    With Clamors of the Deafning Drum,
  Make Peasants bravely hazard Life,
    And quicken those whom Fears benum!
The Clangor of the Trumpet's Sound
Fills all the dusty Place around,
And does the neighb'ring Hills rebound:
Iö triumph when we sing,
We make the trembling Valleys ring.

GRAND CHORUS

*All Instruments and Voices fit the Quire,*
*While we enchanting Harmony admire.*
*What mighty Wonders by our Art are taught,*
*What Miracles by sacred Numbers wrought*
*On Earth: In Heav'n, no Joys are perfect found,*
*Till by Celestial Harmony they're crown'd.⁵*

The opinions of Ernest Brennecke, who writes that 'It is a fairly competent poem, echoing Dryden, of course, but lacking the laureate's [*sic*] mastery of form and language,'⁶ and of A. S. Borgman, who notes that 'Shadwell's poem, although it flows smoothly and is in place rather spirited, suffers in comparison with Dryden's Song . . . and his masterly "Alexander's Feast" (1697). It is, however, not inferior to the odes of D'Urfey and Brady, which were sung in the years 1691 and 1692'⁷ are just, and at first glance adequate, critiques. But the formal relationship between Dryden's ode and its successor is one that should now be re-examined in the light of what has been discovered about Dryden's numerological structure in the 1687 ode.

We have, as far as I know, no explicit statement by any of Dryden's contemporaries about the structure of the 1687 ode, and it would be interesting to know whether the nature of this structure was known – though the lack of contemporary exegesis in this case as in others proves nothing. If Shadwell can be shown to have copied it, not merely reproducing the superficial effects but copying intelligently or redeploying the structural conventions that lay behind it, we would have persuasive evidence that at least one of Dryden's contemporaries was aware of the significance of Dryden's structure, and perhaps, though this is more speculative, might find Shadwell's poem not merely an attempt to emulate Dryden but also a direct response to the preoccupations of musical humanism.[8]

Like Dryden's poem, Shadwell's is in 3 sections: an opening section (Stanzas i-ii in Dryden, i-v in Shadwell) celebrating harmony in both its musical and cosmological aspects; a middle section (Stanzas iii-vii in Dryden, vi-ix in Shadwell) in which a sequence of stanzas characterizes various aspects of music; and a final stanza (the 'Grand Chorus' in both Dryden and Shadwell) concluding the poem.


I

Dryden's opening stanza is of 15 lines, which Brooks and Fowler, and Levine, see as representing though in different ways a double musical octave.[9] The first section of Shadwell's poem also has 15 lines, and these too would seem to represent a double octave. The 15 lines form an ascending scale (each line corresponding to one degree of the scale) that represents in structure the ascending praise of the singers, 'From Earth to Heav'n our warbling Voices raise!' – a scale that ranges from the musicians of the opening triplet singing in Stationer's Hall the praises of sacred Harmony, to the immortal joys above of the final triplet. Like a musical scale this section of 15 lines begins and ends on the keynote, for its key word 'harmony' is sounded in the first and final lines. In a 2-octave scale the central note also sounds the tonic; and here the central line, though not including the word 'harmony', is as a whole a periphrasis for that word: 'Made Qualities most opposite combine', the traditional definition of harmony as *concordia discors*. Furthermore this nodal line is the tonic that joins, combines, or twines (the rhyme words of the central triplet) the lower and upper octaves by acting ambivalently as the last note of one and the first of the other.[10] It is preceded by a line referring to 'the warring Atoms' of chaos and followed by a line referring to the 'pleasing Concords' of divine order, each pointing appropriately to the extremes encompassed, the 'Qualities most opposite'.

'The Scale of Musick from the Sky', which thus links earth and heaven, and which Purcell ascended in a musical apotheosis in Dryden's ode 'On the Death of Mr Purcell',[11] was an established concept having many associations. For this reason it is worth quoting at some length a St Cecilia's Day sermon, preached by Nicholas Brady in 1697, that conveniently reiterates some of these commonplaces, and that because of its occasion, helps to establish the ethos of the St Cecilia celebrations. Its linking of Neoplatonic ecstacy and Jacob's dream is conventional:

> Nothing is so proper or so available as [Church music] . . . for lifting up the soul in devout Contemplation: When we are thus entertained with the employment of *Angels*, our thoughts naturally ascend unto those Mansions of Joy; we have an enter-course, as it were with those Heavenly Inhabitants, and our Conversation seems to be altogether *above*. . . . This Divine Art has such an admirable Secret of uniting Earth and Heaven together, that the Scale of *Musick* appears to be the exact counterpart of *Jacob's Ladder; with one end resting upon the Earth*, in the material Organs that compose it, and *the other end reaching up to Heaven*, in the Life and Spirit of its performances; upon the several *Degrees* of this, *are the Holy Angels*, those Celestial *Choristers*, perpetually *Ascending* and *Descending*; and the Lord himself stands at the top of it, to countenance and encourage the devout employment.[12]

Brady mentions 'several *Degrees*', but had he specified a number the natural choice would have been 15, the number of degrees in the double octave. For a flight of 15 steps linking earth and heaven, or the secular world and the divine, is found in many contexts which commentators have been diligent to relate.

Sometime before 1286 some of these associations were recorded by Durandus, whose classic and eclectic description of ecclesiastical symbolism includes an account of altar steps which properly number 15:

> the fifteen virtues are set forth by them: which were also typified by the fifteen steps by which they went up to the temple of Solomon: and by the prophet in fifteen Psalms of degrees [i.e. Psalms cxx–cxxxv], therein setting forth that he is blest who maketh ascents in his heart.

Durandus' immediate transition to Jacob's ladder implies that it too has 15 degrees:

> This was the ladder that Jacob beheld: 'And his top reached to the heavens.' By these steps the ascent of virtues is sufficiently made manifest, by which we go up to the altar, that is, to Christ, according to that saying of the Psalmist, 'They go from virtue to virtue.' And Job, 'I will seek him through all my steps.'[13]

Although the similarity between Jewish and Christian religious practices was often denied, the attitude of R.T., the author of *De templis* (1638), was representative of informed opinion when he wrote that 'some people are so wise, as they feare lest to build a Christian Church so like *Salomons* Temple, bee directly to bring in Judaisme. But wiser men than they, know that all which the Jewes did, was not Judaisme, Let them remember that for their comfort.'[14] The same author notes that there is 'an ascent of steps' up to 'That famous Temple of Saint *Peters* in Rome . . . the fairest in the whole World' and relates the steps to those of the Jewish temple associated with the 15 gradual psalms.[15] It may be that solomonic proportions were actually imitated in, for example, the north porch of Salisbury Cathedral where, like the temple porch, the floor area is a double square, and where the division of the inside walls on either side of the nave door into an arcade of 15 arches may represent steps.[16]

The divinely ordained measurements of the Jewish temple were commonly held to be significant, to reproduce microcosmically the perfect architecture displayed at large by the whole universe. 'Every part, every pin answered to the Pattern on the Mount, which were the Heavenly Things themselves in the Spirit, in Eternity'[17] wrote Peter Sterry, and Durandus' interest in the symbolism of the Jewish temple, with its porch of 15 steps (so enumerated in the Talmudic book *Succah*) was still very much alive in the seventeenth century. One seventeenth-century book about the temple – there was sufficient interest for several such studies – Samuel Lee's *Orbis miraculum* (1659), in a chapter 'Concerning the Mysteries of the stately Porch of the *Temple*', explains that the 'several steps' of the Porch that it was necessary to ascend before entering 'the holy place' were there 'to shew the divine elevation of the souls of spiritual worshippers, even as *Jacobs* ladder had several rundles; which the ascending Angels were to climb before they could arrive near to God'.[18] To all this Lee gives immediate and universal relevance:

> In like manner, in respect to our drawing nigh to God in divine worship, Soul-exalting humiliation, deep and serious Meditation, searching Examination, self-judging condemnation by reason of our infinite unworthinesse to converse with so holy a Majesty, together with ardent Ejaculations of our hearts in prayer, toward heaven his holy place, are the several steps by which we mount up into the Porch of Præparation; that gives us admission into fellowship and communion with God, in his Sanctuary-worship.

Lee's 'Soul-exalting humiliation' is an oxymoron that may be traced back at least as far as the first half of the sixth century, when St Benedict in Chapter vii of his *Regula* described the 12 steps of humility which a monk should ascend. More generally, the ladder image is an ancient one with an interesting pre-Christian history,[19] but apart from the Benedictine *scala humilitatis* its first important and extended exploitation as an allegory of spiritual improvement was by a Christian writer was by St John Climacus, whose late sixth-century *Heavenly Ladder* is divided into 30 chapters, each corresponding to a rung of the ladder, with the total number corresponding to 'the age of the fulness of Christ'.²⁰ Eventually the two concepts, the Benedictine and the Climacic, seem to have been reconciled in the west in a ladder of 15 rungs. In his *De gradibus humilitatis*, probably written between 1129 and 1135, St Bernard of Clairvaux superimposed on 12 Benedictine steps of humility, which he explains as signifying numerically the 10 commandments plus the double circumcision,²¹ 3 steps of truth, to make an extended *scala* of 15 steps. At about the same time, Honorius Augustodunensis in his *Scala coeli minor* identified each of 15 rungs with a virtue.²² It is this ladder that was illustrated in the *Hortus deliciarum* of Herrad of Landsberg late in the same century, an illustration of special interest for its striking iconographical similarity, in respects other than the number of rungs, with the illustrations of the Climax manuscripts. If, as has been suggested,²³ this picture has a Byzantine model, the number of rungs has perhaps been halved under the influence of certain Climax illustrations that show a pair of hinged stepladders having 15 rungs on each side.

Over 400 years later this concept of a ladder of 15 degrees served as the framework for Cadinal Bellarmino's popular *De ascensione mentis in Deum per scalam rerum creaturarum* (1615), in which the elderly controversialist eschewed debate and 'essayed from the contemplation of creatures, to make a ladder by the which we may in some sort ascend to God. And I have divided it into fifteen steps by [the] which they went up into the Temple of Solomon, and of the fifteen Psalms which are called Graduals.'²⁴ In spite of Bellarmino's ogre-like reputation, which persisted even in Shadwell's time,²⁵ the *De ascensione mentis* was issued in English translation not only in the surreptitious Catholic translation of 1616, but also in Protestant versions in 1638 and 1703 and in an extract in 1684.

The best-known flight of stairs in seventeenth-century English literature is Milton's description in *Paradise Lost*, Bk iii, of the 'steps of gold to heaven gate', and it may perhaps not be fortuitous (it is certainly appropriate) that Milton devotes 15 lines to the passage that begins with Satan's distant sight of the stairway and concludes with Jacob's waking cry that '*This is the gate of heaven.*' The sequence of lines (501–15) is carefully structured, with a steady, minutely controlled ascent, degree by degree, from the tentative half line at the beginning through increasingly more vivid, more forceful words, and an increasingly thick texture, to the delayed verb 'shone', a word that gains emphasis not only from the nature of its preparation, but also from its central position in the 15 lines and from the importance of light imagery in the whole poem. At this mid-point the lines modulate from the sensuous and earthly into the mystical, where description gives way to analogy and where, within this 'spiritual octave', the progression is from the 3-dimensional through the 2-dimensional to a literary simile, and in the simile itself from what 'Jacob saw', through 'Dreaming by night', to his waking comment on the vanished dream. The ambiguities of 'under the open sky' in the penultimate line, which means 'out of doors', 'under an empty night sky' (emphasizing that Jacob's vision was a dream) or 'under a sky that was open and so allowing entrance to heaven', are in remarkable contrast to the 'sparkling orient gems' of a few lines earlier:

> far distant he descries,
> Ascending by degrees magnificent
> Up to the wall of heaven a structure high,
> At top whereof, but far more rich appeared
> The work as of a kingly palace gate
> With frontispiece of diamond and gold
> Embellished, thick with sparkling orient gems
> The portal shone, inimitable on earth
> By model, or by shading pencil drawn.
> The stairs were such as whereon Jacob saw
> Angels ascending and descending, bands
> Of guardians bright, when he from Esau fled
> To Padan-Aram in the field of Luz,
> Dreaming by night under the open sky,
> And waking cried, *This is the gate of heaven.*

The relevance of Milton's simile has been justified in terms of Renaissance interpretations of Jacob's ladder as the way of salvation, and as a *figure* of Christ the Redeemer.[26] In support of this, the centrality of the word 'shone' may be thought of as reproducing the Christocentric structure of the poem as a whole; for light imagery is of special importance in the central lines of the poem.[27] The ladder image is here associated with a door that also suggests Christ ('I am the door: by me if any man enter in, he shall be saved.' John x. 9). Christopher Ricks has ingeniously explained the function of the simile to be that of drawing a limited parallel that involves showing an essential difference between Satan and Jacob. He argues that if Milton is not interested in the relationship between Satan and Jacob 'then to devote more than 5 lines to Jacob is strangely wasteful'.[28] Without denying the relevance of the comparison between Satan and Jacob, it may be suggested that the length of the allusion is a calculated part of its function, that it enables a structural allusion to be made to the *scala* of 15 degrees, and that this allusion is as important as a verbal allusion. If the word 'mysteriously' means both 'in an arcane manner' and 'symbolically', then Milton's next words, 'Each stair mysteriously was meant', may refer both to the arcane nature of the numerological allusion in the preceding 15 lines, and to the allegorical nature of a *scala* such as St Bernard's or Bellarmino's, in which each step has a meaning. Furthermore, just as Satan is excluded from Milton's ladder so, by his nature, he would be prevented from ascending a *scala humilitatis* because of his pride, and a *scala rerum creaturarum* because of his determination to pervert Creation.

Another sequence of 15 lines (Bk iii, 540–54) may also allude numerologically to the ladder. In it Satan, from the vantage point of 'the lower stair', looks not up to heaven, but down to earth. And though he chooses to ignore the steps rising above him, the reader is numerologically reminded of their presence by the 15 lines, so that however gratifying Satan's view may be, 'his sad exclusion from the doors of bliss' makes it worthless.

The lines are largely taken up with a simile that compares Satan with 'a scout' on 'the brow of some high-climbing hill', a simile that can seem confusing because vehicle and tenor are so similar that there may seem to be little point in the similitude, the opposite condition to that of the parallel simile in which Jacob and Satan may seem at first to have very little in common. The momentary confusion is intensified when, having been led to make no distinction between Satan and the scout and what they are both doing, the arresting description of

> some renowned metropolis
> With glistering spires and pinnacles adorned,
> Which now the rising sun gilds with his beams

is seen to be anachronistically inappropriate to Satan; its splendour only serving to draw attention to its inappropriateness. But we should be reminded of other occasions. The first is that recounted in Numbers xiii, when Moses sent men to spy out the land of Canaan. For the Israelites after their journey through the wilderness this was a moment of decision, a turning point much like Satan's. But whereas Satan's apparent courage contrasts with the timidity of the Israelite scouts who advised against invasion because of the strength of the indigenous inhabitants, we know that God's chosen people were not to be withstood as long as their trust remained in God, and conversely that Satan is doomed to ultimate failure, however vulnerable Adam and Eve may seem to be. His promised land is Hell. The Israelite scouts returned with a single bunch of grapes, and this *botrus* was traditionally interpreted as a type of Christ, signifying the presence of the Messiah, which the Jews in their blindness failed to recognize.[29] In a similar way Satan, although he is actually on the ladder, chooses to disregard it and to look elsewhere, the ladder like the *botrus* being a *figure* of Christ unrecognized. Such an interpretation is supported by Milton's own numerologically ordered *De doctrina Christiana* in which the significantly numbered bk i, ch. 15 concerns Christ as mediator, that aspect of Christ typologically prefigured by Jacob's ladder.

If we are reminded of *Paradise Lost* it will be of Adam's ascent 'as in air' to the 'high top' of Eden (bk viii, 300f.), a parallel that gives due significance to the word 'tempting' so disturbingly placed at the beginning of line 308. We may also compare the prelapsarian Adam waking to find his dream true with the post-lapsarian Jacob waking to find the ladder merely a dream, and a reader inhabiting a world where progress is by 'wandering steps and slow' will recognize the contrast between the predicament of fallen man who must laboriously climb the heavenly ladder, and that of unseduced Adam who rises effortlessly by supernatural levitation (l. 302).

The other incident that Milton's simile brings to mind is that treated at large in *Paradise Regained*. We may first be reminded of the temptation of Christ by the use of words such as 'desert ways' (line 544; compare 'the wilderness' in the evangelists), 'high-climbing hill' (line 546, compare 'high mountain' in Luke and Matthew), 'all this world at once' (line 543, compare 'all the kingdoms of the world in a moment of time' in Luke), and 'pinnacles' (line 550, compare 'a pinnacle of the temple' in Luke and Matthew), as well as by a general similarity in the situation. The parallel is significant because this is a period of final resolution at the outset of Christ's ministry, analogous in the scheme of Redemption to that of Satan's moment of reflection on the ladder in his scheme of the Fall. In this way Satan's plan for subversion is seen, by gentle allusion, in the context of its ultimate frustration. Any pretensions of grandeur Satan may have are undercut by our knowledge of his failure when tempting the second Adam.

The structural presence of the ladder extends the parallel. Just as Satan is present on both occasions, first as tempted and then as tempter, so is Christ present on both occasions, on the second as man but with Satan endeavouring to discover his identity, and on the first in the figure of the ladder which Satan ignores. The parallel with Jacob is perhaps still in mind, and, if it is, Satan's blindness my be contrasted with Jacob's frightened realization 'Surely the LORD is in this place; and I knew *it* not. . . . How dreadful *is* this place! this *is* none other but the house of God, and this *is* the gate of heaven.' The ladder also strengthens the parallel with the temptation from the tower, which Milton's use of the word 'pinnacles' brings to mind. In the seventeenth century the porch of the temple, famous for its 15 steps, was associated with the pinnacle of the temple mentioned by Matthew and Luke. Samuel Lee's account of the view from its summit shows how Milton can be seen to stress Satan's sin of vaingloriousness:

> The extraordinary height of this stately and pompous building, (the Porch of the Temple) . . . so famous for its pleasant and capacious Prospect . . . shews forth to us the excellent sublimity of divine contemplation: Wherein the Souls of heavenly Worshippers being intensly conversant, look down upon the Earth as beneath a Saint, and contemn all the Kingdoms of the World and the glory of them. The Heart of a Saint is most humble and lowly, who though exalted into divine communion, yet is the most noble, heroick, high-minded person in the whole world: being such a one as whose heart cannot be filled with the vast Empire of the whole Globe, or the Dominion of all the conceited and imagined worlds in the Universe.[30]

Satan's affections are set on things below, and any appearance he may have of being 'noble, heroick, high-minded' is a sham. In the following passage, which is indebted to Bishop Lightfoote's *The Temple: especially as it stood in the dayes of our Saviour* (1650) (though Lightfoote distinguished between the Porch of the Temple with 12 steps and the Gate of Nicanor with 15 'answerable to the fifteene Psalmes of degrees', a point not brought out by Lee) Lee alludes to the Temptation of Christ:

> Upon the Top of this stately Tower (which the side walls of the Porch sustained), called by the Evangelist *Matthew* . . . *The Pinacle* or wing of the Temple, the blessed body of our Lord possibly was arrived, when he triumphed over the Devil, there tempting him to presumption.[31]

With such commentary in mind, the reader of Milton's description of Satan looking down on the earth is aware of the antithesis of Satan's pride and foolish presumption, and Christ's purpose

> To conquer Sin and Death the two grand foes,
> By humiliation and strong sufferance:
> > (*Par. Reg.*, i. 159–60)

Such a gloss is sustained by the parallel between the Porch of the Temple and the 'kingly palace gate' of Heaven, a parallel that in part relies on the common element of 15 steps.

The precise nature of Satan's sin is perhaps also mysteriously expressed by his position on the ladder. St Bernard describes in his *De gradibus humilitatis* not an ascent through degrees of humility, as his title suggests, but, except for his 3 steps of truth, a descent through the 12 degrees of pride. The bottom step, and that which corresponds with that from which Satan views the world, is 'habitual sinning by which the fear of God is lost and contempt of God incurred.'[32] Bernard explains that 'Only the highest and the lowest fly without hindrance or exertion. . . . In the former *perfect love*, in the latter consummate wickedness, *casteth out fear.* Truth makes one secure, blindness the other.' Satan's bravery is no longer admirable when seen as 'consummate wickedness'. The 'blindness' and 'forgetting . . . his own reason' that Bernard mentions as symptomatic of this step are displayed by Milton's Satan in his failure to look up the ladder, by the scout's delight in the *reflected* light of the rising sun, and by the spiritual blindness of failing to interpret the ladder or realize the divine source of the light that gilds the metropolis and the greater magnificence of its direct rays. 'The spirit malign' corresponds to Bernard's man who 'ponders maliciously, prattles boastfully, or performs viciously,' while Satan's seizure by envy reminds one of Bernard's image of a 'captive given over to the tyranny of vice . . . swallowed up by a whirlpool of carnal desires'.

The ascent of 15 steps to the temple was particularly remembered, at any rate by Catholics, on the ecclesiastical feast celebrated on the eve of St Cecilia's Day for the Feast of the Presentation of the Virgin Mary in the Temple, which had been introduced from the Eastern to the Latin Church by Philippe de Mézières in 1372, and been prescribed for celebration on 21 November by the Universal Church since 1585.[33] The apocryphal gospel of the Pseudo-Matthew, the *Liber de ortu Beatae Mariae et infantia Salvatoris*, and the *Historia de nativitate Mariae et de infantia Salvatoris*, sometimes attributed to St Jerome, both recount how the three-year-old Virgin ascended unaided the 15 steps of the porch of the Temple; and pictorial representations of this event, probably based on the account in the *Legenda aurea,* are often careful to depict the correct number of steps.[34] Sometimes a single flight of very clearly defined steps is shown, as in Orcagna's schematic little sculpture of 1359 in Or San Michele at Florence;[35] sometimes some of the steps are reduced in size so that the full number may be fitted into the picture without taking up too much of the total composition, as in the bottom right-hand panel of the late-fourteenth-century retable of St Anne by Bernardo Puigon in the Museum of Catalonian Art, Barcelona;[36] sometimes the body and clothes of the Virgin conceal a few steps though the total number is not in doubt, as in a miniature of about 1440 in *The Hours of Catherine of Cleves.*[37] The Feast of the Presentation of the Virgin was introduced to the west through Venice, and it is therefore not surprising that 'it was at Venice that the Presentation of the Virgin became', as Venturi thinks, 'the perfect picture; for there Carpaccio and Cima de Congliano prepared the way for the masterpiece of Titian.[38] Cima's picture, now in the Dresden Gallery,[39] shows the 15 steps very clearly, and though Carpaccio shows only 10,[40] Titian's treatment in the Academia at Venice,[41] completed in 1538, probably shows 15 (the last 2 or 3 steps are rather obscure).' Titian's Virgin stands on a wide step forming a platform halfway up the flight: if, as one would suppose, this is *exactly* half way then the flight is of 15 steps. Similarly Tintoretto's representation in Santa Maria dell' Orto at Venice[42] probably shows 15 steps. It is at Florence that the steps are shown in the most elaborate form. Two fourteenth-century paintings at Santa Croce, by Taddeo Gaddi[43] and by Giovanni da Milano[44] show the steps forming a complex composition made up of 3 groups each of 5 steps.

The Virgin's ascent displays, of course, her spiritual precocity: it is a scale of perfection and expresses the humility of the hand-maid of the Lord as clearly as does the Magnificat. In the 'Mary in the Temple' play in the *Ludus Coventriae* collection of the first half of the fifteenth century the incident is dramatized, the Virgin ascending 'þe fyftene grees'[45] while the Episcopus instructs the audience:

Ffrom babylony to hevynly jherusalem þis is þe way
Every man þat thynk his lyff to Amende
Þe fiftene psalmys in memorye of þis mayde say.

The ritualistic ascent is accompanied by the quotation of the first
verse of each of the gradual psalms in turn, and each of these
verses is associated with a virtue, so that each step is 'gostly
applyed', words very close to Milton's claim that 'Each stair
mysteriously was meant'.

The ascent of the Virgin is associated with psalm-singing, and
artists treating this subject frequently show a group of singers and
musicians to make this point, specially noteworthy being the
treatments by Taddeo Gaddi and Giovanni da Milano. The power
of church music to encourage devotion is a favourite topic of St
Cecilia Day sermons: Nicholas Brady has already been quoted as
an example. Another of these sermons, preached in 1698 by
Francis Atterbury, makes the same point, but is worth quoting
because it shows how the analogy between the scale of music and
Jacob's ladder is so well known that it can be evoked without
direct reference. Atterbury argues that church music puts us

in the same State of Mind, that the devout Patriarch was, when
he awoke from his holy Dream; and ready with him to say to
ourselves: *Surely the Lord is in this Place, and I knew it not.
How dreadful is this Place! This is none other than the House of
God, and this is the Gate of Heaven.*[46]

Atterbury goes on to describe devotion through music in words
that echo Bellarmino's title *De ascensione mentis in Deum*, a title
that those who recognized would associate with 15 degrees:

the *Availableness* of Harmony to promote a pious Disposition of
Mind will appear, from the great Influence it naturally has on
the *Passions*, which, when well directed and rightly applied,
are the Wings and Sails of the Mind, that speed its Passage to
Perfection, and are of particular and remarkable Use in the
Offices of *Devotion*: For Devotion consists in an Ascent of the

Mind towards God, attended with holy Breathings of the Soul, and a divine Exercise of all the *Passions* and *Powers* of the Mind. These *Passions* the Melody of Sounds serves only to guide and elevate towards their proper Object.[47]

Although the 'Melody of Sounds' that is called church music is clearly not the same as the musical scale, it is identified with it by the concept of a *scala* of devotional music by which the mind may ascend to God, and through a metonymy by which the scale serves as a symbol for all music derived from the notes that compose it. Furthermore, the ladder of 15 rungs and the musical scale are associated because 15 degrees, in musical terms, span exactly 2 octaves. It is one of those curious correspondences of nature which the seventeenth century tended to speak of as 'mysteries', manifestations of divine order, that the double octave should be particularly appropriate as a link between earth and heaven. In Pythagorean musical thought it was a commonplace that the disdiapason was specially significant. The diapason, or octave, expresses the ratio 1:2, and because it includes the diapente and diatesseron, also includes the ratios 2:3 and 3:4 so that it may be held to be derived from and to express the *tetraktus* ($1+2+3+4=10$), the source of all things. But the disdiapason includes also the ratio 1:3 (diapason kai diapente) and itself expresses the ratio 1:4, thus combining in all possible combinations the 4 small integral numbers in its consonances. The disdiapason is therefore the 'Greater Perfect System' of the Greeks, by virtue of its containing the 3 simple and 2 compound consonances they recognized. More practically, the double octave approximates more closely to the singing range of the human voice than does the single octave.

It is the double octave that Robert Fludd illustrates in his famous diagram of the *monochordum mundi*, which correlates the intervals of 2 octaves with the spheres of the elements, planets and angels in his *Utriusque cosmi . . . historia* (1617), a scheme recalling the scale of nature. Like the 2 octaves of Shadwell's opening 15 lines, which distinguish and link the earthly and the heavenly,

Fludd divides the monochord extending between the Empyrean and the earth into two equal parts, i.e. into two octaves. The centre of the monochord, thus denoting the octave or the ratio 1:2, corresponds to the central position of the *sphaera aequalitatis*. The upper half of the monochord is called the spiritual octave giving eternal life; the lower one is the material octave and represents the transitoriness of the created world.[48]

The way in which the scale of being, Jacob's Ladder, the idea of universal order, the scale of music, and musical composition all cohere in a great hierarchic concept still valid at the end of the seventeenth century is best shown by quotation. A lengthy passage from Peter Sterry's *A Discourse of the Freedom of the Will* (1675) makes the point with infectious enthusiasm:

Being in itself, in its universal Nature, from its purest heighth, by beautiful, harmonious, just degrees and steps, *descendeth* into every Being, even to the lowest shades. All ranks and degrees of Being, so become like the mystical steps in that scale of Divine Harmony and Proportions, *Jacobs Ladder*. Every form of Being to the lowest step, seen and understood according to its order and proportions in its descent upon this *Ladder*, seemeth as an *Angel*, or as a Troop of Angels in one, full of all Angelick Musick and Beauty.

Every thing as it lieth in the whole piece, beareth its part in the Universal Consort. The Divine Musick of the whole would be changed into Confusion and Discords. All the sweet proportions of all the parts would be disordered and become disagreeable, if any one, the least, and least considered part, were taken out of the whole. Every part is tyed to the whole, and to all the other parts, by mutual and essential *Relations*. By virtue of these Relations, All the distinct proportions, of all the parts, and of the whole, *meet* in one, on each part, filling it with, and wrapping it up in the rich Garment of the Universal Harmony, curiously wrought, with all the distinct and particular Harmonies.[49]

Shadwell's series of 15 lines is composed of 5 sets of triplets, the triplets perhaps indicating numerologically the concern with *sacred* harmony or suggesting the harmoniousness of musical triads and the insistent rhyme expressing harmony by its concordance.

2

The second section of Dryden's ode is structurally distinguished by an initial stanza of 8 lines (the octave again) followed by Stanza iv of 4 lines, Stanza v of 5 lines, Stanza vi of 6 lines, and Stanza vii of 7 lines. Shadwell's second section also begins with a stanza of 8 lines, but a sequence of stanzas each one line longer than the last begins from that point, so that Dryden's sequence of stanzas with 8, 4, 5, 6, 7 lines is replaced, or perhaps continued, by Shadwell's sequence of stanzas with 8, 9, 10, 11 lines. This recognition of a regularly incremented sequence ignores the designation of the last 4 lines of Stanza viii as chorus, since the lines seem to belong to the stanza grammatically. I shall return to the significance of the division.

Brooks and Fowler argue that in the corresponding middle section of Dryden's poem the instruments characterized in Stanzas iii–vi are associated with the 4 temperaments; it is appropriate therefore to examine Shadwell's Stanzas vi–ix to see if they have a similar basis or use any consistent number symbolism. The 4 stanzas describe 4 genres (dirges, lovesongs or serenades, epic, and military music), but if these genres were associated by Shadwell with the number of lines in each stanza it is an association that I can not document. 10, the Pythagorean-Platonic number of perfection, is perhaps the natural choice for epic, the pre-eminent genre, and just as the decad includes all other numbers, so the epic here includes lesser genres: 'on cruel Fortune they complain' (dirges), 'how Heroes love' (love songs), 'how puissant Conquerors fight' (martial music). Musical instruments are not mentioned in the epic stanza, though they appear in surrounding ones, and it may be another indication of the perfection of this genre that its music is exclusively vocal, displaying the perfect union of sound and sense. It could also be argued

that the reference to '*sacred Musick*' in the chorus refers back to
'Sacred Harmony' in Stanza i in a way appropriate to the eighth
or octave stanza, and that the sequence of 6 lines which precedes
the chorus numerologically expresses the harmony of the genre
in a way which will become clear when the numerological
significance of Shadwell's final stanza is discussed. But the number
of lines in each of the other stanzas seems less appropriate, and
in so far as Stanza viii does not appear to belong to a coherent
scheme worked out consistently through Stanzas vi–ix it is
necessary to point only tentatively to any supposed number
symbolism.[50] It may be observed that 11, the number that transgresses the decalogue of perfection, could be regarded as appropriate to the destructive energies of war that are the subject of
Stanza ix, and that 8, a number associated with life after death,
could indicate, in Stanza vi, music's power to assuage the grief of
bereavement. But such interpretations require too much special
pleading to be convincing.

More clearly apparent is an effect similar to the symmetrical
rhyme scheme that in Dryden's poem represents the circularity of
the octave. The central section of Shadwell's poem is framed by
pentameter sections, the first 15 and last 6 lines of the poem.
Moreover, in the 4 stanzas of the central section itself, the 2 outer
stanzas mirror each other by being octosyllabic, while the 2 inner
stanzas more subtly mirror each other by being in one case octosyllabic with the exception of 2 pentameters (lines 31–2), in the
other pentameter with the exception of 2 octosyllabic lines
(39–40). These 2 irregularities in the metrically mixed 2 inner
stanzas draw attention to themselves, because the first one is
associated with an irregularity in the rhyme scheme, and the
second comes 2 lines earlier than is expected if the pattern of the
previous stanza is to be repeated. This cyclical structure may be
represented as A (i–v), B (vi), C (vii), C¹ (viii), B (ix), A (Grand
Chorus) the relation of C to C¹ being that of a mirror image –
the only way of providing variety when matching stanzas are
juxtaposed. It may in turn indicate the presence of yet another
structure which counterpoints with those of progressively
longer stanzas and of metrical symmetry.

If this is so, a possible pattern would seem to comprise a self-contained complete octave (Stanza vi); a 2-octave scale beginning 'If Love's gentle Passions' (l. 24) and concluding with 'the Rise and Fall of Kings' (l. 38), with the mid-point 'All chill and panting with the pleasing Pain' indicated as its median tonic by a change of metre to mark a new beginning, and a rhyme to link the line backwards with 'plain' and forwards with 'Strain' and 'complain'; and a further separate 2-octave scale beginning with a change in metre and separated by the designation 'chorus', having as its mid-point 'With Clamors of the Deaf'ning Drum', indicated by an irregularity in the rhyme scheme linking the first octave ('Drum') with the second ('Benumb'). It is fitting that these 2-octave scales should meet in the epic stanza with its 10 lines, for it gives it a centrality appropriate to its number symbolism and

THE STRUCTURE OF SHADWELL'S *A Song for St Cecilia's Day, 1690*

| Sections | Octaves | Stanzas | Line totals | | Metre | |
|---|---|---|---|---|---|---|
| | | i | 3 | | | |
| | | ii | 3 | | | |
| 1 | | iii | 3 | } 15 | Decasyllabics | A |
| | | iv | 3 | | | |
| | | v | 3 | | | |
| | | vi | 8 | | Octosyllabics | B |
| | | vii | 9 | } 15 | Mixed | C |
| 2 | | viii | 6 | | Mixed | |
| | | | | | | } C¹ |
| | | Chorus | 4 | } 15 | Mixed | |
| | | ix | 11 | | Octosyllabics | B |
| 3 | | Grand Chorus | 6 | | Decasyllabics | A |

the genre it celebrates. And it is fitting, too, that it should be singled out for the dignity of including a chorus. If one sees the first of these scales as rising to the 'lofty Epic Strain' perhaps the second scale falls when the strife of warfare and the strident sounds of hautboys, fife, drum and trumpet shatter the harmony of '*sacred Musick*' and 'Some ancient-noble History'. The warfare of Stanza viii is warfare transmuted by art, that of Stanza ix the harsh real thing. That such an image of ascending and descending scales was in Shadwell's mind is perhaps indicated by the reference to the wheel of fortune in one of the two lines at the top of the ascent, 'The Change of Crowns, the Rise and Fall of Kings,' and by the word 'Valleys' in the final line of the stanza.

3

The poem has now been divided into 7 octave scales $(2+1+2+2)$, and it comes as no surprise to find the final Grand Chorus beginning at the point where the eighth octave scale might be expected to begin and so completing a 'great' octave, as it were. But the last section of Shadwell's poem is not after all an 8-line stanza, but a 6-line stanza devoted to harmony. And the lines

> *What mighty Wonders by our Art are taught,*
> *What Miracles by sacred Numbers wrought*
> *On Earth*

are perhaps an invitation to numerological speculation, with the word 'Numbers' having a sense different from the usual one of 'lines of verse' which it has in the St Cecilia odes of Tate and Oldham. Certainly the number of lines is appropriate, for 6, the number of tones in an octave, is associated with harmony – an association documented by Brooks and Fowler.[51] If the first 15 lines of the poem were counted as 1 stanza, the Grand Chorus would form a sixth stanza.

This final stanza appears to be modelled on 6 lines from Book i of Cowley's *Davideis*; and, if this is so, further support is given to the thesis that Shadwell's poem has a numerologically ordered

structure. In the *Davideis*, David is summoned by Saul to cure one
of his recurrent fits of madness through the power of his music,
whereupon Cowley inserts a digression, supported by immensely
full annotation, on the power of music.[52] The essence of music, he
explains, is number, the basis of all Creation from 'Gods Poem,
this *Worlds* new *Essay*' to the microcosm, man, and to man's
artistic creations. Music as we generally think of it, that is 'Sounds
that charm our ears, / Are but one *Dressing* that rich Science
wears.' Of his own poem Cowley boasts:

> Though no man hear't, though no man it rehearse,
> Yet will there still be *Musick* in my *Verse*

and by '*Musick*' he means music as he has just defined it. There are
probable echoes of Cowley's musical digression in Dryden's *A
Song for St Cecilia's Day*, as there are of Cowley's ode on 'The
Resurrection'. What precisely in his own poem Cowley is here
referring to is open to debate, though the presence in a pentameter poem of a line like 'Thou great *Three-One*?'[53] (3 words in
1 line thus representing the Trinity), or having the Almighty
speaking in hexameters[54] are undoubtedly part of it. But it is also
probably more esoteric than that. The digression on music, or
more exactly harmony, is composed of 2 verse paragraphs, the
first an invocation of 6 lines, the second an exposition of $6 \times 6$
$= 36$ lines. The number 6, that of harmony, can hardly be fortuitous in view of the content. The digression is followed by David's
song, a verse paraphrase of Psalm cxiv, in 3 11-line stanzas. The
potency of the psalm is such that '*Sauls* black rage grew softly to
retire' and bearing in mind the preceding digression it seems that
the trinitarian significance of the 3 stanzas, and the total of 33
lines, the number of Christ, are calculated by Cowley to be
numerologically significant and intended to account for the
potency of the song.

Shadwell's final stanza adopts the 3 rhymed pentameter
couplets of Cowley's 6-line invocation. It also echoes some of
Cowley's words, as is evident if the 2 passages are juxtaposed.
Cowley's lines are:

Tell me, oh *Muse* (for *Thou*, or none canst tell
The mystick pow'ers that in blest *Numbers* dwell,
Thou their great *Nature* know'st, nor is it fit
This noblest *Gem* of thine own *Crown* t'omit)
Tell me from whence these heav'nly charms arise
Teach the dull world *t'admire* what they *despise*

and Shadwell's apparent derivative is:

All Instruments and Voices fit the Quire,
While we enchanting Harmony admire,
What mighty Wonders by our Art are taught,
What Miracles by sacred Numbers wrought
On Earth: in Heav'n, no Joys are perfect found,
Till by Celestial Harmony they're crown'd.

Cowley's 'blest Numbers' seems to be echoed by Shadwell's 'sacred Numbers' 'teach' by 'taught', 'admire' is common to both, and Cowley's noun 'Crown' reappears as a verb. Less convincing evidence is provided by the word 'fit', used rather differently in each passage; by 'mighty Wonders . . . Miracles', possibly echoing 'mystick pow'ers' in a similar position in the line (if adjective and noun are reversed 'mystick pow'ers' becomes 'mighty Wonders'); by 'charms' possibly suggesting 'enchanting'; and by 'heav'n[ly]' in the penultimate line of each. The passages are no closer, because no direct allusion is intended, and because their functions are so different: the one introductory and invocatory, the other concluding and asserting; completing in fact the cycle of simple ternary form. Cowley asks for men to be *taught* what they should *admire*, Shadwell asserts what the singers have been taught to admire. But the adaptation, if such it is, is skilful, and Shadwell's workmanship is sound when, for instance, he echoes Cowley's fourth line in his final word: an image also found in line 15, where it is reminiscent of the illustration from the *Hortus deliciarum*; and when Cowley's 'charms' becomes, if it does, '*enchanting*', with its full sense of influencing by the supernatural power of song.

To claim that Shadwell has adapted Cowley's lines skilfully is not to claim any great distinction. Shadwell's poem is a modest success, a suitable gathering of accepted images and poetic cliché with a final stanza from Cowley, some turns of phrase from Dryden, the title of a play by Edward Howard (*The Change of Crownes*: compare Shadwell's line 38), the adaptation in stanza ix of lines from his own catch in *The Squire of Alsatia* Act III, and so on. If the result seems drab or commonplace it should be remembered that the ode was not written as an independent poem, but as the basis for a musical score. ' 'Tis my part to invent,' wrote Dryden in the Preface to *Albion and Albanius* (1685), 'and the musician's to humour that invention,'[55] and Shadwell's bare invention (*inventio*) requires musical development (*amplificatio*), humouring, to bring it to life. Whether Robert King's lost setting succeeded in doing this cannot now be determined, but we can appreciate that Shadwell contrived a suggestive libretto with varied opportunities for musical exploitation. He may even have done more than just provide a libretto if his practice were still what it was 15 years earlier when he wrote *Psyche* and '*chalked out the way to the Composer*' telling him '*which Line I wou'd have sung by One, which by Two, which by Three, which by Four Voices, etc. and what manner of Humour I would have in all the Vocal Musick.*'[56] That is an aspect of Shadwell's work that cannot be considered, but if the Cecilia ode is organized in the way explained in this paper, Shadwell's invention has a dimension hitherto unrecognized. However, it does not therefore follow that the poem is a 'better', more successful, poem than it has hitherto been supposed to be. It is an intelligent response to a literary commission, and it incidentally provides interesting evidence about the way one of Dryden's contemporaries read his first St Cecilia's Day poem. Shadwell's poem remains in itself unmemorable; it sounds perish, only its numbers remain. Take but degree away and the poem 'jangle[s] into *Chaos* once again'.

# NOTES

1 See W. H. Husk, *An Account of the Musical Celebrations on St Cecilia's Day* (1857). The texts of the odes are reprinted in a useful appendix.

2 E. R. Wasserman, 'Pope's "Ode for Musick"', *ELH*, xxviii (1961), 163–86; J. A. Levine, 'Dryden's "Song for St Cecilia's Day, 1687"', *PQ*, xliv (1965), 38–50; and A. Fowler and D. Brooks, 'The Structure of Dryden's "Song for St Cecilia's Day, 1687"', *EC*, xvii (1967), 434–47 reprinted above, pp. 185–200. Besides an obvious debt to these articles I would like to acknowledge the help of many friends, in particular the stimulating and instructive conversation and scepticism of B. F. Nellist and Michael Wilding.

3 Fowler and Brooks, p. 193.

4 See the preface to *Psyche* (1675): 'In all the words which are sung, I did not so much take care of the Wit or Fancy of 'em, as the making of 'em proper for Musick; in which I cannot but have some little knowledge, having been bred, for many years of my Youth, to some performance in it.' (*Complete Works*, ed. M. Summers, 5 vols [1927], ii 280.) Shadwell's highest expectations of a composer setting his words are expounded at some length in his commendatory verses 'To my Much Respected Master and Worthy Friend, Signior Pietro Reggio, On the Publishing his Book of Songs' (1680) in *Works*, v, 239–41. Shadwell also composed and performed. In C. L. Day and E. B. Murrie, *English Song-Books 1651–1702: A Bibliography* (1940), he is recorded as the composer of 2 songs, and in *MacFlecknoe* is advised to 'Set thy own Songs, and sing them to thy lute' (l. 210). See also the note to *MacFlecknoe*, l. 35 in *The Poems of John Dryden*, ed. J. Kinsley, 4 vols (Oxford, 1958), iv 1915–16.

5 My text is from *The Fourth Part of Miscellany Poems*, 4th edn (1716), pp. 93–5, which I have corrected only in l. 15 by replacing a final comma by a full stop, and in l. 6 by removing the *l* from 'conclave', an amendation suggested by Mrs. E. E. Duncan-Jones. This is the text followed, not quite accurately, by M. Summers in his edn of the *Works*, and though it dates from 26 years after the occasion of the poem and 24 years after Shadwell's death it is the earliest edn known to me. The poem would probably have been printed as a broadside on a single half-sheet for distribution at the 1690 St Cecilia celebrations, in the way in which Dryden's poem had been on the previous occasion, but as only a single copy of the first edn of Dryden's poem has survived it is easy to imagine

that because Shadwell's poem was less highly regarded not even a single copy of such an edn would have survived. Tonson might, of course, have used one of these hypothetical lost copies when setting up the *Miscellany*. The 2 other edns I have found are in John Nichols' *A Select Collection of Poems*, v (London, 1780–2), pp. 298–301, where the text agrees substantively with that in Tonson's *Miscellany*, and in Husk's appendix (pp. 154–6). Husk does not disclose the source of his text, only remarking that 'the poem is extant' (p. 25) and that Robert King's music is lost. In Husk's edn the stanzas are not numbered and the last 4 lines of Stanza viii are not designated as chorus or separated from the 6 previous lines. The final word of l. 9 is 'join': see n. 10 below.

6 'Dryden's odes and Draghi's music', *PMLA*, xlix (1934), 31, reprinted in H. T. Swedenberg (ed.), *Essential Articles for the Study of John Dryden* (1966), p. 457.

7 *Thomas Shadwell: His Life and Comedies* (New York, 1928), p. 85.

8 It has been argued by D. T. Mace, 'Musical Humanism, the doctrine of rhythmus, and the Saint Cecilia odes of Dryden', *JWI*, xxvii (1964), 251–92, that Dryden attempted to exploit the rhythmical theories of Isaac Vossius in an attempt to fulfill the ideals of musical humanism. This theory was accepted by F. B. Zimmerman in his 1965 paper on 'Sound and Sense in Purcell's "Simple Songs" ' published in V. Duckles and F. B. Zimmerman, *Words to Music* (Los Angeles, 1967), pp. 43–90 though he notes that 'close examination of Purcell's solo songs reveals that [Purcell] paid no attention whatsoever to the theories of Vossius' (p. 82). The same is probably true of Dryden. In H. N. Davies, 'Dryden and Vossius: a reconsideration', *JWI*, xxix (1966), 282–95, Mace's theory is challenged (and defended by Mace, *ibid.*, pp. 296–310) but if Dryden was indeed interested, and possibly Shadwell too, in musical humanism, it is more likely that they sought to express this through a numerological structure than through Vossius' *rhythmus*.

9 Thomas D'Urfey's ode (1691), and *Alexander's Feast* (1697) also begin with 15-line stanzas. Of the other St Cecilia's Day odes, Smart's is the one most likely, in view of the structure of his *Song to David* (See R. D. Havens, 'The structure of Smart's *Song to David*', *RES* xiv [1938], 178–82), to be numerologically significant. The 8 stanzas of his ode may relate to the octave. The 'mystery in numbers' is celebrated also in Smart's *Jubilate Agno* (W. H. Bond (ed.) [1954], pp. 125–7).

10 In Husk's edn the median tonic is highlighted by being enclosed by the only identical rhyme in the poem: 'You did at first the warring atoms join, / Made qualities most opposite combine, / While discords did with pleasing concords join.' Because this makes perfectly good sense, and because it draws attention to the structure, albeit rather crudely, it is tempting to believe that Husk was faithfully following an authentic copy. Curiously, the 3 lines are echoed in verses by R.G. 'On the death of the late famous Mr Henry Purcell' in Bk ii of the third edn of *Orpheus Britannicus* (1721). It is a poem very largely of rhymed couplets, but includes the following triplet: 'How in that mystic order cou'd he join / So different notes! make contraries combine, / And out of discord, cull such sounds divine.' See F. B. Zimmerman, *Henry Purcell 1659–1695: His Life and Times* (1967), p. 345. Unfortunately R.G.'s version supports neither Tonson's 'twine' or Husk's 'join', though it is just possible that his 'divine' represents an attempt to avoid an awkward identical rhyme, and that Tonson for a similar reason corrected what he thought was a misprint in his copy.

11 Dryden may have known that the scale of music was a particularly appropriate image to associate with the *Orpheus Britannicus*, as ladders were associated with the Orphic mysteries: the Thracian women, by whom Orpheus met his death, are shown decorated with ladders on Greek vases. See A. B. Cook, *Zeus: a study in ancient religion*, II. i (Cambridge, 1925), pp. 121–40. But although Dryden uses the image of the scale of music in this poem, he does not, apparently, attempt to represent it structurally. This may be because he was more concerned to write words suitable for musical setting, an aim in which he succeeded magnificently (see Wasserman, pp. 164–5), or because after the structural ideas of his first St Cecilia ode had been copied by Shadwell he felt disinclined to use them again.

12 *Church-Musick Vindicated. A Sermon preach'd At St Bride's Church, on Monday November 22, 1697. Being St Cecilia's Day*, pp. 11–12, 13, in J. E. Phillips (ed.), *Two St Cecilia's Day Sermons (1696–1697)*, Augustan Society Reprints, xlix (Los Angeles, Calif., 1955). The early synthesis of Neoplatonic and Christian concepts of ascent is described in H. Musurillo, *Symbolism and the Christian Imagination* (Dublin, 1962), ch. v.

13 B. Webb and J. Mason (ed.), *The Symbolism of Churches and Church Ornaments. A translation of the Rationale divinorum officiorum written*

*by William Durandus* (1906), p. 37. See also p. 156 for a similar but earlier passage from Hugh of St-Victor's *Mystical Mirror of the Church*. Hugh of St-Victor also tabulated in his *De arca Noe morali* 'fifteen steps by which wisdom arises and grows in the hearts of the saints', though the image he has in mind is that of a tree, not a ladder. See his *Selected Spiritual Writings*, tr. a religious of C.S.M.V. (1962), p. 93. See also pp. 120–1 for a chapter 'Of the mystery of the numbers seven and eight that make fifteen'. See E. S. Greenhill, 'The Child in the Tree', *Traditio*, x (1954), 323–71, for the association of ladder and tree.

14 Pp. 57–8.

15 Pp. 186–7.

16 I Kings, vi. 3. The north porch at Salisbury seems to demand some such explanation, for as Britton remarked, 'both in the ground plan and general views, it appears a discordant and extraneous object. It neither assimilates with the elevation, nor is it supported by any corresponding appendage. As a simple architectural object it is however beautiful, both internally and externally' (J. Britton, *The History and Antiquities of the Cathedral Church of Salisbury* [1836], p. 71.) The fine pinnacles may also, for reasons which will become clear later in this paper, imitate the Temple. The city of Salisbury lies to the north of its cathedral, and the lateral porch serves to connect the worldly city with the house of God. (Cf. 'Ffrom babylony to hevynly jherusalem þis is þe way,' see p. 217, and Jacob's ladder.) For the significance of a position on the *north* side of the cathedral see E. Panofsky, *Abbot Suger* (Princeton, N.J., 1946), pp. 208–12, G. S. Tyack, *Lore and Legend* (1899), pp. 65–7, and Tyack, *Ecclesiastical Curiosities* (1899), p. 24.

17 V. de S. Pinto (ed.), *Peter Sterry: Platonist and Puritan 1613–1672* (Cambridge, 1934), p. 159.

18 P. 210.

19 See Cook, *loc. cit.*, and, for later developments, the Byzantine 'Guide to Painting' in A. N. Didron, *Christian Iconography*, tr. E. J. Millington and M. Stokes, ii (1886), pp. 380 and 390.

20 St John Climacus, *The Holy Ladder of Perfection by which we may Ascend to Heaven*, tr. Fr Robert (1858), pp. 432–3.

21 *The Steps of Humility*, tr. G. B. Burch (Cambridge, Mass., 1940), pp. 126–7.

22 See A. Katzenellenbogen, *Allegories of the Virtues and Vices in Medieval Art* (New York, 1964), pp. 22–6; E. Mâle, *The Gothic*

*Image*, tr. D. Nussey (1961), pp. 105–8; and G. W. Whiting, *Milton and this Pendant World* (Austin, Tex., 1958), pp. 59–87. Louis Reau, *Iconographie de l'art chretien*, II. i (Paris, 1965), p. 147, records that 'D'après Honorius d'Autun suivi par Herrade de Landsberg dans *l'Hortus Deliciarum*, les 15 échelons de l'Échelle de Jacob symbolisent les vertus.'

23 J. R. Martin, *The Illustration of the Heavenly Ladder of John Climacus*, Studies in Manuscript Illumination, v (Princeton, N.J., 1954), p. 19.

24 *A most learned and pious treatise, full of divine and humane philosophy, framing a ladder, whereby our mindes may ascend to God, by the Stepps of his Creatures*, tr. T.B. [i.e. Francis Young] (Douay, i.e. secretly in England, 1616), ed. J. Brodrick as *The Ascent of the Mind to God by a Ladder of Things Created* (1928), pp. xxii. The scale of *nature* as ladder for man's ascent is studied in A. O. Lovejoy, *The Great Chain of Being* (Cambridge, Mass., 1936). The scale of *meditation* is discussed in L. L. Martz, *The Poetry of Meditation*, 2nd ed (New Haven, Conn., 1962), where reference is made to the Dominican rosary 'of 150 "Aves", divided into fifteen "decades"' (p. 101).

25 Shadwell, *Works*, v, 350.

26 Whiting, *op. cit.*; C. A. Patrides, 'Renaissance Interpretations of Jacob's Ladder', *Theologische Zeitschrift*, xviii (1962), 411–18. D. C. Allen, '*The Scala Religionis in Paradise Lost*', *MLN*, lxxi (1956), 404–5; and W. G. Madsen, *From Shadowy Types to Truth* (1968), pp. 113–44.

27 See *The Poems of John Milton*, ed. J. Carey and A. Fowler (1968), p. 441, and the nn. on *Par. Lost*, vi, 749f. All Milton quotations are from this edition.

28 *Milton's Grand Style* (Oxford, 1963), p. 128. Cf. Fowler's Introd. to *Par. Lost*, p. 435.

29 See Mâle, p. 144.

30 P. 211.

31 P. 211. See also E. M. Pope '*Paradise Regained*,' *the Tradition and the Poem* (Baltimore, Md., 1947), p. 84 n.21. In Herbert's 'The Church-porch' advice on the rejection of temptation is given to one 'whose sweet youth and early hopes inhance / Thy rate and price, and mark thee for a treasure' (ll. 1–2), and the use of church porches by penitents and as schoolrooms may have been in Herbert's mind – as might the temptations of Christ. The poem has been interpreted numerologically by Martz, p. 291, who writes that 'It is a typical Herbertian touch that these stanzas, after undergoing drastic

revision, should at last emerge with the "perfect number", seventy-seven: signifying, no doubt, that the man thus regulated has at last reached a degree of perfection sufficient to permit him to partake of the "mystical repast" which we have glimpsed from the very first stanza.' To justify his description of 77 as a 'perfect number' Martz refers to Sabin Chambers, *The Garden of our B. Lady* (St Omer, 1619), pp. 20–2, where, in a flourish of *occupatio* following some specious calculation, Chambers writes of the 'signification' of the supposed 77 words in the Creed in 'all vulgar tongues'. But if Herbert's choice of 77 stanzas is significant, and it may well be, for there has to be some reason to end at one point rather than another in a poem like 'The Church-porch', it surely signifies the remission of sins after penitence, and the coming of Christ, according to St Luke's genealogy in the 77th generation, to abolish all sins. See P. Bongo, *Numerorum mysteria* (Bergamo, 1591), s.v. *LXXVII*.

32 Tr. Burch, p. 225.

33 Sister Mary Jerome Kishpaugh, *The Feast of the Presentation of the Virgin Mary in the Temple: An Historical and Literary Study* (Washington, D.C., 1941).

34 See A. Venturi, *The Madonna. A pictorial representation of the life and death of the Mother of Our Lord Jesus Christ by the painters and sculptors of Christendom*, tr. A. Meynell (n.d.) pp. 107–21 and J. Lafontaine–Doscogne, *Iconographie de l'enfance de la Vierge dans l'Empire Byzantin et en Occident*, ii (Brussels, 1965), pp. 112–28.

35 Reproduced in Venturi, p. 114; Lafontaine-Doscogne, Fig. 53.

36 Lafontaine-Doscogne, Fig. 9.

37 *The Hours of Catherine of Cleves*, ed. J. Plummer (1966), Pl. vi, reproduced from f. 23v of the portion of the MS preserved in the Guennol Collection, New York.

38 Venturi, p. 118.

39 *Ibid.*, facing p. 120.

40 *Ibid.*, p. 117.

41 *Ibid.*, p. 107.

42 *Ibid.*, p. 121.

43 *Ibid.*, p. 112.

44 *Ibid.*, p. 113; Lafontaigne-Doscogne, Fig. 6.

45 K. S. Block (ed.), *Ludus Coventriae* (1922), pp. 74–7.

46 Atterbury, *Sermons and Discourses on Several Subjects and Occasions*, iv (1751), p. 249.

47 *Ibid.*, pp. 249–50.

SHADWELL's *A Song for St Cecilia's Day, 1690*

48 P. J. Ammann, 'The musical theory and philosophy of Robert
Fludd', *JWI*, xxx (1967), 202. Ammann reproduces the diagram,
Pl. 23b, and so does J. Hollander, *The Untuning of the Sky: Ideas of
music in English poetry 1500–1700* (Princeton, N.J., 1961), foll. p. 242.
49 Pinto (ed.), *Peter Sterry*, p. 152. A contemporary composer, John
Joubert, has described how a reference to Jacob's ladder (signifying
the church) in his choral work *Urbs Beata* is expressed in the music
by a 1-octave scale. See P. H. Davison, 'The Composer, the
University, and Society: John Joubert interviewed', *Alta* ii, 7
(1968–9), pp. 12–13. For a modern exposition of the traditional
interpretation of Jacob's ladder see Nicolette Gray's scholarly
children's book, *Jacob's Ladder, a Bible picture book from Anglo-
Saxon and 12th Century English MSS.* (1949).
50 M-S. Røstvig, 'Renaissance Numerology: Acrostics or Criticism?'
*EC*, xvi (1966), 10–11, rightly insists that
> When engaging in numerological analysis it is never enough to
> state that one feels 'reasonably sure' of a particular interpretation
> of a given number. *All* one's interpretations must be backed by
> specific references to established sources and must form part of a
> coherent system. Indeed, the system must be so coherent that
> once it has been established one should be able to *predict* how the
> poet will proceed in passages that still remain to be investigated.

My interpretations of 8, 10, and 11 are all taken from P. Bongo,
*Numerorum mysteria* (Bergamo, 1591). The danger of numerological interpretation is exhibited earlier in my essay. By confining my
attention to ladders with 15 rungs I did not mean to imply there
are not other established ladder concepts associated with numbers
other than 15, the ladder of love of St John of the Cross with
10 rungs, or St Augustine's 4-runged ladder. And I do not suggest
*all* flights of 15 steps (e.g. the steps from the chamber in Haggard's
*King Solomon's Mines*, ch. xviii) are numerologically significant.
51 See their n. 35, and also Wasserman, pp. 167–9. A more technical
approach may be found in William Holder, *A Treatise of the Natural
Grounds, and Principles of Harmony* (1694), pp. 193–4.
52 Cowley, *Poems*, ed. A. R. Waller (Cambridge, 1905), pp. 253–4.
53 *Ibid.*, p. 251.
54 *Ibid.*, p. 373.
55 Dryden, *Of Dramatic Poesy and Other Critical Essays*, ed. G. Watson,
ii (1962), p. 41.
56 *Works*, ii, p. 280.

# Symbolic numbers in Fielding's *Joseph Andrews*

DOUGLAS BROOKS

On the face of it, a numerological analysis of an eighteenth-century novel might seem a laughable undertaking; doubly so, perhaps, since any kind of structural analysis of the early novel is still a somewhat perfunctory matter.[1] Thus, we are accustomed to hearing *Joseph Andrews* – along with *Moll Flanders* and a host of other works – dismissed as being structurally inadequate. To quote a recent critic: in *Joseph Andrews* 'the ordering of events [is] as chaotic as life itself . . .'.[2] But such a statement is demonstrably untrue, and in the following pages I want to move from general formal analysis to specifically numerological analysis, in an attempt to show that Fielding's first novel is, in fact, rigorously patterned, and possesses a structure of literally mathematical precision.

## I

The novel falls into 3 parts: Books I and IV, largely static, frame 2 central books of picaresque movement.[3] The frame effect is further reinforced by the echoes of *Pamela*, which are concentrated in Books I and IV.[4] The 2 framing books are, in addition, linked by similarity of episode. Thus, I. v–x, the chapters in which Lady Booby reveals her passion for Joseph, are recapitulated in IV. i; while the discussion between Lady Booby and Slipslop about Joseph in I. vii is matched by the longer discussion between the two on the same subject in IV. vi. Again, in I. xiv Adams arrives at the Dragon Inn and recognizes Joseph (who is in difficulties with Mrs Tow-wouse); in IV. xv there is a series of arrivals, all having to do with the 'recognition' of Joseph, the establishing of his true parentage. While in IV. ii Adams, referring to Joseph and Fanny, tells Lady Booby that ' "This Couple were desirous to consummate long ago, and I dissuaded them from it," '⁵ advice which he gave them in I. xi ('Mr *Adams* had with much ado prevented them from marrying; and persuaded them to wait').

Most important of all is the pairing of part of the Dragon Inn episode with the final chapter of Book IV. In IV. xvi Joseph and Fanny are married and go to bed 'to enjoy the private Rewards of their Constancy; Rewards so great and sweet, that I apprehend *Joseph* neither envied the noblest Duke, nor *Fanny* the finest Duchess that Night'. This has been seen – rightly, I think – as an allusion to *Pamela*'s subtitle, 'Virtue Rewarded': here Joseph and Fanny receive *their* reward.⁶ But the full harmony of this union can be fully appreciated only if we recall its comically-discordant anticipation in I. xvii. Mrs Tow-wouse has just discovered her husband in bed with Betty the chambermaid, and in the 'most hideous Uproar' that ensues, her voice is heard, 'like a Bass Viol in a Conert',

to articulate the following Sounds.——'O you damn'd Villain, is this the Return to all the Care I have taken of your Family? This the Reward of my Virtue? Is this the manner in which you behave to one who brought you a Fortune, and preferred you to so many Matches, all your Betters?'

But though comic, this is full of irony as well. For Mrs Tow-wouse's emphasis on the monetary side of marriage is a fine dig at the mercenary Pamela, serving to stress the innocent, un-mercenary nature of Joseph's and Fanny's union and 'reward'; while the reader is left with the impression that Tow-wouse's adultery with the open-hearted Betty is a more fitting relationship than his marriage to his uncharitable wife and that it does, in fact, mime, on a lower level, the marriage of Joseph and Fanny. An additional point links the 2 episodes: Betty satisfies herself on Tow-wouse only after she had been rejected by Joseph, who is saving himself for Fanny.

2

If Books I and IV are paired, so are II and III, and so closely that
the similarities cannot be regarded as fortuitous. A noteworthy
feature here is that parallel episodes appear in the *same chapter*
of their respective books. Thus, in III. ii Adams and Joseph,
together with Fanny, encounter what they think are ghosts or
murderers (they turn out to be sheep stealers), and manage to
escape under cover of darkness. They arrive at a river bank:

> *Adams* here made a full stop, and declared he could swim, but
> doubted how it was possible to get Fanny over; to which
> *Joseph* answered, 'if they walked along its Banks they might be
> certain of soon finding a Bridge, especially as by the number of
> Lights they might be assured a Parish was near.' 'Odso, that's
> true indeed,' said *Adams*, 'I did not think of that.'

In terms of Joseph's developing maturity,[7] this episode is
important in itself; his common sense is set over against Adams'
blindness to things practical. The main force of the incident in
contrasting the two, however, derives from the fact that it is an
almost exact repetition of one in II. ii: Adams

> soon came to a large Water, which filling the whole Road,
> he saw no Method of passing unless by wading through,
> which he accordingly did up to his Middle; but was no sooner
> got to the other Side, than he perceived, if he had looked over
> the Hedge, he would have found a Foot-Path capable of
> conducting him without wetting his Shoes.

In this, the earlier, episode Adams is alone. By the method of
episode parallelism, therefore, Fielding illustrates Adams' un-
changing blindness to practical matters: only the presence of
Joseph in III. ii prevents him from getting a second dousing.

A similar relationship exists between II. ix and III. ix. In the
former, Adams rescues a woman (who, he discovers later, is
Fanny) from rape; in the latter the agents of the 'roasting'

squire arrive and, after a battle, abduct Fanny for their master.

She is rescued in III. xii, and this leads to a reunion between her and Joseph at an inn: 'O Reader, conceive if thou canst, the Joy which fired the Breasts of these Lovers on this Meeting'; which recalls Chapter xii of Book II, where Joseph and Fanny are reunited at another inn:

> But, O Reader, when this Nightingale, who was no other than *Joseph Andrews* himself, saw his beloved *Fanny* in the Situation we have described her, can'st thou conceive the Agitations of his Mind? If thou can'st not, wave that Meditation to behold his Happiness, when clasping her in his Arms, he found Life and Blood returning into her Cheeks.

Such, then, is the basic structure of *Joseph Andrews*; and perhaps a schematic outline is useful at this point:

BOOK I
Lady Booby and Joseph.
Dialogue: Lady Booby and Slipslop.
Arrival of Adams.
Virtue rewarded.
Joseph and Betty.

        BOOK II
        ii   Adams and water.
        ix   Rescue of Fanny (near-rape).
        xii Reunion.

        BOOK III
        ii   Adams and river.
        ix   Fanny abducted (near-rape).
        xii Reunion.

BOOK IV
Lady Booby and Joseph.
Dialogue: Lady Booby and Slipslop.
Various arrivals.
Virtue rewarded.
Joseph and Fanny.

## 3

But in addition to this, the novel reveals a more pervasive pattern of episode parallelism. In Book I, for instance, there is a superb irony in the fact that Joseph should be dismissed for failing to be seduced (Chapter x), while the Betty in the Booby household should be dismissed for supposed improper relations with Joseph (I. vii). And of course, corresponding to this last dismissal is that of the other Betty in Chapter xvii (note the numerical chime, vii, xvii).

The similarity between the situations of Joseph and Betty is made more apparent by the physical similarities of the two: like Joseph, Betty is good-natured; like him, she has undergone sexual temptation in her vulnerable position as a servant; but unlike him she has, while escaping 'pretty well', not emerged unscathed. Finally, like Joseph (who 'was now in the one and twentieth Year of his Age' [I. viii]), Betty 'was but one and twenty' (I. xviii).

Soon after his dismissal, Joseph is robbed and stripped (I. xii). The focus now is on theft and charity; but we see how judiciously Fielding has constructed the book: robbery for money is sandwiched between the attempted sexual 'robberies' of Lady Booby and Slipslop in the first half, and that of Betty in the second.[8] (He derives an additional irony from the fact that it is actually Betty who exemplifies charity by clothing Joseph when he arrives at the 'Dragon'.)

The 'Dragon' episode overlaps the division between Books I and II. Fielding employed this enjambment in the interest not only of thematic continuity but of structural symmetry; for by ending Book I as he did he was able, as we have seen, to balance Joseph's dismissal for continence against Betty's dismissal for incontinence.

Furthermore, 2 important themes of the novel – the sexual and the monetary – are united by this division of the 'Dragon' episode: over against Joseph's dismissal in Book I (motivated by frustrated lust) is placed his retention in Book II by Mrs Tow-wouse (motivated by avarice; he has not paid the bill for the horse's board, and she knows he possesses a gold piece). It is a fine bit of irony that Joseph's bill should be paid by the amorously-motivated charity of Slipslop (II. iii).

The principle of echo and parallelism is continued in II. iii, where Joseph is refused entry into the stagecoach by a lady because he wears livery, recalling the prudish lady's refusal to let him ride in the coach in I. xii. The theme is repeated in II. v, where Joseph, injured this time by a fall from Adams' horse, is refused entry into the coach by Miss Grave-airs. The parallel with I. xii here is reinforced by the fact that Joseph is injured on both occasions, though the motives leading to the refusal differ.

Book II seems to be relatively free of cross-references after this until Chapters ix and x, which serve as complex parallels to certain chapters in Book I. A parallel with I. xii is introduced fairly early on when the gentleman who is accompanying Adams, hearing shrieks from behind some bushes, assumes that a robbery is taking place (both incidents occur at night). But this hint at theft of money is immediately countered by the revelation of the robbery's sexual nature: Adams, 'on coming up to the Place whence the Noise proceeded, found a Woman struggling with a Man, who had thrown her on the Ground, and had almost overpowered her'.

II. ix thus subsumes, in addition to I. xii (Adams' willingness to come to the rescue contrasts, of course, with the behaviour of the stagecoach passengers), I. v and vi, the attempts on Joseph by Lady Booby and Slipslop. Fanny, as yet unnamed, serves here as a surrogate for Joseph in his absence from this part of the novel;[9] and Adams' rescue of her underlines the inseparability of charity and chastity again: the parson, representing the former, rescues Fanny, exemplifying the latter.

The parallel between the attempted seductions of Joseph and Fanny is made explicit when Fanny tells Adams that her would-be ravisher

desired her to stop, and after some rude Kisses, which she resisted, and some Entreaties, which she rejected, he laid violent hands on her, and was attempting to execute his wicked Will, when, she thanked G——, he timely came up and prevented him.

Compare I. vi: 'so did Mrs *Slipslop* prepare to lay her violent amorous Hands on the poor *Joseph*, when luckily her Mistress's Bell rung, and delivered the intended Martyr from her Clutches'.[10]

A substantial passage added to the Beginning of II. x in the second edition starts:

> THE Silence of *Adams*, added to the Darkness of the Night, and Loneliness of the Place, struck dreadful Apprehensions into the poor Woman's Mind: She began to fear as great an Enemy in her Deliverer, as he had delivered her from.

This fulfils a deliberate thematic function by stressing Adams' chastity: he has the opportunity for rape but the thought never enters his head. Hence the irony when, with the arrival of the bird batters in the same chapter, the ravisher, who has by now recovered from Adams' blows, accuses him of being a robber and Fanny of being his whore – a parody of I. xii, with the ravisher now taking Joseph's part of the injured and robbed innocent.

The bird batters' debate over the sharing of the reward money gives Adams, had he been 'a dextrous nimble Thief', a chance to escape: 'but *Adams* trusted rather to his Innocence than his Heels'; which recalls I. xvi, the escape from the 'Dragon' of one of the men who had robbed Joseph. The escape occurred, it is hinted, because the constable guarding him had succumbed to a bribe, as 'not being concerned in the taking the Thief, he could not have been entitled to any part of the Reward, if he had been convicted'. (The bird batters instead to exclude 'the young Fellow, who had been employed only in holding the Nets' from any share in the reward.)

But the parallel extends even further, stressing again, structurally, the intimate relationship between sexual and monetary in the novel. For just as the man who robbed Joseph is caught and then escapes, so is the would-be ravisher caught by Adams, succeeds in 'escaping' by deception (accusing Adams of theft),

then escapes properly by slipping away from the justice's house
when the identities of Adams and Fanny are revealed (II. xi).

4

The method of repetitive structuring is continued in Book III,
though the most obvious instances of its use – in Chapters ii, ix
and xii – have already been discussed. Nevertheless, before
passing on to Book IV, I should like to examine III. xii a little
more closely; for it serves to unite several thematic strands. In it,
Fanny is rescued from the captain who had abducted her on the
'roasting' squire's orders by the arrival of Lady Booby's steward,
Peter Pounce. Later in the chapter he offers to take Adams in his
chariot, 'finding he had no longer hopes of satisfying his old
Appetite with *Fanny*'. This last piece of information is meant to
stir the reader's memory: Fanny's rescue by the lustful Pounce
(who desires are never to be satisfied) echoes Joseph's redemption
from the 'Dragon' by Slipslop, who, we remember, fails in her
attempts to get Joseph into the stagecoach with her, and is again
doomed to perpetual frustration.

But if, as I have argued, the reunion of Joseph and Fanny here
recalls a similar reunion in II. xii, the rescue of Fanny from rape
by the arrival of Pounce in his chariot broadly parallels, in
addition, the rescue of the robbed Joseph by the passengers in the
stagecoach in I. xii. Once more, sexual counterpoints monetary,
attempted rape echoes robbery.

It is this recurring pattern in Chapter xii of each of the first 3
books, indeed, that is one of the most noticeable features of the
novel's structure. In I. xii Joseph is robbed and rescued; in II. xii
he and Fanny are reunited; in III. xii Fanny is rescued from rape
and reunited with Joseph. The pattern is, in fact, a cumulative one:
III. xii combines the motifs (robbery, reunion) that occur separ-
ately in I. xii and II. xii. And so insistent is it that it almost forces
us to predict what Fielding has in store in IV. xii, if we bear in
mind the clues laid in I. ii (Joseph 'was esteemed to be the only
Son of Gaffar and Gammer *Andrews*'), and I. viii and II. xii, the
physical twinning of Joseph and Fanny. For if Fielding is to

remain true to his scheme, there must again be a robbery and a reunion. And so there is. But with a superb twist; for Joseph and Fanny are united by becoming brother and sister and are thus apparently prevented forever from attaining the ultimate union, marriage. Fate, it seems, has stolen Fanny from Joseph this time; so that the scene ironically echoes the robbery-rape motif as well as containing a 'reunion' which is actually the reverse of a reunion.[11]

The final chapter to participate in the system I have been outlining (apart from IV. xvi, already considered, and a minor case in IV. vii),[12] is xiv, containing the night escapades at Booby Hall. Mark Spilka has made out a convincing case for the climactic force of this episode;[13] but it is a force that derives largely from its heavily recapitulative nature, a point which Spilka failed to note.

Thus, when Adams leaps naked from bed and rescues the soft-skinned Didapper from the amorous clutches of the bearded Slipslop – mistaking the man for the women and *vice versa* – he is unwittingly parodying his rescue of Fanny in II. ix. And when Lady Booby appears on the scene and, seeing him struggling with Slipslop, immediately accuses him of 'Impudence in chusing her House for the Scene of his Debaucheries, and her own Woman for the Object of his Bestiality', the parody is extended and the comedy heightened; for here is an echo of II. x, the robber's false accusation against Adams. The echo resounds even louder when the parson, acquitted by the discovery of Didapper's 'Diamond Buttons for the Sleeves', makes his way back to his room. Taking a wrong turning in the dark, he ends up in Fanny's bed and sleeps with her, to her horror in the morning. He is still almost exactly where he was in II. x; and once again comes the false accusation, this time voiced by Joseph: ' "How! . . . Hath he offered any Rudeness to you?" '

5

The above analysis should be sufficient to indicate the care with which Fielding constructed his novel. With this established, I now want to proceed to a numerological exploration of its structure.

The first thing to consider is the division into 4 books. It is easy to assume that Fielding is here glancing at Part I of *Don Quixote*, which is similarly divided; but I suspect this to have been a fortunate coincidence rather than a planned allusion. In fact, it may well be that the novel is organized on a four-book plan because 4 was traditionally regarded as symbolizing concord, friendship, and justice. The former meanings derived from the harmonizing of the 4 elements to create the world order. Plato expresses it thus in the *Timaeus*:

> what brings solids into unison is never one middle term alone but always two. Thus it was that in the midst between fire and earth God set water and air, and having bestowed upon them so far as possible a like ratio one towards another – air being to water as fire to air, and water being to earth as air to water, – he joined together and constructed a Heaven visible and tangible. For these reasons and out of these materials, such in kind and four in number, the body of the Cosmos was harmonized by proportion and brought into existence. These conditions secured for it Amity, so that being united in identity with itself it became indissoluble by any agent other than Him who had bound it together;[14]

while the significance of 4 as justice is intimately related, as F. M. Cornford has explained: 'Justice . . . completes the tetrad, and assures that the opposite tensions of the contraries shall be held together in harmony. It is easy to see why later authorities also identify the square number with φιλία.'[15]

Concord and harmony are achieved with the marriage of Joseph and Fanny: Andrew Wright has well remarked that 'marriage is the matter of Book IV'[16] since it contains, in addition to the concluding marriage, the arrival of the recently-married Pamela and Mr Booby in Chapter iv, and the debate between Adams and Joseph on marriage in Chapter viii, etc. And justice triumphs explicitly, too, when, in IV. xvi, Adams encounters

> the Justice of Peace before whom he and *Fanny* had made their Appearance. The Parson presently saluted him very kindly;

and the Justice informed him, that he had found the Fellow who attempted to swear against him and the young Woman the very next day, and had committed him to *Salisbury* Gaol, where he was charged with many Robberies.

(At the end of the chapter it is mentioned that the pedlar has been 'made an Excise-man; a Trust which he discharges with such Justice, that he is greatly beloved in his Neighbourhood'.) But it is also implicitly just that Joseph should finally obtain Fanny, despite the attempts of Lady Booby, and the law ('justice') in the persons of Lawyer Scout and the Justice of IV. v, to prevent the union of the two.

Furthermore, as the *Timaeus* passage makes clear, the peculiar stability of 4 arises from the fact that it possesses 2 means. This is apparent in Plato's first example, 'air being to water as fire to air', which can be expressed diagrammatically as follows: water : air : : air : fire; or, more simply, ABBA, the pattern deliberately reproduced in the saying attributed to Pythagoras by Iamblichus and Porphyry, φιλότης ἰσότης, ἰσότης φιλότης (friendship is equality, equality is friendship).[17]

Now it will be recalled from the first and second sections of this essay that the 4 books of *Joseph Andrews* are arranged in just this way; that Books I and IV are linked by echo, repetition, and the *Pamela* parody, as are, even more closely (by the use of identical chapter numbers), the 2 central books, II and III, thus giving us the replicative scheme ABBA.

But the novel's numerology does not function solely to direct us to the 'harmonious' marriage of Joseph and Fanny, and ultimate justice. It seems to me, indeed, that Fielding's use of this overall replicative scheme brings into focus the basic theme of the novel, which is not so much charity or chastity as *friendship*. The title page makes this quite clear by telling us that we are about to read *The History of the Adventures of Joseph Andrews, And of his Friend Mr. Abraham Adams.* And Fielding has emphasized his concern with friendship in several ways. Most noticeable, apart from the title itself, is the interpolated tale in IV. x, '*The History of two Friends, which may afford an useful Lesson to all those Persons, who happen to take up their Residence in married Families'*, which, I have argued elsewhere,[18] is an integral part of the novel because it shows us dissension between the 2 friends Leonard and Paul, and thus underscores by contrast the perfect amity of Joseph and Adams in the chapter immediately following, where Adams comes to Joseph's aid against Didapper despite his wife's and Lady Booby's objections. The notion of friendship appears through literary allusion here, too, for both this tale and its counterpart in Book II, *'The History* of Leonora' (Chapters iv and vi) are modelled on 'The Novel of the Curious Impertinent' in *I Don Quixote*, IV. vi–viii,[19] the beginning of the first paragraph of which reads: 'Anselmo and Lothario, considerable gentlemen of Florence . . . were so eminent for their friendship, that they were called nothing but the Two Friends.'[20] And so that the reader will not miss the allusion to Cervantes Fielding drops a broad hint by referring in III. i to 'the impertinent Curiosity of *Anselmo*, the Weakness of *Camilla*, the irresolute Friendship of *Lothario*'. The notion of friendship thus permeates the novel explicitly and implicitly.

At this point, I think, we can take a more inclusive view of the subject matter of Book IV than that suggested by Andrew Wright and quoted above. Not only is it about marriage; it also marks the culmination of the theme of friendship, and, most fittingly (since 4 is the number of concord and union) it is the book of *re*-unions, where Adams is reunited with his young son who is thought to have been drowned (IV. viii); Joseph and Fanny are reunited with their rightful parents, and so on.

But 4 possesses yet another meaning. It signifies virtue, since square numbers are particularly virtuous, and the square consists of 4 right angles, each of which symbolizes 'right reason, and right reason is the perennial fount of virtue'.[21] And it seems to me that Fielding exploits this meaning of 4 as well in the marriage that concludes the novel. For, as we saw above, the marriage of Joseph and Fanny is nothing other than a 'reward' for 'virtue', a re-enactment of the marriage – which itself symbolized 'virtue rewarded' – in Richardson's *Pamela*.[22]

This is underlined in yet another way: the marriage occurs in the *sixteenth* chapter of Book IV, and 16 – as the square of the just and virtuous 4 – possesses the meanings of 4, only more so – it is doubly virtuous since it is the square of a square.[23] Equally significantly, 16 is specifically connected with love-making and marriage, an association which arose from the biological fact that at the age of 16 *incipiant homines veneri indulgere generareque*.[24] And Plato associated the number with marriage when he wrote that 'The limit of the marriage-age shall be from sixteen to twenty years.'[25]

Finally, according to Bongo 16 *est numerus felicitatis*, the number of felicity;[26] a meaning which Fielding may well have been alluding to in the final chapter when he entitled it '*the last. In which this true History is brought to a happy Conclusion*,' and wrote in it of 'The happy, the blest Moment' (when the time came for Fanny to undress); 'this happy Couple'; 'a State of Bliss scarce ever equalled'; and of the fact that 'The Happiness of this Couple is a perpetual Fountain of Pleasure to their fond Parents.'[27]

Yet even this is not all. For we might say that the whole movement of the novel is *towards* 16 and all that it signifies – justice, virtue, and so on – since the total number of chapters is 64, and Book IV is the only book to possess its 'just' (or mean) share of 16.[28] The actual chapter totals for each book are (in order) 18, 17, 13, and 16, and it will be apparent that the descent towards 16 is made sufficiently clear by the 18–17–16 movement of Books I, II and IV.[29] Thus the very arithmetic of the novel's structure enacts a just sharing of rewards; and the reader who has followed my argument thus far will not be surprised to learn that 64 itself possesses meanings relevant to the theme of the novel. Like 16 it symbolizes justice (because it can be divided into equal halves until the monad is reached),[30] and it is, in addition, dedicated to Mercury,[31] the god of 'peace and concord',[32] whose zodiacal house is Gemini, the Heavenly Twins (again symbols of concord),[33] and who is the guardian of the fourth day of the planetary week.[34]

## 6

I began this paper by demonstrating what might be termed the abstract symmetry of *Joseph Andrews*, and then went on to suggest an interpretation of its basic structural numbers, 4, 16, and 64. I hope it will be agreed that there is a striking correlation between the meaning of the novel and the symbolic significance of the numbers concerned – so striking, indeed, that one would hesitate to put it down to coincidence. I want to go further in my numerological reading of *Joseph Andrews*; but before doing so I should like to point out 2 places where I think Fielding actually hints to the reader that he should indulge in the pastime of book and chapter counting.

The first occurs – significantly – right at the beginning, in I. iii, when Adams, among other questions, asks Joseph 'how many Books there were in the New Testament? which were they? how many Chapters they contained? and such like'. Now the number of books in the Old *and* New Testaments of the Authorized Version and the number of chapters in *Joseph Andrews*, though they do not tally exactly, are in fact curiously close – 66 and 64 respectively; a point that Adams' questions draw attention to.[35]

The second occurs in II. i where Fielding, in jocular vein, employs an arithmetical analogy when referring to the division of his novel into books and chapters: 'These several Places therefore in our Paper, which are filled with our Books and Chapters, are understood as so much Buckram, Stays, and Stay-tape in a Taylor's Bill, serving only to make up the Sum Total, commonly found at the Bottom of our first Page, and of his last.'

It seems to me, then, that we have Fielding's own authority for regarding *Joseph Andrews* numerologically, and I should like to continue by shifting my focus slightly and taking up a suggestion of M. C. Battestin's that *Joseph Andrews* is to be related to 'the tradition of the Christian epic'.[36] This suggestion has not, so far as I am aware, been developed, and since it has a direct bearing on the novel's numerology it deserves brief consideration here.

As Battestin has shown, Fielding's 2 heroes, Joseph and Adams, are based (via the writings of Latitudinarian divines) on the figures of the biblical Joseph and Abraham, and 'an adaptation of the stories of Joseph and Abraham – already on the Continent the subjects of several epic poems – would be in accord with theories of the biblical epic then prevalent in England'.[37] Moreover, Barabara Lewalski's recent study of the genre has brought to light 2 points relevant for *Joseph Andrews*. The first is that the Book of Job provided the pattern for the brief biblical epic, having been regarded from patristic times 'as an analogue of the classical epic';[38] the second is that the brief biblical epic was almost invariably divided into 3 or 4 books, the former originally in honour of the Trinity, the latter after the 4 Gospels.[39]

In view of this, it might have been with specific allusive intent that, in IV. viii, Fielding compared Joseph's patience to that of Job: 'The Patience of *Joseph*, nor perhaps of *Job*, could bear no longer';[40] and it certainly gives us one reason – if not the primary one – for the division of *Joseph Andrews* into 4 books.[41]

But Fielding's novel is an answer to Richardson's *Pamela*; and however much *Pamela* may owe to spiritual biography or autobiography, and be related Puritan traditions,[42] it is easy to see how it also suggested the biblical epic to Fielding, prompting him to cast his novel in that form. (In fact what he has effected is a modification of the introspective mode of spiritual autobiography into the extrovert mode of the comic epic.) For example, Pamela's passivity in the face of her adversary might well have reminded Fielding (and Richardson's other readers) of the passive heroes of biblical epic, Job and Christ.[43] (Characteristically, Adams and Joseph recall that active warrior hero – and type of Christ – Hercules, as they brandish crabstick and cudgel.)[44] Then again, as the conflict between Pamela and her master develops, the one becomes an angel and the other a devil, offering her temptation.[45] General echoes become more particular once Pamela is moved to B.'s Lincolnshire estate, however, where she is implicitly identified with Christ: a procedure that would appear to be completely at odds with the conventions of spiritual biography as J. Paul Hunter has analysed them, but is perhaps more understandable in terms of biblical epic. The point has been well made by M. Kinkead–Weekes:

In the second movement Pamela is imprisoned. This is a period of 'persecutions, oppressions and distress', but it is also a period of spiritual growth. It lasts, pointedly, for forty days and forty nights, and the presence of biblical language in the prayer which opens it, and in the scene by the pond at its heart, should indicate that the new conflict within Pamela herself has a religious dimension.[46]

The identification seems to be reinforced by another echo that sounds when Pamela, recounting her life story to Mrs Jewkes, tells her that she was brought up by her parents '"till I was almost twelve years of age"' (i. 175), at which time she entered the service of the B. family (hinting at Jesus' break from his parents at the same age, when he disputed with the doctors in the temple (Luke, ii. 42)). And it is confirmed by what appears to be the novel's one instance of typology among an abundance of other biblical allusions which possess less thematic relevance.[47] This occurs when Pamela has been walking with Mr B. in the garden: 'But I trust, that that God, who has delivered me from the paw of the lion and the bear, that is, his and Mrs Jewkes's violences, will soon deliver me from this *Philistine*, that I may not *defy the commands of the living God!*' (i. 184). Pamela is misquoting I Samuel, xvii (David's encounter with Goliath), verses 26, 'who is this uncircumcised Philistine, that he should defy the armies of the living God?' and 37, 'The Lord that delivered me out of the paw of the lion, and out of the paw of the bear, he will deliver me out of the hand of this Philistine.'[48]

The point of the allusion is that David's victory over Goliath was traditionally interpreted as a type of Christ's victory over Satan in the wilderness;[49] and Richardson makes the identification, implicit in the allusion, explicit when, on the same page, he has Pamela physically struggling with B. and saying, '"to be sure you are Lucifer himself, in the *shape* of my master, or you could not use me thus"' (i. 184).

Finally, even though *Pamela* contains no direct references to Job, it is possible that Job's material rewards once his trials are over (Job, xlii. 11–12) might have been at the back of Richardson's mind when he gave his heroine's virtue an equally temporal reward.[50]

Having placed *Joseph Andrews*, via *Pamela*, in the tradition of
biblical epic, it is worth noting that many such works show
evidence of numerological organization.[51] But what is particularly
interesting, and might well have been noticed by the arith-
metically-minded Fielding (see his remarks in *Joseph Andrews*, II. i,
quoted above), is that Milton's 'brief epic', *Paradise Regained*,
written in the almost-canonical 4 books (like *Joseph Andrews*),
makes prominent structural use of 64, the number, as we have
seen, of the overall chapter total of *Joseph Andrews*.

It appears, in fact, at the poem's mathematical centre,[52] and
provides the line total for Christ's speech rejecting Satan's offer of
military fame and glory, and his substitution of the *Paradise
Regained* ideal of 'the just man', the prime example of which is
Job (iii. 62ff.). The speech contains, in addition, a condemnation
of those who 'all the flourishing works of peace destroy' (iii. 80),
and his exaltation of the glory achieved 'without ambition, war
or violence; / By deeds of peace' (iii. 90–91).

In short, Milton seems to be exploiting here two primary meanings of 64 which we encountered earlier on in connection with
*Joseph Andrews*: justice and peace.[53] The coincidence is striking; it
becomes even more so when we recall that in Book IV of *The
Faerie Queene* prominent structural use is again made of 64.[54]


7

*Joseph Andrews*, is, then, a comic biblical epic, and my suggestion that it is organized on numerological lines appears to be
confirmed by Milton's use of numerology in *Paradise Regained*
and (to a lesser extent) by Richardson's use of substantive number
symbolism in *Pamela*, his heroine's 40-day period of imprisonment and trial.

But the question arises, since the journey of Joseph and Adams
is Fielding's version of Pamela's trial, might we not reasonably
expect to find number symbolism here – more so, perhaps, than
anywhere else? It takes only a moment, however, to determine
that there is no simple correspondence, as we might have supposed: the journey does not last 40 days; it takes only 11.[55] And if

we follow Fielding's hints about chapter totals we soon discover that it does not occupy 40 chapters – another possibility – but 38.[56]

In fact, though, 38 is more relevant to Fielding's purpose than 40 would have been. Like 40, *it is specifically associated with the wanderings of the Israelites in the wilderness*, as Moses reminds them in Deuteronomy, ii. 14, when recapitulating their journey 'in the fortieth year, in the eleventh month, on the first day of the month' (Deuteronomy i. 3): 'And the space in which we came from Kadesh-barnea, until we were come over the brook Zered, was thirty and eight years.'

And, moreover, according to Bongo, 38 is not only evil in holy writ; it signifies (to quote his index) 'imperfect and grudging charity' (*imperfectae, et languidae charitatis significativus*) as well,[57] both of which meanings could not relate more closely to the wretched wanderings of Joseph, Adams, and Fanny, in which, at almost every point, charity is tested and found wanting.[58]

There is a gentle irony in Fielding's use of biblical numbers here – irony directed at that Puritan habit of mind which could accept the symbolic significance of Pamela's forty days and nights, and see in 'Crusoe's twenty-eight years of isolation and suffering' a parallel to 'the Puritan alienation between the Restoration and the accession of William and Mary'.[59] And yet Fielding intends it seriously, too; so that in *Joseph Andrews* number symbolism takes its place alongside other – what we regard as more conventional – allegorical features.[60]

## 8

Further minor instances of numerological decorum may be noted in conclusion. The first occurs in III. xi, the scene of Joseph's despair over the abduction of Fanny, or, as the chapter heading has it, '*Containing the Exhortations of Parson* Adams *to his Friend in Affliction*'. The allusion here must be to 11 as the number of grief and mourning.[61]

The number 11, and this brings me to the second instance, is often discussed in connection with 12 (a number of perfection and completion) since its imperfection is vividly expressed through the fact that it falls 1 short of 12. This is the case in Cornelius Agrippa's *Three Books of Occult Philosophy*:

> The number eleven as it exceeds the number ten, which is the number of the commandments, so it falls short of the number twelve, which is of grace and perfection. . . . Now the number twelve is divine. . . . There were . . . so many Apostles of Christ set over the twelve tribes, and twelve thousand people were set apart and chosen.[62]

If 11 is the number of lamentation, then, 12 is, among other things, the number of salvation, because Christ chose to elect as many disciples.[63] This might well account for the pattern of rescue – or salvation – and reunion that I have traced in the twelfth chapter of each of *Joseph Andrews*'s 4 books, and particularly for pattern centring round the eleventh *and* twelfth chapters of Books II and III, in which suffering yields to joyful reunion.[64]

Thirdly, and finally, it is worth remarking on Fielding's use of mid-point symbolism in the novel. The central position was often characterized by an image of elevation and/or kingship;[65] so that it should come as no surprise when we encounter, at the end of the central chapter – vii – of Book III the erection of a 'throne' (a blanket over a tub of water) on either side of which stand 'the King and Queen, namely, the Master of the House, and the Captain', with Adams sitting in the centre between them (until he falls into the tub).[66] This complements the central action of Book II – Adams's encounter with the coward (vii to ix) – which takes place on 'the Summit of a Hill' (II. vii).[67]

This essay has not exhausted the possible numerological implications of *Joseph Andrews*. My aim has been to interest (and perhaps amuse) the reader, rather than to bore him. But I also hope that, once the novelty and apparent eccentricity of the approach have worn off, it will be seen that something new and, maybe, valuable, has been said, and that the preceding pages may have contributed something to our slowly growing understanding of the considerable complexities of the early novel.

# NOTES

1 Among the few exceptions to this generalization must be mentioned F. W. Hilles' interesting essay, 'Art and Artifice in *Tom Jones*', in *Imagined Worlds: Essays on Some English Novels and Novelists in Honour of John Butt*, ed. Maynard Mack and Ian Gregor (1968), pp. 91–110, and M. C. Battestin's '*Tom Jones*: The Argument of Design', forthcoming in the Louis Landa Festschrift.

2 Robert Donovan, *The Shaping Vision: Imagination in the English Novel from Defoe to Dickens* (Ithaca, N.Y., 1966), p. 86.

3 Andrew Wright, *Henry Fielding: Mask and Feast* (1965), p. 60, states that in Book I 'of a total of 18 chapters, 9 (2–10) are devoted to Joseph in London, and 9 (11–18) to Joseph on the road'. But Joseph does not arrive in London until Ch. iv, and from Chs xii to xviii he is at the Dragon Inn; so that Book I's main matter is contained in 2 static 7-chapter units.

4 See Donovan, Ch. iv; and my 'Richardson's *Pamela* and Fielding's *Joseph Andrews*', *EC*, xvii (1967), 158–68.

5 Quotations are from the Wesleyan *Joseph Andrews*, ed. M. C. Battestin (Oxford, 1967).

6 Maurice Johnson, *Fielding's Art of Fiction* (Philadelphia, Pa., 1961), p. 56.

7 Dick Taylor, Jr, 'Joseph as Hero in *Joseph Andrews*', *Tulane Studies in English*, vii (1957), 91–109, has made out a case for the novel as a growth allegory on the lines of *Tom Jones*.

8 Thus dramatically illustrating the intimate relationship between charity and chastity and their obverse (on which see M. C. Battestin, *The Moral Basis of Fielding's Art* [Middletown, Conn., 1959], Ch. iii).

9 Her function in this respect is brought out by the physical similarities between her and Joseph. The two are, in fact, identical (compare their descriptions in I. viii and II. xii).

10 Not too much importance can be attached to the recurrence of the 'violent hands' phrase, however. It is a particular favourite of Fielding's (see *Tom Jones*, IV, xii; VI. ii; IX. vii; XII. i, iii and vii).

11 An analogous pattern appears in *Jonathan Wild*, where similar events occur in Chs ix and x of all 4 books. Thus, in I. ix Wild makes an attempt on Laetitia Snap's chastity and is repulsed; in II. ix we are presented with his plans for seducing Mrs Heartfree; and in IV. ix Mrs Heartfree is nearly raped by Count La Ruse. In

I. x Laetitia, having rejected Wild, yields to Tom Smirk the apprentice; in II. x Mrs Heartfree withstands, and is rescued from, Wild; in III. x there is a reference to Wild in the boat in which he was cast away at the end of II. x, and also to Laetitia's infidelity with Fireblood; finally, in IV. x Wild catches *'Fireblood* in the Arms of his lovely *Laetitia'*. (In referring to Bk IV I use the revised chapter numbering of the 1754 edn. The 1754 text omits IV. ix of the first edn (1743), so that IV. ix and x (1754) were originally numbered x and xi.)

12 In IV. vii Joseph rescues Fanny from one of Didapper's servants, and the fight recalls that of Adams in II. ix. Interestingly, although there is no identification of chapter numbers at this point, the 2 fights occur in the same position in their respective volumes in the early editions of the novel. Thus, in the 1st edn the fight in II. ix covers vol. i. 224–7, and that in IV. vii, vol. ii. 225–7 (2nd edn, i. 224–6; ii. 225–6).

13 'Comic Resolution in Fielding's *Joseph Andrews'*, reprinted from *CE* in the Twentieth Century Views *Fielding*, ed. Ronald Paulson (Englewood Cliffs, N.J., 1962), pp. 59–68.

14 *Timaeus*, 32 B–C, tr. R. G. Bury, Loeb edn (London and New York, 1929), pp. 59–61.

15 'Mysticism and Science in the Pythagorean Tradition', *CQ*, xvii (1923), 4.

16 *Henry Fielding: Mask and Feast*, p. 68. The concept of marriage as concord and harmony is, of course, a commonplace. See, e.g., Sir John Davies' *Orchestra*, Sts. 110–11; and Jonson's masque *Hymenaei*: 'the *rite* was to joyne the marryed payre with bands of silke, in signe of future *concord'* (*Ben Jonson*, ed. C. H. Herford and Percy and Evelyn Simpson, vii [Oxford, 1941], p. 210).

17 Cornford, p. 4, n. 6.

18 'The Interpolated Tales in *Joseph Andrews* Again', *MP*, lxv (1968), 208–13.

19 See Homer Goldberg, 'The Interpolated Stories in *Joseph Andrews* or "The History of the World in General" Satirically Revised', *MP*, lxiii (1966), 295–310, and also my 'Interpolated Tales'.

20 Tr. P. Motteux (London and New York, 1943), i. 262. Cervantes's 'novel' – and hence the two tales of Fielding's based on it – take their places in the long tradition of tales about friends: Chaucer's *Knight's Tale*, for instance, and 'The wonderful history of Titus and Gisippus, and whereby is fully declared the figure of perfect amity,' as re-

counted in Sir Thomas Elyot's *The Book named The Governor*, II. xii.

21 Pietro Bongo, *Numerorum mysteria* (Bergamo, 1599), p. 195 (where 4 as justice is also mentioned).

22 This is made abundantly clear immediately after the wedding when Mr Williams tells Pamela: ' "I will say, that to see so much innocence and virtue so eminently rewarded, is one of the greatest pleasures I have ever known" ' (ed. M. Kinkead-Weekes, 2 vols. [London and New York, 1962], i, 309–10).

23 On 16 as justice see Bongo, p. 415; Vitruvius, *De Architectura*, III. i. 8, also points out that 16 is 'the most perfect number' since it is obtained by adding the perfect 6 to the perfect 10 (tr. M. H. Morgan, [New York, 1960], p. 74) (echoed by Bongo, p. 411). Did Fielding notice that Pamela is 16 when she marries (i, 176 [' "I have lived about sixteen years in virtue and reputation" '], 357 and 369)?

24 Bongo, p. 411.

25 *Laws*, vi, 785 B; tr. R. G. Bury, 2 vols, Loeb edn (London and New York, 1926), i, 501.

26 Bongo, p. 413.

27 It is probably another instance of numerological decorum that Spenser should mention 'felicity' in the sixteenth stanza of *The Faerie Queene*, IV. viii.

28 I am indebted to Alastair Fowler for pointing this out to me.

29 Bk. III is the odd man out here, but Fielding needed it to complete his structural *chiasmus* – the ABBA scheme outlined above – and also to bring the overall chapter total to 64.

30 On p. 413 Bongo discusses 4, 16 and 64 together. The principle of equal division is mentioned on p. 486.

31 In the well-known tradition of planetary squares. Bongo, p. 345 makes passing mention of the fact. For a more expansive treatment see Cornelius Agrippa, *Three Books of Occult Philosophy*, tr. J. F. (1651), II. xxii; p. 241. In this tradition 16, attributed to Jupiter, still retains associations similar to those already outlined above for that number ('love, peace, and concord': *ibid.*, p. 240).

32 The words are Agrippa's (II. xliii; 302).

33 The twins were not only depicted as males in calendrical art, but also as male and female, and even as bride and bridegroom (see Alastair Fowler, *Spenser and the Numbers of Time* (1964), p. 167, nn. 1 and 2). What Burlingame in *The Sot-Weed Factor* calls ' "the Two as One" ' (Part III, Ch. ii) is well expressed in the physical twinning of Joseph and Fanny, mentioned above.

34 The notion of reconciliation and concord at the end of the novel appears in a more subtle way still. For there is, in effect, a double marriage, since the wedding of Joseph and Fanny is an exact re-enactment of that between Richardson's Pamela and Mr B., who are present at the *Joseph Andrews* wedding (see my 'Richardson's *Pamela* and Fielding's *Joseph Andrews*', p. 159). Fielding is in this way symbolically reconciling his novel with Richardson's.

35 Alastair Fowler drew my own attention to this. I have in my possession a copy of *The Holy Bible . . . with Practical Observations on Each Chapter, by the Late Rev. Mr. Ostervald* (Newcastle-upon-Tyne, 1793), vol. i of which contains a prefatory table giving the number of books, letters and words in the Old and New Testaments, and the central book, chapter and verse in each: proof of eighteenth-century numerological interest in the Bible, and an interesting sidelight on one of the preoccupations of the Age of Reason.

36 *The Moral Basis of Fielding's Art*, p. 41.

37 Introd. to *'Joseph Andrews' and 'Shamela'* (1965), p. xxx; and see *The Moral Basis*, Ch. iii. One may note, as an instance of Fielding's precise attention to numerical detail, that Joseph is 17 when he becomes Lady Booby's footboy (I. ii), the age of the biblical Joseph when he was sold to Potiphar (Genesis xxxvii. 2 and 36).

38 *Milton's Brief Epic: The Genre, Meaning, and Art of 'Paradise Regained'* (Providence, R.I. and London, 1966), p. 11. On pp. 32ff. will be found references to seventeenth-century biblical epics which used Job as a structural model.

39 *Ibid,*, p. 67. References to four-book epics appear on, e.g., pp. 43, 82, 85, 89, 91, and 102.

40 This follows 2 other references to patience under affliction, in III. xi and IV. viii.

41 It is difficult to determine priorities in a case like this. But it seems obvious – from *The Faerie Queene* and *Paradise Lost*, for instance – that adherence to a canonical number (here, 12) by no means hindered far more elaborate numerical symbolism: it was merely fortunate for Fielding that 4 was so rich in meanings.

42 These are usefully described in J. Paul Hunter, *The Reluctant Pilgrim: Defoe's Emblematic Method and Quest for Form in 'Robinson Crusoe'* (Baltimore, Md., 1966), Chs ii to v. See also G. A. Starr, *Defoe and Spiritual Autobiography* (Princeton, N.J., 1965).

43 See Lewalski, p. 36 for Richard Blackmore's comments on, and

defence of, the heroic nature of Job's passivity, in contrast to the 'very active' heroes of Homer and Virgil. The Introd. to the second edn of *Pamela* (February 1741) referred to 'the poor passive PAMELA' (*Samuel Richardson's Introduction to 'Pamela'*, ed. Sheridan W. Baker, Jr, Augustan Reprint Society Pub. No. 48 [Los Angeles, Calif., 1954], p. xxvi).

44 Their version of the club of Hercules. Hercules is mentioned several times in the novel (e.g. I. xvii), but the full function of the allusions must await exploration elsewhere.

45 E.g. i. 24, 43, 47, 72, 89 (angel and devil); i. 15, 51, 58 (temptation).

46 Introd. to *Pamela*, i, p. ix. In fact, Pamela's 'worst trial' (i. 174), when the disguised B. climbs into bed with her, occurs on Sunday, the 38th day of her imprisonment, though it is true that she recounts it on Tuesday, the 40th, which is also the day of her interview with B. when the movement towards reconciliation begins. The 40 *days* recalls Christ; but it was a Puritan commonplace to seek identification with the wandering Israelites (see J. Paul Hunter, *op. cit.*, pp. 109 and 174 for Defoe's use of such allusions in *Robinson Crusoe*).

47 As Lewalski points out (e.g., p. 86), typological symbolism was a feature of biblical epic, though it was also fundamental to the Puritan world-view (Hunter, pp. 99ff.). The biblical allusion in *Pamela*, i. 217, incidentally, reinforces the suggestion of the number 40. It is to Numbers, xi. 5 and is related contextually to the Israelites' 40-year sojourn in the wilderness.

48 Pamela also mentions the lion and bear (among other animals) on p. 146; but it is unlikely that she has this passage in mind.

49 Lewalski, p. 279 (and p. 230 on the analogy with Hercules's victory over Antaeus). Goliath oppressed the Israelites for 40 days (I Samuel xvii. 16). Are B.'s articles – which offer Pamela clothes, money, servants, etc. – a parallel to Satan's offering Christ 'all the kingdoms of the world' (Luke, iv. 5, Matthew, iv. 8).

50 Lewalski, pp. 20–1: eventually 'God declares Job victor in all his combats and gives him due reward.' But see Hunter, p. 43, on the spiritual guide tradition, which described 'the frequent (but by no means certain) temporal rewards brought by piety and godliness'.

51 Gunnar Qvarnström's *Poetry and Numbers* (Lund, 1966) discusses Benlowes' *Theophila* (1652) in detail; and see his passing reference to Alexander Ross's *Virgilii Evangelisantis Christiados* (1638) on pp. 79–80. On *Paradise Lost*, see the same author's *The Enchanted*

257

*Palace: Some Structural Aspects of 'Paradise Lost'* (Stockholm, 1967).

52 On the symbolic significance of the central position see Alastair Fowler, *Spenser and the Numbers of Time*, pp. 45–6, and Qvarnström, *The Enchanted Palace*, Ch. ii. The exactly central line of *Paradise Regained* is iii. 47 (1035th out of a total of 2070).

53 This is the only 64-line speech in the poem. Qvarnström, *The Enchanted Palace*, pp. 114 and 157, has already noted another case of this type of numerology in the poem, involving the number 33.

54 It is the stanza total for Canto viii. But although the meanings peace and concord are generally relevant here, the sequence IV – viii – 64 is specifically illuminated by Fowler's comment on the function of cubic numbers in Bk IV (*Spenser and the Numbers of Time*, p. 186; where, however, no mention is made of Canto viii's stanza total).

55 F. Homes Dudden, *Henry Fielding: His Life, Works, and Times*, i (Oxford, 1952), pp. 344–50. As Dudden remarks, 'the time-scheme has been carefully worked out'.

56 Joseph's journey begins in I. xi after his dismissal by Lady Booby, and he and Adams return home at the beginning of IV. i. To the chapter totals for Bks II and III (17 and 13 respectively), therefore, must be added the final 8 chapters of Bk I. (I include the 2 prolegomenous chapters, II. i and III. i in my count.) The allusion may well be to the precise period of Pamela's trials (see n. 46 above), though as nn. 47 and 49 indicate, Richardson seems to have had 40 in mind as the significant figure.

57 Pp. 499–500, and Appendix, pp. 48–9, citing, among other texts, John, v. 5, I Kings, xvi. 29, and II Kings, xv. 8.

58 The individual totals for Bks II and III are equally meaningful. The number 17 is evil and unfortunate in Pythagorean, Roman, and Jewish thought (Bongo, pp. 416–17, 420); and 13 signifies transgression of divine law (*ibid.*, p. 401), because it goes one beyond the total of the disciples, and impiety and irreverence (*ibid.*, p. 400). It might also be relevant that 18 (the chapter total for Bk I) was regarded by divines as 'unhappy' (Cornelius Agrippa, *Three Books of Occult Philosophy*, II. xv; p. 222) because 'the children of Israel served Eglon the king of Moab eighteen years' (Judges, iii. 14).

59 Hunter, p. 204.

60 In my 'Abraham Adams and Parson Trulliber: The Meaning of *Joseph Andrews*, Book II, Chapter 14', *MLR*, lxiii (1968), 794–801, I try to show the allegorical depth of what is, from this point of view, perhaps the most rewarding scene in the novel.

61 Bongo, p. 383 (classified in the index as *luctui sacer*; Lewis and Short define *luctus* as '*sorrow, mourning, grief, affliction, distress, lamentation,* esp. over the loss of something dear to one'). This accounts, too, for the 11 stanzas of Milton's 'On the Death of a Fair Infant' and the 11 paragraphs of *Lycidas*. Note, in addition, that the journey in *Joseph Andrews* takes 11 days (see n. 55 above). If we read this symbolically it accords well with the interpretations I have offered of the other journey numbers, 38, 17, and 13. It is interesting that Deuteronomy, i. 2 (the chapter immediately preceding that containing the reference to 38) reads: 'There are eleven days' journey from Horeb by the way of mount Seir unto Kadesh-barnea.'

62 II. xiii; p. 216.

63 See also Vincent F. Hopper, *Medieval Number Symbolism* (New York, 1938), p. 86.

64 In II. xi Fanny and Adams are wrongly accused before the justice, and in II. xii they are reunited with Joseph; in III. xi Joseph laments Fanny's abduction, and in III. xii she is rescued and he is reunited with her.

65 See refs in n. 52 above.

66 The notion of *falling* at the centre had been anticipated by Marvell's 'The First Anniversary of the Government under O.C.', the central line (201) of which reads, in part, 'Thou *Cromwell* falling . . .' (Alastair Fowler first mentioned this to me.) The central chapter (ix) of *Joseph Andrews*, Bk I, terminates with the image of a balance, recalling the balance image in the centre of *The Rape of the Lock*, Canto v. Morris Golden, *Thomas Gray* (New York, 1964) has noted several instances of central-line symbolism in Gray's poetry.

67 Anticipating the central chapter of *Tom Jones* (IX. ii), which has Tom standing on the top of Mazard Hill (104th out of 208 chapters). (The significance of this episode has been convincingly explored by M. C. Battestin in his 'Fielding's Definition of Wisdom: Some Functions of Ambiguity and Emblem in *Tom Jones*', *ELH*, xxxv (1968), 188–217, especially 214ff, though without reference to the mid-point tradition to which it also relates.) But this is only a minor aspect of *Tom Jones*'s formal organization, some pointers to the mathematical rigour of which should lend support to the above reading of *Joseph Andrews*.

Thus, while *Tom Jones* appears to contain little Pythagorean-Biblical number symbolism, Fielding's interest in abstract numerical patterning (for its own sake, perhaps, but also as an expression of a universe still felt to be ordered by 'number, weight, and measure') is more readily apparent here than anywhere else. It is obvious, in fact, that Fielding wanted the reader of the novel to do two things when he first approached it: (i) note the chapter totals for each book, and (ii) deduce from this operation that books having the same number of chapters will, in all likelihood, bear a special, echoic, relationship to each other. Furthermore, it is beyond doubt that Fielding requested the 6-volume format of the first and second editions of the novel from his publisher so as to emphasize, as clearly as possible, its arithmetical scheme, which runs as follows (it is helpful to imagine this superimposed on F. W. Hilles' diagram of *Tom Jones*, in *Imagined Worlds*, ed. M. Mack and I. Gregor, p. 95 [see n. 1, above]): volume I (Bks I, II, III; 13, 9, and 10 chapters) answered by volume VI (Bks XVI, XVII, XVIII; 10, 9, and 13 chapters – the opening sequence reversed); volume II (Bks IV, V, VI; 14, 12, and 14 chapters) answered by volume V (Bks XIII, XIV, XV; 12, 10, and 12 chapters), flanking volumes III and IV (Bks VII to XII), where the numerical patterning becomes less regular (15, 15, and 7; 9, 10, and 14 chapters respectively).

The question I have opened here is large, and I hope to go into it thoroughly elsewhere. But if we can conceive the possibility of volume divisions (as well as book and chapter divisions) occasionally having a definite formal significance in the eighteenth-century novel, then one final suggestion emerges concerning *Joseph Andrews*. I have already shown that Fielding uses mid-point symbolism in Bks I, II, and III; and the central chapter of the novel as a whole (II. xiv) also partakes of this symbolism (it begins with Adams being thrown into the mire when he visits Trulliber). *Joseph Andrews*, however, was originally published in 2 volumes, 2 books per volume; so that the middle point of the narrative actually *appears* to be at the beginning of volume II (it is only after we have done some arithmetical calculation, of however simple a kind, that II. xiv is seen to be exactly central). It is here, then, that the contemporary reader might not unreasonably have expected his image of elevation. And Fielding gives him one – but characteristically reversed again – when, in III. ii, Adams, Joseph, and Fanny find 'themselves on the Descent of a very steep Hill. *Adams*'s Foot slipping, he instantly disappeared . . . rolling down the Hill . . . from top to bottom, without receiving any harm.'